UNSTEADY CROWNS

About the Author

The late A.W. Purdue was Reader in British History at the Open University. He was the author of sixteen books, including the histories of prominent North-East families. His book publications include *The Monarchy and the British People* (Batsford, 1998), *The Civilisation of the Crowd: Popular Culture in England, 1750–1900* (Sutton Publishing, 1999) and *Newcastle: The Biography* (Amberley Publishing, 2011).

★★★

In memoriam
A.W. Purdue 1941–2020

UNSTEADY CROWNS

WHY THE WORLD'S MONARCHIES ARE STRUGGLING FOR SURVIVAL

A.W. PURDUE

The History Press

Cover illustration © imageBROKER/Alamy Stock Photo.

First published 2005
This paperback edition first published 2022

The History Press
97 St George's Place, Cheltenham,
Gloucestershire, GL50 3QB
www.thehistorypress.co.uk

British Library Cataloguing in Publication Data.
A catalogue record for this book is available from the British Library.

ISBN 978 07509 9932 8

Typesetting and origination by The History Press
Printed and bound in Great Britain by TJ Books Limited, Padstow, Cornwall.

Trees for LYfe

CONTENTS

INTRODUCTION

THE POWER OF KINGSHIP

At the beginning of the twentieth century, monarchies were the normal form of government and, with the exception of Central and South America, they were to be found throughout the world. By the end of the century, there were fewer than thirty left and many of the remaining monarchs reigned over small states. The form of government that had been universal since early in human history had become a rarity.

It is tempting to see this development as the inevitable result of broad historical forces such as modernisation, industrialisation and secularisation, but in the nineteenth century the institution of monarchy had proved resilient and adaptable in the face of the emergence of sweeping economic and social change. Nor do we find that countries that retain monarchical systems are necessarily the least modern, for Sweden, Norway, Denmark, the Netherlands, Japan and Britain are far from synonyms for backwardness.

The twentieth century's wars were the major reason for the end of so many monarchies. In 1918 three emperors departed, and the Second World War was to see a further cull of kings.

Yet few regimes of any sort were able to survive defeat in total war. Only a handful of monarchies with long traditions and sturdy roots were overthrown for other reasons, with only a few disappearing because of popular discontent expressed via the ballot box. The demise of one of the most ancient empires, China, came about largely because of a century of pressure from without, which the imperial system was unable to withstand, and after a succession of humiliations.

The onward march of democracy and the progressive widening of franchises would seem a possible reason for the demise of so many monarchies had such a march taken place, but the twentieth century can scarcely be claimed to have been a heyday for democracy. Regimes far more autocratic and illiberal than most monarchies came and went, and in the early twenty-first century only a fraction of the world's states can be considered liberal democracies. Most of the surviving monarchies are among them.

This book sets out to consider, within a comparative framework, whether there were structural reasons for the demise of monarchies or whether the end of each has to be explained in terms of national histories and traditions, together with the misfortunes and mistakes of individual monarchs.

It is important at the outset to analyse what is unique about monarchical systems and whether, despite the diversity of monarchies throughout history, we can find common denominators. Were the monarchies of medieval Europe different in essence from their oriental or Arab counterparts, or was monarchy so in tune with universal human needs and instincts that it transcended individual cultural contexts and boundaries? There are many names for monarchs; emperors, ruling princes and dukes, sultans, emirs and even African chiefs are or have been monarchs. The essential characteristic of monarchy is royal authority, with the monarch, at least in theory, exercising ultimate authority by virtue of the special form of legitimacy.

It is conventional to divide modern monarchies into specific types: constitutional, autocratic or theocratic. Such divisions are useful and important, but we must remember that they are not polarities or even discrete, and that monarchies are positioned on a spectrum with the greater or lesser degrees of political power at the extremes, while all monarchies have some religious dimension. The three main characteristics of monarchy are religious sanction, political power and the hereditary principle, and all modern monarchies continue, if only residually, to be defined by them.

The modern British monarchy is often seen as not only constitutional, but largely symbolic and ornamental, yet the coronation of Queen Elizabeth II made clear the importance of its religious and mystical dimension:

> Then shall the Queen go to her Throne and be lifted up into it by the Archbishops and Bishops and other Peers of the Kingdom; and being enthroned, or placed therein, all the Great Officers, those that bear the Swords and the Sceptres, and the Nobles who carried the other regalia, shall stand round the steps of the Throne; and the Archbishop standing before the Queen shall say;

> STAND firm and hold fast from henceforth the seat and state of royal and imperial dignity, which is this day delivered unto you, in the Name and by the Authority of Almighty God, and by the hands of us the Bishops and servants of God, though unworthy. And the Lord God Almighty, whose ministers we are, and the stewards of his mysteries, establish your throne in righteousness, that it may stand fast for ever-more. Amen.[1]

What is not always recognised is that coronation and con-secration divest the monarch of his or her individuality and past identity. The monarch becomes separate from the run of humanity. Most early artistic portrayals of monarchs are iconic and impersonal; they concentrate upon the crown rather than the man. The separation of the person from the office is shown most clearly in the naming of kings. Eastern traditions demonstrate a greater continuity here, with, as in China, the emperor's former name never mentioned, or, as in Japan, the emperor's reign being given a special auspicious name, which becomes the monarch's name after his death. Even in Europe, the monarch chooses the name by which he will be known as king, with, in Britain, Alberts and Davids becoming Georges or Edwards.

Royal authority has been the norm for the greater part of human history, and the idea of the monarch as head of a family, the head of an organic community of which he or she is the expression, remains as true of monarchy today as at its beginnings. The early origins of monarchy lie in literal kinship with the rule of the chieftain, who was the patriarch of the family, the leader in war and the priest. Such relations between ruler and ruled can still be found today in Africa and parts of the Middle East. The chieftain's office was not necessarily based on primogeniture but was hereditary in that rulers were usually chosen from a leading family. The early monarch was the lawmaker or law interpreter, the general or protector, and the intermediary between the spirits and the living, the past and the present. Early peoples felt perpetually threatened, and, it has been argued, the beginnings of kingship were probably located in their quest for protection 'against myriad hostile forces – natural, supernatural and human'.[2] Among German tribes, as among the African, the whole clan was believed to have a spiritual power, which ensured good crops, victory in battle and the power to cure diseases. Such powers were expressed through the king, but if he failed could he really be a true king?

The magical origins of kingship are demonstrated very clearly by the importance attached to the regalia and treasures

of monarchies. The crown, sword and sceptre became standard symbols of monarchy in Europe and have their origins
in its earliest history. The stewardship of the three items that
comprise the Japanese regalia, the sacred mirror, the jewel and
the sword, is essential to legitimate sovereignty. In the Malay
sultanates, regalia include musical instruments and weapons;
such symbols of greatness have supernatural powers. Thrones
may seem to be merely symbols of power or secular authority,
setting the sovereign physically above the courtiers, but they
also project the spiritual or magical dimension of kingship.

In Burma, the throne in the main hall of audience in the
royal palace of Mandalay was placed exactly under the tall
spire that surmounts the roof and seems to pierce the heavens,
and it was thought to occupy the 'centre of the world', like
the cosmic mountain on which Indra, the king of the gods,
is seated.[3]

The Golden Stool of the Asante, supposedly a seventeenth-
century gift from Heaven, was so sacred that even the king
could not sit upon it, but guarding it was an essential condi-
tion for his legitimate rule.

An anthropological study of kingship finds that two characteristics stand out:

> The first is that the same highly ritualised elements appear
> consistently, albeit with different permutations, in societies
> that have no obvious connection. The second is the extra-
> ordinary range of monarchical societies – from the smallest
> Pacific islands to the complex city-kingdoms of South and
> South-East Asia to modern European democracies.[4]

The power and authority of early kings were not unqualified.
In the very earliest stages of kingship the association between
the king and fertility meant that 'kings must die' either at
the end of a fixed period of power or when they were no
longer young and virile.[5] Even later, the very breadth of their

responsibilities and the extent of their claims as protectors rendered them vulnerable to failures in matters both within and outside their control. Failure in battle, bad harvests or epidemics could suggest that this was not the legitimate king or that the spirits or the divinity had withdrawn approval. Kingship in sub-Saharan Africa exemplifies this well. Kings were associated with divine power, and their priestly functions were crucial to their power, for these were designed to ensure the spiritual and earthly well-being of subjects. Their semi-divine status and closeness to the ancestors of their lineage group were the reason why many did not appear in public. The importance of their religious role and the ceremonies only they could perform meant that old or infirm monarchs could be retired or killed: 'In the small kingdom of Ankole in East Africa ... the ailing monarch was expected to take poison prepared by his own spiritual advisers.'[6]

The heads that have worn crowns have always been uneasy. Monarchs received the credit for good times and were the scapegoat for the bad times. Essentially, power was lent or exchanged in return for results. Kings exercised charismatic power, but charisma could not long survive successive failures. As Reinhard Bendix has put it: 'As long as the ruler and his people share the belief in the ruler's intercession with the spirits on behalf of the community, the exchange relations of authority is sustained.'[7] The problem of maintaining charisma, especially in the face of misfortunes or defeats, has troubled monarchs throughout history, while the alternative problem for the 'loyal' subject has been when to decide that the 'bad', weak or unlucky king has forfeited his mandate.

Monarchy emerged deeply anchored in religious belief. The act of consecration performed by priests who validated the authenticity of the monarch and had special knowledge of the mysteries, ceremonies and ritual by which he was consecrated was crucial to his acceptance as legitimate. This led in many cultures to a sharing of royal power with some sort of priestly order, and everywhere to an ultimate check upon kings who no longer seemed to have the support of divine providence.

In the West, two different patterns developed. In the eastern part of the Roman Empire, there was no real division between Church and State, and ultimate religious and secular authority was lodged in the person of the emperor. In a sense not found in western Europe, the emperor represented God on Earth, the symbol of the Kingdom of Heaven. The Byzantine Empire lasted for over a thousand years. In many ways the position of its emperors was closer to the position of oriental monarchs than to west European counterparts. The Patriarch was clearly subordinate to the emperor, and though he looked after internal Church affairs, the charge of maintaining the Christian nature of the Empire was the Emperor's. In the western part of the Empire, Germanic tribal traditions and the expanding influence of the Catholic Church came together. On the one hand, there was the tradition of tribal chiefs representing the principle of leadership in war and election by acclamation, while the Church represented principles of hierarchy and law. These two principles merged when Carolingian kings were consecrated by the Pope, but that very act revealed limitations upon royal authority. Whereas the Eastern Church accepted the emperor as the representative of God on Earth, Western kings were expected to rule under God's laws as interpreted by the Church. Indeed, west European monarchs had constraints on their power from both above and below, for if consecration demonstrated the superior position of the Church, acclamation represented the consent of the nobility. The Carolingian Regent, Pepin, was elected king by nobles and then anointed by Bishop Boniface. Charlemagne managed to elevate his association with the divine by adding to his consecration ceremony the words 'by the Grace of God', but it was, nevertheless, by ecclesiastical authority that he was consecrated. Kingship had, however, mystical or religious dimensions. The need to be victorious in battle might be a secular duty, but the power to cure certain diseases pointed clearly to a God-given position.

The division of authority in medieval Europe between kings and popes or bishops, and between State and Church, was not general throughout the world, though in Japan an inversion of this developed, with emperors for centuries having a largely mystical, symbolic and priestly role, while secular power was invested in shoguns. In Islamic society, the caliph was not forced to share authority with anyone and had a dual religious and temporal role; he wore the mantle of the Prophet's authority. In China, the emperor was accepted as the mediator between the Middle Kingdom and the Divine, and had a mandate from Heaven; his position was underpinned by the belief that, with the assistance of learned advisers, he alone could perform the ceremonies and rituals necessary to the continued success of society. China was not a confessional state, but there was acceptance of the emperor's divine role which was founded on animist beliefs and traditions. There was no Church to support or thwart him, while the Confucian influence that came further to support his authority was not a religion but rather a philosophy that sought harmony and order in the relations between ruler and ruled, authority and subject, and past and present. Although simple subjects might confuse the position of emperors, who had a special sacerdotal role in being able to influence heavenly authority, Chinese and Japanese emperors were not gods.

The two related and overlapping conceptions of kingship, the priest and the warrior, could thus be contained in the one office or be divided into a dualism, sometimes harmonious, sometimes fractious. Even republics were affected by the tension between secular and religious authority with the Roman Republic, after the expulsion of the Tarquins, finding it necessary to maintain a *rex sacrorum* whose duties were confined to the carrying out of religious rites. The Dalai Lama of Tibet is often cited as coming closest to the early origins of kingship and to theocracy. He is held to possess unlimited spiritual and secular authority, as he is recognised as the reincarnation of Avolokitesvara, the legendary founder of Tibet. The Dalai Lama did not, however, become sovereign of Tibet until the middle of the seventeenth century, and Dalai Lamas shared power with the Panchen Lama and for a while with temporal kings. Such dualism was found in most states under Tibetan influence, such as Nepal, Sikkim and Bhutan, where the tradition was to have a spiritual and a temporal ruler. Even after the Gurkha conquest of Nepal and the coming of Hinduism rather than Buddhism as the dominant religion, this division was revived in the nineteenth century with the creation of hereditary Prime Ministers, the Ranas.

Religion reinforced monarchy and legitimised it, but it could also be a brake upon monarchical power. This has been held to be the case in India, where the combination of religion and a priestly caste, the Brahmins, has been seen as effectively limiting secular and kingly power. Even kings regarded as divine depended upon priests for all religious functions, and the social order was ordained by religion, with the result that 'politics, bereft of much opportunity to organise social life, had such shallow roots that it was fundamentally unstable'.[8] Although this view that the state in India was epiphenomenal is longstanding and was held, among others, by Marx and Weber, it has been challenged by Nicholas B. Dirks, who, using the small southern Indian kingdom of Pudukkottai as a detailed case study, has argued that its *Kallar* kings *ruled* and that the ideas 'of royal authority and honor, and associated notions of power, dominance and order' were well established.[9] Nevertheless, most Indian states and monarchies do seem to have been relatively weak and short-lived, and Indian civilisation has been united politically only three times, by the native Mauryans, the Muslim Mughal Empire and the British.

The principle by which a monarch came to be invested in his position was not always a clear-cut case of primogeniture within a hereditary system. The Islamic world came to be divided in the century after Muhammad between the majority view that successors should be chosen from among the companions of the Prophet by a process of acclamation (the view of the Sunni Muslims) and a minority (Shi'ite), which argued for direct hereditary descent within the Prophet's Umayyad clan. Islamic monarchy had, save under the strongest rulers, an ineradicable tendency to instability, whether under the early Arab caliphs or under the great sultanates which later ruled over the Ottoman Empire, India and Persia. One factor in this was the problem of succession. A hereditary system based upon primogeniture was difficult to establish when rulers had large numbers of wives and vast harems, and even the practice of fratricide by the established heir was unable to prevent challenges from within the dynasty. Indeed, most monarchies where kings were permitted a number of wives and concubines had succession problems. Native Chinese dynasties normally looked to the empress's eldest son as the heir, but the emperor had the right to nominate whomever he chose, while the Mongols originally chose their leader by election. In Europe, the hereditary principle was a medieval innovation, and even when the king's son was the heir he had to be acclaimed; Bohemia and Hungary long persisted with the election of kings, and, as late as the eighteenth century, Polish kings were elected. If the hereditary principle had the obvious disadvantage that the heir might make an unsuitable monarch, it had the advantage of being straightforward and of minimising the chances of struggles for the throne. Over time, it added to the charismatic and mystical qualities of kingship, making royalty a special caste above the greatest nobles.

At the core of monarchy as a model of civil authority over the last 1,000 years is the implicit assumption that one individual is somehow privileged over all other members of the population both to formulate and to enforce a vision of communal good, a set of collective values and a concept of social well-being. Often exercising judicial, administrative, legislative, priestly and military command, monarchy implied the existence of an irrevocable chasm between the maturity of the leader and the immaturity and natural incapacity of the subject.[10]

If it was, whether by primogeniture or a looser system of inheritance, the blood line that determined the privilege to rule, how was the purity of this line to be assured? Essentially, monarchies that had royal harems or numerous wives or concubines placed the stress upon the male line of descent. The mother of a future king or emperor might well be a slave-girl, and that the child was of the blood line had to be ensured by the close guarding of the king's wives and concubines by palace eunuchs. The general insistence in the Western world on the necessity for queens to be of royal blood was a more secure system for ensuring that heirs were royal in a general sense. There can be less doubt as to who someone's mother is than to who the father is, though the care taken to ensure that royal births were public and witnessed by officials and ministers, and the doubts expressed, for example, over the provenance of James II's son, the 'Old Pretender', demonstrate that even the maternal line can be questioned. In much of Africa it was the maternal line that was given priority. The aim in monarchies with kings and queens as in western Europe was, nevertheless, to ensure that an heir to the throne was clearly the offspring of their lawful union. The tale of King Candaules of Lydia, so proud of his queen's attractions that he exhibited her naked to his trusted general, Gyges, may be mythical, but the consequences – the murder of the King by the favourite, and the subsequent marriage of Gyges and the Queen and ascent to the throne of Gyges – demonstrate the necessity of guarding the sexual mystery of queens. Kings had to be careful that their consorts consorted only with them. By the eighteenth century the 'off with her head' fates of Anne Boleyn and Catherine Howard had given way to less severe penalties for the adultery of queens. George I's wife, Sophia Dorothea, and George III's sister, Queen Caroline of Denmark, both of whom were accused of adultery, were confined to the castle of Celle in Hanover; outside western Europe the punishment remained harsher.

The importance of the maternal line in many African societies and the universal importance attached to legitimacy via birth raise the important question of queens who rule, as opposed to queen consorts. Despite the suggestion that it was the priestess rather than the priest who exercised the real power and inspired awe in early human societies and the view that it was the female, she who gave birth, rather than the male, he who impregnated, which best symbolised fertility, the language and practice of monarchy have been predominantly male. If the notion that 'the king must die' in order that the fields might flourish and the crops grow while the queen bee continued to rule was ever widespread, it seems to have survived as at best a Jungian collective memory into the times of recorded history. We tend to talk of *kingship*, even though ruling queens have punctuated lines of male monarchs in many cultures. We have only to consider European history to be aware of the charisma of ruling queens: Queen Elizabeth I of England, Queen Christina of Sweden, Catherine the Great of Russia or Queen Victoria.

In many cultures the possibility of reigning queens was legally impossible, as with much of Europe where Salic law provided for the succession of males alone. Almost everywhere the primacy of male heirs made the accession of a queen an unusual occurrence, generally occasioned by the lack of male heirs, though there are several instances of the rule of widows. The traditional inequality of the sexes within monarchy largely reflected the relations between the sexes within societies and the realities of comparable physical strength where monarchs were expected to fulfil the role of warrior leaders. When a queen married, it would inevitably be to an inferior or a foreigner, and she would presumably come under his influence. Then there was the question of the priestly role of monarchs, which in many cultures ruled out females as less pure or otherwise unfitted for such a religious role. It is surprising in this regard that Japan, where the sacerdotal dimension of monarchy was so central, had eight empresses regnant and that one of the first *de facto* rulers of the nation as a whole was a woman known to Chinese chroniclers in the third century AD as Queen Himiko; it was not until 1889 that an Imperial House Law provided for the adoption of Salic law. Reigning females are scarce in the history of Islamic societies, but the Muslim Maldives had three women in succession on the throne between 1347 and 1388, while the Muslim port-state of Pasai in South-East Asia had a tradition of powerful queens. Indeed, two other Muslim states in southern Asia seem to have adopted a system of favouring queens, even in defiance of the hereditary system and the *Sharia* or Holy Law. It has been argued that the appeal of these female monarchs was that they encapsulated the charisma of kingship in the 'gunpowder empires' of South-East Asia without the bellicosity and tyranny,[11] but peace and order have not inevitably characterised the rule of queens. What seems evident is that queenship usually worked better when the queens were virgins or widows. Mighty male subjects could more easily give allegiance when there was no male consort around. As leaders in war, virgin queens or the widows of charismatic male rulers could be potent indeed. The image of the 'wicked queen' parallels that of the 'bad king', but it has been seen as more disturbing and is embedded in mythology and popular culture. The tyrannical queen was supposedly an unnatural inversion of femininity, and her transgression aroused fear and psychological antipathy. Whereas ruthlessness could be viewed as a necessary corollary of strength in a king, it could be portrayed as a more sinister quality when it characterised a queen.

As we have seen, the power of monarchs was on the whole greater in the East than in the West. This was true not only as regards the spiritual power of kings but as regards their power in relation to the nobility. Medieval kings were, in western Europe, part of a system based on the concept of mutual obligations, duties and loyalties between kings, nobles and knights. The realms of kings were often scattered, making central control difficult, and the terms on which they ruled might be different in different parts of their kingdoms. The nobility tended to enjoy a long and close association with their estates, which continued when dynasties ended. Towns had special privileges granted them by kings in charters, and if this usually made burghers loyal to the king as opposed to the great nobles of the locality, it also limited royal power. In contrast, the power of landlords was limited in China, in part by multiple inheritance, but also because with a change of dynasty estates were usually reallocated. While west European monarchs relied upon the nobility both for support in war and to maintain order in time of peace, Chinese emperors had what amounted to a vast civil service and bureaucracy to administer their dominions. Islamic states were usually organised upon military lines, with governors or pashas wielding great power, but deriving it personally from the sultan, and with many administrative posts being held by non-Islamic groups.

Throughout the world, all monarchs served in a sacral capacity until at least around AD 1500. Whether they ruled under a direct divine mandate or under spiritual leadership, they held their power as a divine gift. Ironically, in view of the close association of monarchy with religion, it was the decline in the power of the Church and the division of Christendom with the Protestant Reformation that provided the opportunity for west European kings to claim greater power. Kings not only attempted to enforce religious uniformity in their realms but laid claim to a divine right to rule, while some, as with the English monarchy, became heads of national churches. The early modern period saw a tendency for European monarchies to increase their power, not only at the expense of the Church but at the expense of the nobility as well.

With the rebirth of the territorial state and the development of the idea of political sovereignty, monarchical authority put an end to political and military feudalism. Claiming the monopoly of coercion, the dynasties presided over expanded standing armies and centralised bureaucracies loyal to the crown. They also secured the fiscal independence needed to pay for this large and growing state apparatus without excessively bending to the nobility.[12]

The idea of absolute monarchy represented two different developments: an increase in the aspirations of monarchy; and the improved communications, more efficient central administration and standing armies that facilitated these aspirations. The power of the state grew and the power of the monarch over the state grew with it. Absolute monarchy, associated most closely with Louis XIV of France, seems at first sight a simple concept, that there should be no limits to the power of the monarch, but even the proponents of absolute monarchy accepted that there were indeed limits, and drew a distinction between absolute and arbitrary power. Thus Jacques Benigne Bossuet, one of the great theorists of absolute monarchy, wrote that 'The Prince is accountable to none for what he commands', but went on to argue 'but it does not follow from this that the government is arbitrary since, besides everything being subject to the will of God, there are laws in states and anything done contrary to them is legally null'.[13]

Monarchy in seventeenth-century Europe was essentially a modernising force, anti-feudal and, to a degree, anti-aristocratic, while its opponents' ethos was a mixture of the defence of traditional and provincial and civic rights, joined, where religious cohesion had broken down, by different forms of protestant dissent. The Civil War in the British Isles and Ireland saw the monarchy challenged by a temporary alliance of these forces and led to the ultimate expression of disloyalty, the execution of a king. It is significant, however, that it was not parliament that demanded the trial of the monarch, still less his execution, but Cromwell and the commanders of the parliamentary army, plus the 'Rump' of the House of Commons, while the execution was widely regarded as an illegal and even sacrilegious act. Charles, as Robert Tombs has written, 'was to be more successful as a martyr than as a monarch'.[14]

There is an irony in the fact that the European monarchy that moved closest to absolute monarchy was at the end of the eighteenth century to be overthrown by revolution, while the monarchy that saw its efforts to increase royal power thwarted was to be the firm bastion against revolution. After the Glorious Revolution of 1688, Britain posited a very different model of monarchy from that of France. British monarchs ruled rather than merely reigned, but did so in conjunction with a powerful aristocracy and with the support of gentry and mercantile interests. What has been called the British 'military-fiscal state' had an economic dynamism and a military potential that relative to size and population exceeded that of France.

If an initial effect of the forces that we may loosely summarise as modernisation was to strengthen monarchy, these same forces would in the long run make monarchies in the West adapt to them. Because they resulted in an enormous increase in the power of Europe, these forces would threaten every aspect of civilisation elsewhere in the world, including systems of government. Secularisation, technological development and the relative decline of the importance of agriculture and the countryside as opposed to commerce and towns challenged the existing balances of economies and societies. Inevitably, they also challenged systems of government. Sovereignty and government came increasingly to be seen as contractual rather than divinely ordained within the most economically advanced states. At the same time western Europe moved from being defensive, embattled over centuries facing successive waves of actual or putative conquerors spilling out of Asia, to becoming aggressive and expansionist.

Despite the trauma of the French Revolution, the institution of monarchy proved resilient. Napoleon Bonaparte's Empire represented a new interpretation of monarchy, which was to prove both successful and influential. His was a truly modern monarchy, which skilfully wove meritocracy and tradition into a potent projection of both the Emperor and France. The Napoleonic Empire demonstrated the capacity of monarchical charisma to dampen animosities and reconcile past and present. If it looked forward to the dictatorships of the twentieth century with its centralism and its harnessing of nationalist feeling, there was also something of the ethos of Louis XIV's France about the Empire. At his most arrogant when he set up his relatives and generals as the monarchs of subsidiary states, he was at his most conservative when he secured a degree of royal legitimacy in marrying Marie Louise of Austria, joining a Habsburg lineage to a self-made monarchy. The temporary restoration of the Bourbons foundered on the anachronistic view of monarchy of Charles X, but France's subsequent history demonstrated the degree to which France was in symbolic and psychological disarray, torn between not simply monarchism and republicanism but a variety of pasts and allegiances, Republican, Legitimist, Orleanist and Bonapartist.

From henceforth, however, Western monarchies had to struggle with, adapt to or align themselves with social orders other than aristocracy and with the concept of the nation. Kingship continued to be imbued with charisma but had consciously to project such charisma to a wider audience. It was no longer enough to dazzle and impress small numbers of nobles and courtiers and be a distant if awesome figure to peasants who had a vague if vital image of their ruler. Subjects had to be turned into subject citizens who gave positive and conscious assent to king and state. The notion of its divine ordination did not disappear even in the most urbanised and industrialised societies, but it was increasingly harnessed by the ruler's bonds with the nation.

Historians have, in recent years, devoted considerable attention to the ways in which monarchies refashioned themselves during the course of the nineteenth and early twentieth centuries. The ceremonies and rituals of monarchy became more magnificent and public, capital cities became great theatres for the projection of kings and emperors and were designed for military reviews and triumphal progresses, while there was a new emphasis upon kings and emperors as the personification of the nation.

David Cannadine drew attention to this phenomenon in his study of the transformation and rituals of the British monarchy, and has been followed by T. Fujitani in his book on the Japanese monarchy and Maurizio Peleggi in his treatment of the refashioning of the Siamese monarchy.[15] All concur that this was part of a wider process by which states reached out to secure not just the obedience but the positive commitment of peoples to the nation and nation state. Modern states required such commitment and needed the populace to feel part of the wider community of the nation and to empathise with it through its symbols, rituals and ceremonies. Thus, republics as well as monarchies placed an enormous emphasis upon national flags and anthems, national days that saluted the nation's past victories and achievements and public buildings and monuments that crystallised the ethos of the state. In monarchies the kings and emperors were the centrepieces of such ritual and pageantry and had the added advantage of standing for continuity and succession, binding the nation's present to pasts real and imagined. Republicanism occurred when state and nation were seen as new-born and as rejecting what pasts they had, as with the United States and Latin America, or as with Switzerland, where it permitted a loose federation. Its great success was in the USA, where the ghosts of the British constitution became two houses and an elective, albeit transient, monarch, the President. That in general republicanism continued to be aberrant and monarchy remained the normal form of government was demonstrated by the appearance of new monarchies in eastern Europe in the wake of the shrinking Ottoman Empire. Here nations reborn, searching in mists for half-remembered and idealised pasts, found in kingship a suitable institution with which to symbolise their rebirths.

There can be little doubt as to the remodelling of monarchy on a world scale in the nineteenth century, but questions arise. Can we speak of it as the *invention* of tradition or was it merely a refashioning of state and monarchy to meet the needs of the modern age? The concept of invented tradition is supposedly an oxymoron and, as with the headmaster of a Victorian public school who is supposed to have announced that 'from tomorrow the tradition of the school will be …', trembles on the brink of absurdity. Yet, all traditions had presumably to have their beginnings. There may be only a fine line between the invention of a tradition and its considerable reworking, but the main innovations in the late modern period were essentially a reprojection of monarchy towards peoples as opposed to small elites. Royal rituals, whether religious or secular, had always been important, but had in sizeable states been witnessed by only the inner circles of power, with glimpses afforded to the populace of capital cities. Modern communications made it possible and modern socio-political contexts made it necessary to project on a grand and national scale. So far as the major ceremonies and rituals of monarchies are concerned, a thoroughgoing reworking of rituals already extant and in some cases revived seems more apposite than invention. Genuinely new rituals did, of course, emerge, especially in the context of royal relationships with the armed forces, as did new orders of chivalry and complex honours systems, and even new ranks of nobility, as with Meiji Japan's marquises and barons.

If the emergence of mass societies and the need to involve whole populations in the cause of national cohesion was a challenge to Western monarchies, the impact of an administratively, commercially and militarily superior West placed great strains upon states and their monarchies in the rest of the world. The declines of the Ottoman Empire and of imperial China were only the most spectacular examples of this process. It must be noted, however, that, as the power of Ottoman sultans declined, it was not only their erstwhile European subjects who opted for new monarchies, for their Muslim satraps, as in Egypt, sought to become monarchs in their own right. Eastern and African emperors, kings, princes and chiefs did not on the whole meet the spectacular and rapid demise of the Central and South American Aztec and Inca Empires in the sixteenth century. Some did disappear, as with the Kingdoms of Madagascar and Hawaii, the latter essentially deposed by the USA, but African kings and chiefs, like Indian princes and Indo-Chinese kings, retained degrees of autonomy under colonial rule. Others strove, like the Chinese emperors, alternatively to keep the Western powers at bay or to learn selectively from the West in order to defy it. Only Japan, forced out of its isolation by a US naval squadron under the command of Commodore Perry, was able rapidly to transform its economy and armed forces and become a great power on the Western model.

Nationalism posed problems for monarchies. In western Europe monarchy had traditionally been based on a relationship between rulers and subjects, with sovereigns often ruling over a heterogeneous collection of territories and nationalities. For the Habsburg Empire there could be no question of an alignment of monarchy and nation; indeed, the Empire's survival into the twentieth century was based on the older concept of emperor as above nations. The British, French and Spanish monarchies had, however, increasingly associated themselves with national feeling. The monarchies ruling the new united states of Italy and Germany were products of nationalism, though the German Empire was essentially a federation with the King of Prussia becoming Emperor, while the Kings of Bavaria, Wurtemberg, and Saxony retained their crowns. Everywhere in Europe, save in the Habsburg dominions, monarchs found it necessary to associate themselves with national identity. Elsewhere in the world, monarchy could associate itself with the defence of national culture and tradition in the face of Western hegemony or, as with Japan, be the means of importing Western ways under the mantle of an age-old institution.

Central and South America was the one area where monarchy disappeared, but the rapidity of its demise has been exaggerated. The connection of the Spanish and Portuguese monarchies with their Central and South American colonies was interrupted by the French Revolutionary Wars and Spain, much weakened, found control of its Latin American possessions opposed by nationalist movements. It was not at first clear what form of government would be adopted by the number of new states which emerged in the wake of successful revolts. Monarchy and Spanish rule were closely identified, while there was to the north the model of the USA, which, having achieved independence from Britain, had opted for a republic. It was, however, by no means certain that republics would become the normal form of government in Latin America and there were in America several influential proponents of monarchism and examples of attempts to form new monarchies.

Three centuries of Spanish rule had shaped society and government along authoritarian and aristocratic lines, and there was little basis for democratic government or liberal institutions. It was soon apparent that Spanish rule had been replaced by strong personal leadership in the form of either dictatorships or elected presidents, who, once established, tended to rule for extended terms and even, as in Paraguay and Guatemala, establish home-grown dynasties. Such leaders had a flimsy legitimacy, their governments were often unstable and there was usually a crisis of succession. In these circumstances there were many who felt that, if monocratic rule was the only option, monarchy would be the better version, as it would solve the problems of legitimacy and would be in harmony with tradition. General José de San Martin, the Argentinian hero of independence, supported monarchist proposals in Argentina and Peru during the struggle for independence, and even Simon Bolivar was attracted by the possibility of monarchies.[16] The problems monarchists faced, however, were that independence had been achieved *from* a monarchy and that kings were difficult to find. Princes of the Spanish house were tainted by association with the old regime (though overtures were made to them), while Britain discouraged overtures to British royals and, in any case, non-Spanish princes would not fit in culturally.

Despite the fiasco of the brief reign of Augustin de Inturbide, who had himself crowned Augustin I, monarchism lingered in Mexico; General Mariano Paredes planned a monarchy in the 1840s, and this was followed by the ill-fated reign of Emperor Maximilian in the 1860s, which ended with this Habsburg facing a firing squad, and finally put an end to the aspirations of Mexican monarchists. General Juan José Flores and Garcia Moreno were involved in various clandestine monarchist projects for Ecuador, Peru and Bolivia in the 1840s and 1850s, but the failure of their schemes and the end of Maximilian's venture in Mexico saw the end of monarchism as a serious option in Spanish America.[17]

Portuguese America had a different and happier history, for the endurance of monarchy in Brazil until 1889 made for a more harmonious relationship with the colonial past and for relatively peaceful development. The emigration of the Portuguese Regent (later King John VI) and the court to Rio de Janeiro in 1807 in the face of the threat to the monarchy from Napoleon inverted the previous order and made a 'tropical Versailles' the centre of the Portuguese Empire.[18] This development proved a spur to Brazil's economic progress. The British Royal Navy had escorted the Regent to Brazil, and under British pressure the country's ports were open to free trade, thus encouraging trade with Europe and leading to Brazil becoming Latin America's largest exporter by the mid-nineteenth century. Brazil became an independent monarchy in 1822. John VI returned to Portugal, but his son Dom Pedro became Emperor of Brazil. The continued rule by the royal house did much to ensure that a country with a considerable slave population and with an enormous divide between rich and poor enjoyed a degree of stability. The legitimacy that came with monarchy ensured the qualified support of the Brazilian land-owning elite, but Emperor Pedro abdicated in 1831 after military failure in the war to prevent Paraguay becoming independent and dissatisfaction among the elite at the Emperor's desire to put an end to the slave trade. It was the attempt by his son, Emperor Pedro II, to abolish slavery without compensation to slave owners that forced his abdication in 1889 after a *coup d'état* by ambitious army officers and disaffected plantation owners. That there was little opposition to the overthrow of the monarchy suggests that it enjoyed little real support, though it might be more accurate to say that it had lost the support of key elite groups.

Its lack of monarchies, save for the Dominion of Canada, made the American continent the exception in a world dominated by monarchies. Any survey of the world's governments in 1900 had to begin with monarchy as the first word in the vocabulary. Kingship, which had been common to humanity since the beginning, was still all but universal. Monarchy might be qualified as constitutional or autocratic, but kings reigned throughout much of the world. All the scientific, rational, utilitarian and mechanistic outlook associated with modern Europe had failed to budge monarchy. It flourished amid mass societies with their newspapers and football teams as well as in the peasant economies of Asia. The new century would put it to the test.

PART ONE

A WORLD FIT FOR KINGS

1

THE FAR EAST: CELESTIAL EMPIRES

As we have seen, all monarchies have had a spiritual or religious dimension. Kings were not just symbolic figures, representative of the peoples and cultures they ruled over, but were held to connect the fate of their peoples with the divinity or the cosmos. Nowhere was this aspect of monarchy more pronounced than in the Far East and in the Chinese and Japanese Empires, yet the two monarchies developed in very different ways. In both the priestly roles of the monarchs were pronounced, with the rituals they alone could perform seen as essential to the prosperity of their realms, but while in China the sacerdotal aspects of the emperors reinforced and went hand in hand with executive authority and autocratic power, in Japan the emperors, for great stretches of Japanese history, were confined to a priestly and cultural role, with executive authority lodged in other hands.

Both imperial systems claimed origins in times before recorded history. China is the world's oldest civilisation, and its monarchical system was inextricable from its continuous existence over more than 3,500 years. The history of the

Chinese emperors can be traced from the times of the Shang dynasty, later named Yin, of northern China, which existed, though the dates are contestable, from the eighteenth to the twelfth centuries BC. There was, however, a misty and largely mythical tradition of powerful rulers existing long before the Shang, the five rulers of 2852–2205.

Japanese claims as to the origins of kingship were more extravagant. The Chronicles of the eighth century tell of the Sun Goddess (*Amaterasu Ōmikami*) who sent the God-child, Jimmu, to rule Japan. Descending to the island of Kyushu, he conquered the East and established his capital in Yamato. In theory, therefore, Japanese emperors not only enjoyed the mandate of the Gods and were able to intercede with them, but were descended from them.

A significant distinction between the Chinese and Japanese monarchies is that, while the Chinese monarchy had an institutional continuity – dynasties came and went and some of them were dynasties imposed by foreign conquerors – the Japanese have had, theoretically, only one dynasty, an umbilical cord connecting the monarchy to the very origins of the people and the beginnings of time. A second distinction is the greater perseverance among the elite as well as the common people of animist traditions. In Japan Shinto placed an extraordinary emphasis upon purity, and a complementary emphasis upon the removal of impurities, in which the emperor, who could intercede with the spirits, had a unique role.

In China, the symbolic and religious significance of the emperors, who were held to be in communication with divine forces, was crucial to the cohesion of the vast territory and population of the Middle Kingdom. The idealised and sacerdotal position of the ruler was firmly established during the reigns of the later kings of Zhou. This position continued to reflect nature and ancestor worship and the need to keep society in harmony with the universe, the stars and planets.

It received further and distinctive support from the teachings of Confucius (traditional dates 551–479 BC), who saw the monarch as reigning under the mandate of Heaven and in accordance with a morality and code of behaviour that made for a stable society.

The continuities of a Chinese kingdom or empire were never given. The tensions between imperial rule and centrifugal tendencies were always evident, and the early history of China is one of contending rulers and peoples. The first regime that could claim to be the sole effective authority in China was that of the King of Qin, who by 221 BC had forced all other kings to submit to him and adopted the title *Huangdi*, usually translated as 'Emperor'. Under the short-lived Qin and the succeeding Han dynasty, institutions and practices that would continue to mark imperial rule into modern times were developed: cadres of officials; the standardisation of economic practices; the enforcement of imperial laws throughout the land; and the attempt to establish secure frontiers. There followed, however, the 'centuries of disunity', a time of competing kingdoms, fragmented authority and internecine warfare, that lasted from the third to the sixth century AD.

Invasion by non-Chinese peoples was another threat to the stability of China and the continuity of the imperial throne. Under the Tang dynasty, Chinese frontiers grew wider, despite external threats. The population of China was and was to remain overwhelmingly composed of the Han people, but conquests on the perimeter were usually maintained by reliance on non-Chinese regional commissioners and troops who made uneasy subordinates and were a potential source of rebellions. After the deposition of the last of the Tang emperors in 907, there followed a further period of disunity in which short-lived dynasties struggled for power. The Song dynasty (960–1127) proved incapable of holding the north, and though it survived in the south for a further century and a half, non-Chinese rulers held the north-east and north-west. With Mongol invasion came the first foreign invaders capable not only of setting up a northern kingdom but of establishing themselves in the south as well. The Yuan dynasty (1279–1368) set up by Kublai Khan left a permanent impression upon China, a capital in the north-east that was to become Beijing, and territorial and administrative divisions that survive in the People's Republic. The long period of the Ming dynasty (1368–1644), founded in the south, ended with a further invasion from the north. The new invaders, the Manchu, established China's last imperial dynasty, the Qing ('Pure') which was to endure into the twentieth century.

What characterised the Chinese Empire through all the centuries of internal division and foreign invasion was a continuity in the essentials of the imperial system. Even foreign dynasties repeatedly reinvented the status, duties and style of the emperor, just as they maintained similar administrative systems and did not seek to disrupt the social order.

The institutions of government and administration were developed and refined. The Song period in particular was one of institutional innovation in which the monarchical state became more centralised, autocratic and professional in its administration. The opportunities for imperial absolutism had been increased by the decline of the aristocracy, which had been much weakened during the wars and rebellions during and after the reigns of the later Tang emperors. The absence of a powerful landed aristocracy facilitated the enhancement of the position of emperors. Their lives became ever more ritualised and formal, and their distance from even the higher classes increased. There was nothing of the *primus inter pares* about the position of the emperor, no reliance upon feudal vassals, no acclamation by the warriors, no uneasy relationship with a Church and no concept of a law above or separate from the imperial will. The Song, Yuan and Ming periods therefore witnessed the development and refinement of characteristics that were already pronounced, the perfection of a system rather than any radical departures from it.

There were both religious and secular reasons for this persistence. There was a continued belief in the divine appointment of emperors and their enjoyment of a heavenly mandate. The power of the emperor was held to be unlimited, and there was no body of law and no ecclesiastical or secular authority to challenge his power. He was indeed the father of his people, the patriarchal head of a patrilineal society.

Emperors were, in many ways, hardly regarded as persons. In all monarchical systems the symbolic nature of the king or emperor was significant in that the character of his realm was inherent in him and its fortunes entrusted to him, but in China the symbolism almost obscured the living being with his capabilities and weaknesses. There are indeed few biographies of Chinese emperors. The mystical position of the emperor was a source of great strength, for he alone could perform the rituals necessary to ensure fertility and security. The perseverance of animist traditions contrasted with the inability of any organised religion to secure the adherence of the whole of society and establish itself as a counterweight to imperial authority. Religion in China had to be essentially quietist; tolerated so long as it eschewed pretensions to come between emperor and people; sternly chastised when it forgot its place. Confucian beliefs and tenets further buttressed the imperial position, considering submission and obedience to the emperor as part of a moral order in which respect for the head of the family was central.

Unlike Western rulers, Chinese emperors had no turbulent aristocracies to rely on, cater for and fear, and no popes or other prelates to challenge their authority. There was therefore no need to turn to towns or merchants as counterweights to aristocratic or ecclesiastical influence. As Barrington Moore has commented:

> Imperial Chinese society never created an urban trading and manufacturing class comparable to that which grew out of the latter stages of feudalism in Western Europe, though at times there were some starts in this direction. Imperial success in uniting the country can be advanced as one of the more obvious reasons for the difference. In Europe the conflict between Pope and Emperor, between kings and nobles, helped the merchants in the cities to break through the crust of the traditional agrarian society because they constituted a valuable source of power in this many-sided competition.[1]

Moore's diagnosis may underestimate the degree to which trading skills, particularly in south China, existed and were honed. The success of twentieth-century Shanghai and Hong Kong and the all-too-evident domination of economic life by the Chinese diaspora in parts of South-East Asia suggest a long history of engagement in commerce. He is clearly right, however, in suggesting that commerce was undervalued and even resented in imperial China, that Confucian ethics rather despised the merchant and that the state did little to encourage or protect townsmen and business. There was no tradition of urban or city rights and legal privileges such as characterised the development of towns in Europe.

Landowners owed the titles of their land to the imperial government, and rather than the government being dependent on the support of landowners, it was they who depended on the government. Mandarins bought land with the rewards for their work for government, but those who inherited land usually needed to pass examinations to prove their gentility and could hope to further increase income and landholding by being given an imperial post. Partible inheritance was a further barrier to the rise of mighty landowners.

The very size of China and the problems of its agrarian economy favoured the imperial system, with its ability in good times not only to ensure order but to undertake great public works. The need for water-control systems for transport, irrigation and the prevention of flooding worked in favour of a centralised government and bureaucracy. While European monarchs struggled to free themselves in the early modern period from dependency on mighty aristocratic subjects on whose support their predecessors had relied upon and had their power limited by, Chinese emperors ruled by means of a bureaucracy that penetrated into every corner of the Empire, while, as officials were regularly moved from post to post, there was little chance that they could establish local power bases.

The major problem of all regimes in both East and West was how to raise sufficient money by taxation to maintain the court, expand government and pay armies. The Chinese had devised a more effective system than Western monarchies. The latter might elevate humble subjects – Cardinal Wolsey, Thomas Cromwell or Colbert – as their administrators and taxation overlords, appoint their tax farmers and find new goods to tax, but the imperial Chinese bureaucracy with its legions of officials was a much more effective instrument.

A class of officials, drawn mainly from the elite with leisure enough to prepare for a complex examination process but open to the occasional bright son of a poor family, had an ethos and identity in which cultural pride, elitism, corporate spirit and loyalty to the font of patronage and the guarantor of continuity and stability provided faithful servants of the regime. This class provided the maintenance of law and order, the implementation of imperial decrees, the architects and administrators of great schemes and the collection of taxes. They were not, for the most part, well paid, and were therefore corrupt, but provided the corruption was retail rather than wholesale, provided the peasants were not squeezed so hard that they would revolt, and provided the tax gatherers handed over sufficient to the imperial treasury, the system worked rather well.

Chinese ethics and practice placed a great emphasis upon stability. China's frontier problems and the threat of invasion from central Asia were not dissimilar to Europe's perennial problem of invasion by the same nomadic hordes from the East. The great size of China, its cultural superiority and its numerous population made it an effective bulwark against such incursions: it could occasionally be conquered, but its ethnic homogeneity, social structure and culture remained substantially intact. To concentrate upon invasions or even periods of internal instability underestimates the much longer periods of internal peace.

Under the early Ming emperors, China reached the apogee of its civilisation. Active emperors promulgated reforms and closely scrutinised the activities of the civil service. Although southern in origin, the Ming established the capital at Beijing, building a complex of palaces that Western monarchs could not hope to emulate. The early fifteenth century saw great imperial naval expeditions to India, Africa and South-East Asia. Significantly, however, the Ming Empire soon lost interest in the outside world and adopted a defensive posture to it. China seemed at the height of its superiority to the rest of the world, a gilded, stable and harmonious civilisation. A central question, however, is whether equilibrium, stability and harmony created a sort of steady-state civilisation that lacked capacity for further development. To contemporary Chinese such a question would have seemed inappropriate. Harmony, balance and a sort of perfection had been achieved. Developments taking place far away in barbaric Europe were, at the best, like the clocks brought by Jesuit missionaries, amusing but unimportant.

The fall of the Ming dynasty came not at the hands of distant Europe but from a more familiar quarter. Invaded by the Manchu, who in common with the Mongols were nomadic warriors from the north-east, the last Ming emperor hanged himself in the palace grounds at Beijing and the imperial throne was taken over by a new Manchu dynasty. As tended to be the pattern with new dynasties, early emperors were dynamic and forceful individuals. A conquering foreign administration, the Manchu imposed themselves on China, maintained their armies of Manchu bannermen and matched every senior Chinese official with a Manchu shadow. The queue and the kow-tow symbolised the elevation of the emperor and the Manchu as a whole above their Chinese subjects, while Manchu conceptions of monarchy reinforced the autocratic power of the emperor. As ever, the new regime had nevertheless to adapt itself to the ways and traditions of the vast country it presided over, though some historians have, in recent years, argued that the assimilation of the Manchus has been exaggerated.[2]

The power, dignity and separation from ordinary mortals of the long-lived Emperor Kangxi (1662–1722) is effectively summarised by Jonathan D. Spence:

> the mediator between heaven and earth, in Chinese terms the 'Son of Heaven', who ruled the 'central country'. Much of his life had to be spent in ritual activity: at court audiences in the Forbidden City, offering prayers at the temple of heaven, attending lectures by court scholars on the Confucian classics, performing sacrifices to his Manchu ancestors in the shamanic shrines. When he was not on his travels, he lived in the magnificent palaces in or near Peking, surrounded by high walls and guarded by tens of thousands of troops. Almost every detail of this life emphasised his uniqueness and superiority to lesser mortals: he alone faced south, while his ministers faced the north; he alone wrote in red while they wrote in black ...[3]

Just as China succumbed to conquest from central Asia, western Europe, armed with newly developed military technology and efficiently administered fighting forces, was bringing to an end its own vulnerability to the long cycle of threats from nomadic peoples. The triumph of the West was imminent and was to bring down imperial China. More than a century separated the haughty reception of the British mission led by Lord McCartney in 1793 and the last desperate attempts by the Dowager Empress Cixi to modernise a regime, now clearly subordinate to the Western powers, a few years before the final fall of the imperial system in 1911. The intervening period saw successive humiliations in the face of Western military and technological superiority, limitations upon Chinese sovereignty as colonies and treaty ports were established along the coastline, messianic internal rebellions and unsuccessful attempts to modernise along Western lines.

By the beginning of the twentieth century, it was becoming clear that the mandate of Heaven had been withdrawn from the Manchu or Qing dynasty. The effective ruler of China from 1861 – when her husband, the Emperor Xianfeng, died – until her death in 1908, was the Dowager Empress, Cixi. This era was one of dark melodrama and steep decline. Perhaps the wickedness of the 'Old Buddha' has been exaggerated by princes, officials and generals, only too pleased to blacken the name of the strong woman they feared. It remains a fact that all who stood in her way, including her own son Tongzhi, were killed or met mysterious deaths, and that until the last years of her life she was an implacable opponent of reform and westernisation. It is also the case that features of the imperial system that had always threatened its efficiency, the many wives and concubines, the lack of a clear line of succession in the absence of primogeniture and the influence of powerful eunuchs, made the court a hot-house of intrigue, decadence and cruelty.

Perhaps the last chance for the Qing dynasty came with Emperor Guangxu's reform programme in 1898. Conservative forces prevailed and the Emperor became virtually the prisoner of his aunt, the Empress Cixi, who once more became Regent. The occupation of Beijing by the army of the great powers that crushed the anti-foreign Boxer rebellion marked the further humiliation of China and caused the Empress finally to change course and embrace reform. By the time of her death in 1908, a constitution had been promised, Western dress been adopted by officials and the military and the 2,500-year-old examination system abolished. The end of the examination system in 1904 was crucial, for examinations had been the sinews that connected the imperial government and the regional elites.[4] This rush of reforms was too sudden, too late and perhaps too little considered. In any case, the regime had long lost real support.

The revolution of 1911 saw the end of Qing rule with the deposition of the child-emperor Puyi. It may well be that the alien aspects of the Qing regime meant that, once its authority was in question, its lack of support among the mass of Chinese quickened its end. Heaven having withdrawn its approval, it would have been in accordance with precedent for a new dynasty to have emerged. The impact of the West had, however, discredited not just the dynasty, not just the rule of the disliked Manchu, but the age-old monarchy itself.[5]

It would be simplistic to blame successive emperors and their advisers for the lengthy diminuendo of imperial China. It was the very strength of Chinese culture and tradition that proved its weakness, and there were no obvious constituencies for reforms along Western lines. Students, technocrats, westernised intellectuals and businessmen enjoyed little popular sympathy. Populist movements tended to be xenophobic. It was, perhaps, impossible to reform a proud civilisation, but, certainly, any reform programme with a chance of success would have had to come from above. A foreign dynasty, dependent on a bureaucracy, which had become ossified and corrupt, was in no position to implement one.

China was not alone in her unsuccessful attempts to preserve her institutions and culture and yet strive for modern armies with which to defend them. There are parallels with the Ottoman Empire, and even with that Empire's enemy, Tsarist Russia. The Korean Kingdom, for long a Chinese satellite, shadowed China in her decline. The great exception was, of course, imperial Japan.

Why was Japan the odd man out, the only country to experience a comparatively smooth adoption of Western technology, methods of administration and even aspects of the Western mindset, without enormous dislocation, large-scale civil war and rebellion or national trauma? The paradox of Japan is the combination of strong national feeling and the ability to adapt. The Japanese monarchy played a crucial role in the process of adaptation.

Japan was aware earlier than China of the dangers of the West. For all Japanese pride in ancestry and uniqueness, Japan was not the Middle Kingdom but a collection of islands on the outer periphery of the Chinese Empire. Like Korea, Japan was for centuries a tributary power of China's, 'even if Japan's incorporation into the tributary system was more ambiguous than Korea's'.[6] It had managed to absorb Chinese characters and Confucianism and learn to drink tea with even more ceremony than eighteenth-century English ladies. What was remarkable was that it was Japan's most ancient and revered institution, its imperial dynasty, which was to provide the mechanism for an accommodation of Western influence.

Sharing with China the lack of any independent or rival religious authority to their claims, the Japanese emperors were the source of the highest religious as well as, in theory, the highest secular authority. They never achieved, however, the degree of centralised control over their realms that Chinese emperors often enjoyed and ruled over powerful clans whose leaders had considerable autonomy. Many historians have seen the Japanese socio-political structure as close to European feudalism, with strong lord–vassal relationships on top of a rural peasantry that made up the vast majority of the population.

The contrast with China is that the mandate of Heaven was never withdrawn from the Japanese imperial dynasty, though their earthly power was for centuries almost non-existent. As David Montgomery Earl has argued:

> According to Chinese theory and practice, the sovereign might be removed or the dynasty changed under certain conditions. In Japanese theory, on the other hand, regardless of how unreasonable the sovereign might be, the subjects could never forget their duty to act as subjects. Although this rule was partly vitiated in practice by forced abdications, there was no recorded instance of dynastic change in Japanese history.[7]

In China there were many changes of dynasty, but emperors ruled while, for well over a thousand years until the late nineteenth century, secular power in Japan tended to be vested in hands other than the emperor's. In 794 Emperor Kammu commissioned the first *Sei-i-tai-shogun*, or 'Barbarian-quelling General'. Kammu himself never allowed holders of this title to detract from his authority, but in the ninth century the powerful Fujiwara family took over much of the emperor's executive power, and during the Kamakura period (1192–1333) Japan was dominated by the Minamoto clan. Yorimoto Minamoto was the first shogun to hold the office for life and to make it hereditary. During the Ashikaga Shogunate (1338–1573) Japan experienced a period of endemic civil war, which has been compared to England's Wars of the Roses. The latter part of this turbulent period coincided with European penetration into south Asia and the introduction of muskets and cannon. It was brought to an end by the decisive victories won by Tokugawa Ieyasu, who initiated a shogunate that lasted for two and a half centuries.

The Tokugawa period saw an extraordinary effort to isolate Japan in an attempt to create a stable society. Essentially a conservative regime, the Tokugawa sought to preserve the social hierarchy and in particular the positions of the nobility, or *daimyo*, and the *samurai*. They also sought to centralise political authority and preserve internal peace. Comparisons have been made between the 'absolute monarchy' of Louis XIV and the Shogunate of the Togukawa period: both extended central power and forced the nobility to be resident for long periods at the courts of Versailles or Edo respectively.

Emperors remained important, and indeed essential, to the regime because of their enormous symbolic and religious significance, but the shogunate, or *bakufu* (shogunal government), ruled. Exactly what the justification for a hereditary shogunate was was a vexed question, and one that it was dangerous to ask for most of the Tokugawa period. Was the shogun a legitimate ruler in his own right, with the emperor a revered figure who should not concern himself with government? This was the theory favoured during the years when the Shogunate was most powerful and secure. Was the emperor the rightful sovereign and the shogun his deputy or proxy? The question few dared to ask openly until the last years of the Shogunate was whether the Tokugawa had usurped the emperor's position.

In the long run the attempt to stabilise and control the semi-feudal system faltered on the very success of the Tokugawa in maintaining a long period of peace and prosperity. In such circumstances the very *raison d'être* of the *samurai* and the feudal position of the *daimyo* became obsolete, while peace and the spending power of a nobility enjoying aristocratic privilege but with fewer duties made for an increase in the numbers and wealth of a merchant class. There was a slow erosion of authority, but there is little reason to believe that, had it not been for the jolt to Japan's esteem delivered by Commodore Perry's 'black ships' in 1853 and the subsequent forced opening of Japan to Western influence and commerce, the Tokugawa Shogunate would have been in any danger of collapse.

As it was, the regime was fatally weakened by the humiliation of having to accept unequal treaties. The fall of the *bakufu* in 1868 was largely the result of its inability to cope with foreign pressure. The alliance of forces that brought the Shogunate to an end included many who wished to reject Western influence and Western ways. The 'restoration' of the emperor's political authority could well be seen as a conservative measure invoking the very spirit of Japanese identity and tradition. Yet the relatively peaceful revolution was followed by the abolition of the old feudal structure and purposeful moves towards modernisation. As Hugh Cortazzi has put it:

> In the 1850s it seemed to some observers that Japan might, like most other oriental states, succumb to western pressures and become a colonial or semi-colonial dependency. Yet by 1894 equality of status with the western powers had been largely achieved.[8]

The Japanese achievement in the final decades of the nineteenth century was indeed remarkable. The role of the monarchy was essential to its success. The emperor embodied *kokutai*, an inner or mystical force that bound the Japanese together and underlay Japan's distinctiveness. That Japan's programme of modernisation on Western lines was implemented under the authority of the emperor was crucial in ensuring that conservative opposition was muted.

The restoration was, however, the work not of the emperor but of a group of able young *daimyo* and *samurai*, who realised the necessity of transforming Japan. It has been argued that Japan's previously 'feudal' structure made it more promising ground for rapid modernisation than bureaucratic China.[9] A further factor was the relative sophistication of the pre-industrial economy. Japan may have had a 'rice and merchant economy', but it would not be too inapposite to describe the eighteenth-century British economy as a 'corn and merchant economy'. The point is that both were well-developed pre-industrial economies, the major precondition for becoming successful industrial economies. Nothing, however, completely explains the vigour and vitality of a ruling elite, or at least a section of it, that was radical enough to make a revolution from above. Men like Ito Hirobumi, sometimes called 'Japan's Bismarck', Okubo Toshimichi, who transformed the image of the emperor, and Iwakura Tomomi, who led Japan's fact-finding mission to Europe in 1871, took a conservative revolution, whose watchword was 'revere the Emperor and destroy the barbarians', and turned it into a radical movement dedicated to 'civilisation and reform'.

Marxist historians convinced of the need for a bourgeois revolution as a precursor of modernisation have seen the modernisation/Westernisation of Japan as flawed by its top-down nature and, in particular, by the centrality of the new emphasis upon the authority of the emperor. Yet, the emperor with his redefined position was central to the creation of a new Japan, a Japan that founded a dynamic present upon a semi-mythical past. An influential analysis of the Meiji Restoration has seen a process of pure invention at work, a deliberate creation of national myths so as to forge a modern nation. T. Fujitani has claimed that in the Tokugawa period:

> the common people's knowledge of the emperor, potentially the most powerful symbol of the Japanese nation, was non-existent, vague, or fused with folk beliefs in deities who might grant worldly benefits but who had little to do with the nation. Thus, the leaders of the Meiji regime needed novel and powerful means of channelling the longings of the people for a better world and the inchoate and scattered sense of identity as a people in the direction of modern nationalism.[10]

To claim that the common people had no knowledge of the emperor seems rash. That their knowledge was both vague and fused with folk beliefs seems likely. Knowledge of their king in medieval and even early modern European villages was probably such, but no less potent for being so. It seems likely that the architects of the Meiji Restoration of 1868 reinterpreted the national past, synthesised folk beliefs into a suitable historic framework and reified useful myths. The Meiji statesmen made use of the arguments of some late Tokugawa scholars that the emperor's powers had been wrongly taken from him by the shoguns, and the superficial manifestations of the restoration, the new ubiquity and visibility of the emperor clad in European uniform, suggested an emperor who ruled. Their brilliant insight was, however, that the emperor's spiritual authority could be projected as the essence of a new national consciousness. The monarchy continued in Richard Storry's words to be '"above the clouds" – in other words above the storm and stress of daily government', and emperors 'whatever their powers have been in theory, have acted only on the advice of ministers and officials'.[11]

The centrepiece of the restoration, Emperor Mutsuhito, better known by his reign name, the Emperor Meiji, was an unlikely candidate for a movement that would see Japan import many Western ways. Only 16 years old when he came to the throne, he revered his father, the Emperor Komei, who hated all foreigners and had the traditional imperial Kyoto upbringing, the syllabus of which was culture, religion and ritual. Yet within a short time he was on a horse and in Western-style uniform, had a Western haircut, had stopped blackening his teeth, and appeared the very model of a major modern monarch.

To some degree, the position of the emperor was, indeed, westernised rather than restored, but the process reconciled Western ways with Japanese spirit. The Meiji constitution of 1889 was formally a gift from the Emperor, and articles promulgated the unique nature of the Japanese people and the divine nature of the imperial house. Yet the very notion of a constitution was a Western innovation, and there was much borrowing from the constitution of the German Empire, with the Emperor being given a special authority over the armed forces and reserved powers when it came to declarations of war and the conclusion of treaties.

The changes that accompanied the Meiji Restoration were profound. They involved a reinterpretation of Japanese identity, the turning of Shinto into a state religion and, above all, an emphasis upon the emperor as the fount of all authority and the embodiment of the essence of the nation. A major question is whether these changes should be seen as a refurbishment of the symbols and icons of the nation and an insistence upon an official version of the nation's past, or whether, as has been claimed, the changes amounted to the invention by the ruling elite of a new Japan complete with new traditions.[12]

A problem for all governments in the age of the nation state has been the need to engage the bulk of the population, hitherto often peasants with horizons limited to the village or locality, in the concept of the nation. From the late nineteenth century, state after state found it necessary to assist the developing 'imagined communities' by an emphasis upon national flags and symbols, the designing of national rituals and the observance of national days and festivals. The turning of peasants into Frenchmen was assisted by the tricolour, Marianne and Bastille Day, just as the turning of immigrants into Americans was assisted by venerating the Stars and Stripes and the celebration of Thanksgiving. In monarchies there was an enhancement of the ceremonial surrounding the monarch, an emphasis upon coronations, royal weddings and funerals and the beginning of regular royal visits to all corners of the realms.

In Japan it was necessary to build national consciousness in a previously decentralised society, to make outlying provinces associate with state and nation and bring peasants with varied folk beliefs into a nation with a standardised set of institutions and a single self-image. Central to this nation building was the dissemination of the image of the emperor. Ancient ceremonies were refashioned, new imperial rituals developed, and great state ceremonies organised. At the centre of the most important was the figure of the emperor:

> From the late 1880s … the Meiji regime's public rituals took on their full-blown modern form, with Tokyo and to some extent Kyoto used as central and open stages for a dazzling new assortment of imperial pageants. All of these were influenced by western models, even the most archaic looking of them, and some of them – such as imperial weddings and wedding anniversary celebrations – had no precedent whatever in the ceremonial vocabulary. The most spectacular pageants of the late nineteenth and early twentieth centuries included celebrations of political accomplishments such as the promulgation of the Meiji Constitution, war victory ceremonials, and imperial funerals, weddings and wedding anniversaries.[13]

It is important, however, not to see the refurbishment of the Japanese monarchy as unique in terms of the international tendency to remodel the style and ritual of monarchies that has been discerned in the nineteenth century. Nor should we see this broader nineteenth-century development as unique in the long history of monarchy. Monarchies have always acted as important agents of cultural transmission, both in the way they have imported ideas, fashions and art forms from abroad and in their role in assisting popular cultural forms to rise and become part of court culture, while, conversely, the cultural fashions of the court have moved downwards and become embedded in popular culture. What was special about the transformation of the Japanese monarchy was the rapidity and radical nature of the change and the brilliance and daring of a project that used the institution that embodied the very essence of Japanese tradition to persuade Japan to open itself to Western ways.

Okubo Toshimichi is said to have seen Louis XIV's monarchical style as a suitable model for an intermediary stage that would be followed by constitutional monarchy.[14] After Okubo's assassination, however, the initiative passed to Ito Hirobumi, whose model was that of the 'social monarchy' developed by Lorenz von Stein, a monarchy that would:

> arbitrate the competing interests of different groups in society, that is, would personify the general will and remain 'transcendentally' above the class struggle, preventing the exploitation of the weak by the strong and ensuring social harmony.[15]

The borrowings for the new Japanese style of monarchy must be regarded as eclectic. In its transitional stage there were bizarre contradictions with the Emperor's consort, the childless Empress Haruko, taking on many of the attributes of a Western consort, while there continued the practice of highborn concubines being in rotation serviced by the Emperor in order to provide successors to the throne. It was not until the time of Emperor Hirohito that such an oriental practice was discontinued. Full of contradictions and contrasts, at once a symbol of an embroidered national consciousness and imported institutions and rituals from various European monarchies, the transformed monarchy was successful as the guardian and personification of the new Japan.

The incredible success of Japan's efforts to modernise her economy and institutions led to a position at the beginning of the twentieth century where Japan was no longer vulnerable in the face of Western expansion but was almost an honorary Western power and a potent and militarily formidable force.

Japan's victory in the Sino-Japanese War of 1894–5, her part in the suppression of the Boxer Rising, her alliance with Britain in 1902, her victory over Russia in the war of 1904–5 and the annexation of Korea in 1910 all marked Japan's progressive moves to great-power status.

Japan can be said to have become not only a great power but a colonial power by 1914, absorbing the Kingdom of Ryukyu and its major island, Okinawa, in 1878, annexing Taiwan in 1895 and firmly established in Manchuria after the Russo-Japanese War. This expansion was achieved at the expense of China and Russia and with the acquiescence of Britain and the USA. Faced with a choice between becoming an ally of the Western powers or a defender of Asian powers against the expansionist West, Japan opted for the former. During a visit to Japan in 1881, King Kalakaua of Hawaii suggested the formation of a league of Asian powers headed by Japan to guard against the hegemony of European powers, and a marriage between his niece and chosen successor, Princess Lili'uokalani, and the Japanese Prince Sadamaro. The Emperor Meiji turned down both proposals.[16] It was to be some sixty years before Kalakaua's suggestion was partially taken up with the Japanese plan for a Greater Asia Co-prosperity Sphere drawn up in 1941.

The enhanced glory of the Japanese monarchy can be contrasted with the demise of the Chinese monarchy, in which Japan played a part, and the end of the Korean monarchy, for long China's satellite, for which Japan was directly responsible. There were great similarities between the Chinese and Korean monarchies: a court of concubines and eunuchs, Confucianism overlaying Buddhism and an attachment to Chinese traditions, which was epitomised by the retention of the Ming style of dress long after the Qing dynasty had taken over China. A further similarity was the role played in the twilight years of the Yi dynasty by a powerful and cunning woman, Queen Min, who bears some similarity to the Dowager Empress. The emergence of such women in the unlikely soil of late and post-Confucian societies is interesting.

Korea's position was unenviable. Traditionally within the political and cultural spheres of China, it now found itself threatened by Japan, and then by Russia, and opened to American cultural influence. Nor was the monarchy sturdy. There was the combination of misgovernment and a dysfunctional royal family with a weak king or emperor who temporised and was alternatively under the influence of his father and his wife, Queen Min. Pro-Chinese and traditionalist factions, Japanese sympathisers and supporters of Russia machinated against each other. Disorder gave the Japanese the excuse for intervention, which in turn provoked China. The outcome of the Sino-Japanese War gave Japan enormous leverage in Korea, but this was not enough, and the Meiji government wished for administrative control. Finding in Queen Min a major obstacle, the Japanese contrived her murder, a grisly affair, with similarities to the murder on the other side of the world of Queen Draga of Serbia. A group of some thirty Japanese burst into the royal palace and cut down the queen with their swords, stripped her naked and burnt her body in the garden.

As with many events in modern Japanese history, it is difficult to establish whether the Queen's death was the outcome of a formal decision made in Tokyo. Neither Japanese foreign nor military policy was distinguished by firm and clear lines of command. It is clear that Miura Goro, the minister plenipotentiary extraordinary, had been appointed because the Japanese government expected a man with his military background to take strong actions against Japan's enemies in Korea, foremost among whom was Queen Min, and that Miura planned the assassination, hoping to fix the blame on the Korean faction opposed to the Queen, which was led by the king's father, the *taewon'gun*. The emperor and his principal ministers were both unaware of the plot and disturbed by its consequences, but it is significant that, although the government arrested Japanese officers who had participated in the murder and instituted courts martial, and Miura himself was arrested and charged, and that the proceedings against the accused made their guilt abundantly clear, all were acquitted.[17] Today, Queen Min is regarded as a patriotic heroine by many Koreans.

In 1896, however, the hitherto weak king revolted, sought refuge in the Russian Embassy and promoted himself to emperor. A subsequent period of Russian influence came to an end with Japan's victory in the Russo-Japanese War, and thereafter Japan progressively tightened its grip on Korea. In 1907 the 'Emperor', as he had declared himself, was forced to abdicate in favour of his imbecile son, and in 1910 Korean independence and its ancient monarchy met their demise. Perhaps as a gesture to Korean feelings, or perhaps out of monarchical solidarity, the last monarch, King Yi, was granted a substantial pension.

An initial, if broad, distinction between Far Eastern monarchies and, indeed, cultures is between those subject to Chinese and those under Indian influence. The latter can be subdivided into those that remained Buddhist or Hindu and those that were Islamised. A further difference is between those that remained at least technically independent and those that became the colonies or protectorates of the European powers or Japan.

Indian concepts of monarchy, like Indian religions, have proved to be influential and exportable. Yet the apparent paradox is that Indian monarchical systems have been seen as at once charismatic and weak. India, unlike China, had no history of a continuous great empire uniting the whole sub-continent. Indeed, before the invasions of Islamic outsiders, there were only three examples of a large proportion of India coming under the rule of single centralised monarchies: under the Mauryan emperors (322–185 BC), the Guptas (AD 320–550) and under King Harsha (606–647). This has been explained by the dominance and the nature of religion in India, which made the material world and its ambitions and pretensions of less importance than the spiritual. The state was, therefore, a secondary concern and was to a degree an illusion compared with the duty of living according to morality (*dharma*). The general tendency was for Indian kingdoms to be weak in Western or Chinese terms, in the sense of lacking centralised administration and allowing devolution to their peripheries. If, as we have seen, the secular and religious aspects of kingship are always present in monarchies, though one may predominate over the other, India gives us an instance where kings simply fitted in with a religious, moral and social order and took their place within it. To Marx, Weber and, more recently, Louis Dumont, the state was because of the Indian religious mindset essentially unimportant and irrelevant, and the natural order was that of towns or villages held together by religion and caste. The priestly caste, the Brahmins, with its otherworldly and spiritual principles, was at least as important as kings. As Roger Kershaw has written with regard to the Indian influence on South-East Asia:

> although the king exercises danda [the infliction of punishment] as punisher, and although force resides in him, he is not the sole or the most important wielder of power and possessor of authority. Authority is dual: the guarantors of the social order are the Brahman as archaya (teacher) and the ruler together.[18]

It may well be that, in their transmission to South-East Asia from India, Indic models of monarchy underwent a change of emphasis and the charismatic elements became the basis in many instances for absolutism and 'God-Kings', though, if Geertz assessed pre-colonial Bali rightly, it could also provide the basis for a largely ceremonial 'theatre monarchy'.[19] India's other religious export, Buddhism, may, via a concept of the sovereign as regulator in accordance with universal cosmic law, have been even more conducive to monarchical absolutism in its exported form than Hinduism.

Right across Asia along the line of China's southern and India's northern borders, and then across Indo-China, lay areas where indigenous cultures were overlaid by competing Chinese and Indian cultural influences. In Tibet, Bhutan, Sikkim and Nepal were monarchies whose traditions and rituals bore the marks of these cultural and religious layers with Lamaist Buddhism in Tibet, Sikkim and Bhutan, and Hinduism in Nepal, giving the monarchies their dominant characteristics of intense spirituality and theocracy. The Muslim conquest of north-east India had the effect of cutting off these kingdoms from Indian influences after the twelfth century, with the result that later cultural imports tended to come from China and Mongolia.

The societies of South-East Asia were remarkably open to external cultural influences, and this left their religious and monarchical traditions wonderfully syncretic, with indigenous, Chinese or Indian and Buddhist, Hindu, Confucian and Islamic concepts melding into complex and individual forms. In the Indo-Chinese Peninsula, only Vietnam can be said to have come under Chinese influence from the very beginnings of its history and to have retained the stamp of Chinese civilisation thereafter. The other Indo-Chinese states were deeply influenced by Indian cultural influences, one of the most important effects of which was the rise of monarchies organised on the lines of Indian kingdoms from as early as the third century AD. Essentially, an Indian superstructure was imposed upon an indigenous substratum. Such monarchies, like Indian kingdoms, consisted of an inner kingdom surrounded by vassal states. Indo-Chinese monarchies were not, however, clones of the Indian model of monarchy, and differences can be explained by the absence of a ubiquitous

Brahmin caste despite Brahminic influence, the continuity
of indigenous traditions, the perseverance of Buddhism after
its defeat on its home soil in India and competing Chinese
influence. Between the sixth and the thirteenth centuries,
three great civilisations, the Vietnamese, the Khmer and the
Burmese, succeeded each other as the dominant forces on
the Indo-Chinese Peninsula. Although the Mongol invasion
of the peninsula brought about the decline of the Indianised
kingdoms and of Indian culture, the legacy of the Sanskrit cultural tradition and of Mahayana Buddhism and Hinduism was
profound, not least in leaving their mark upon royal ritual and
ceremony and the very conception of monarchy:

> The Indian conception of divine kingship was adopted by
> the Indo-Chinese peoples who came within the orbit of
> Indian culture ... The king was regarded as a god on earth,
> uniting in his person the guardian spirits of the cardinal
> points, and escaping the cycle of rebirth after death ... The
> adoption of Sinhalese Buddhism as the official religion by
> kingdoms where Hinduism had formerly predominated did
> not deprive the king of his divine nature; on the contrary it
> made him a sort of living Buddha.[20]

From the end of the thirteenth century, Islam made major
advances in what is today Malaysia and in much of the
archipelago including Sumatra and Java. Islam was, however,
superimposed on Buddhist and Hindu cultures, and monarchical traditions reveal strong continuities. Enthronements in
Perak still, for instance, display strong Brahmin influence, with
Hindu ritual covered by a Muslim veneer: 'A Malay sovereign
has to sit immobile on his throne, rigidity being evidence in
Hindu ritual of incipient godhead.'[21]

In the nineteenth century South-East Asia came under
increasing European influence and pressure, with the kingdoms of what became French Indo-China gradually becoming

either French colonies or protectorates, while by 1824 the British had acquired Malacca and were soon encroaching on Burma, which became a British colony in 1889.

As European influence penetrated South-East Asia, the European powers discovered a volatile political situation, with the kingdoms of the area engaged in wars of conquest and expansion. During the eighteenth century, Burma threatened Siam, while Siam had expansionist ambitions as regards the territories of Cambodia and Laos, and by the end of the century decades of civil conflict to the north had resulted in a united Vietnamese Empire backed by French influence. The wars between the native kingdoms facilitated the establishment of European colonies and protectorates, for only a monarch of consummate political ability could hope both to defeat the threats to his kingdom from adjacent states and retain independence from the European empires. There was only one dynasty, that of the Chakri dynasty of Siam, which was able to do this.

P'raya Chakri, a successful Siamese general, seized power with considerable popular support in 1782 and was proclaimed king, thus founding the dynasty which still rules modern Thailand. Rama I, as he was known, successfully defended Siam against the Burmese and extended his country's possessions in the Malay Peninsula, and his son and successor, Rama II, was no less effective against the neighbouring kingdoms and sultanates. From the reign of Rama III (1824–51), however, Siam had to face up to not just the problems with adjacent kingdoms but the growing spread of Western economic, cultural and political influence. Burma was increasingly a British sphere, as was the Malay Peninsula, while Vietnam and Cambodia were coming under French protection. It was King Mongkut, or Rama IV (1851–68), a monk before he succeeded his brother at the age of 49, who reformed his country's institutions, opened it up to Western trade and ideas and cleverly played off France and Britain against each other.

By so doing, he maintained his country's independence. The long reign of his successor, King Chulalongkorn, or Rama V, saw continued modernisation of the country and the consolidation of its frontiers.

Siam stands alongside Japan as an isolated instance of a nation which was able to absorb the new reality of Western power and culture and create a modern identity that was a symbiosis of tradition and Western innovation. As with Japan, the monarchy was of crucial importance in this process, though it can be argued that whereas in the Japanese instance the monarchy was the cultural icon vitalising and legitimising change, in Siam the new identity was formed by the monarchs themselves. Siam's monarchical modernisation has been seen as another example of the refashioning or reinvention of monarchy in the nineteenth century. Western monarchical symbols and ceremonies were grafted on to the native equivalents, there was an emphasis upon public theatre akin to the majestic pageantries and parades of late nineteenth-century Europe, and above all an effort was made to reach out to the people in what may be regarded as, if not a democratisation, a popularisation of monarchy as both the link with a half-imaginary past and the personification of the nation in the present.[22] The monarchy became inseparable from the concept of the Thai nation in its uniqueness.

As we have previously remarked, however, neither a remodelling of monarchical style nor the role of monarchy as a conduit of cultural transmission are unusual in the long history of the world's monarchies. Courts have ever been the places by which new fashions, whether in the arts, dress or social mores, have entered countries from abroad. This has often been facilitated by a dynastic marriage with the foreign princess who becomes queen consort, bringing with her the music, the taste in dress or painting, even the religious beliefs of her home country.[23] Crown princes journeying abroad performed a similar function. The dress, the manners and the vices of the foreign culture deemed superior or smarter are inevitably adopted first by kings and courtiers. It is hardly surprising that kings of Siam, like other non-European monarchs in the nineteenth century, introduced Western ways and styles into their country, and that the photographs and portraits of Siamese monarchs and their royal families gradually came to resemble those of European royalty. This was no knee-bending to the West but an affirmation that the kings of Siam were part of an international royal caste eager to identify themselves with the style of the most powerful monarchies in the world. By the middle of the century, King Mongkut was addressing Queen Victoria as 'Our most respected and distinguished friend, and by race of royalty Our very affectionate sister'.[24]

The Chakri kings by their selective importation of Western culture led Siam's modernisation, and in so doing made the monarchy the icon of modernisation and of the nation. Only an institution that could draw upon the past and indigenous tradition for its authority while it remodelled itself and the nation could have achieved this.

By 1914, monarchies in Asia had enjoyed mixed fortunes. The great Chinese Empire was no more. The Islamic Kingdom of Afghanistan remained independent, protected by the inhospitality of its terrain and the ferocity of its peoples from conflicting Russian and British ambitions. Tibet and the small Himalayan kingdoms also survived, though their independence was qualified. Many monarchies survived under the aegis of the colonial powers, enjoying security, status and varying degrees of autonomy. Only Japan and Siam demonstrated that monarchy could not only survive but transform itself into a dynamic modern force inseparable from self-images of the Japanese and Thai peoples.

HEIRS OF THE PROPHET: MONARCHY IN THE ISLAMIC WORLD

Islam began among the Arabs, and the first centuries after the death of Muhammad saw Arab conquests in the name of the Prophet, with Islamisation and Arabisation going hand in hand. With the Koran came the Arabic script, language and culture, together with a considerable degree of intermarriage between conquerors and conquered. These conquests extended far beyond what is today considered the Arab world, and even within that sphere there were substantial minorities, some of them Christian and others that accepted Islam but retained a separate non-Arab identity. Nevertheless, the Arab imprint upon Islam remained strong, if it was less distinct as the Muslim faith spread into Persia, India, South-East Asia and sub-Saharan Africa.

Islam made no provision for the nation and recognised no division between religious and civil or political life. Whereas Chinese and Japanese rulers were sovereign under Heaven's mandate, but were largely untroubled by organised religion, and Western monarchs had to compete with ecclesiastical power, the idea of the caliph was that ruler, judge and leader of public worship were one. Nevertheless, Islam was fractured after the Prophet's death by religious differences between Sunni, the majority, who held that Abu-Bakr, his closest companion, should become the first caliph, and the Shia, who considered that Ali, his son-in-law, should become leader. This and the personal ambitions of successful military leaders, ethnic divides and the perseverance of older notions of monarchy meant that, although Islamic life and society were always deeply permeated by religion, the Islamic world was as fissiparous as any. There were rival caliphates, revolts by provincial governors and wars between Islamic leaders, while even the caliphs' religious authority was questioned by the *ulema*, specialists in the interpretation of religious law.

The Arabian origins and the continued Arab influence upon the Muslim world were not positive when it came to creating states that could be stable when they were not expanding. There was a certain inbuilt puritanism born of Islam's desert origins that predicated waves of reform movements bent upon keeping the religion pure and opposed to the town and worldly comforts and pleasures. States were set up by conquering tribes imbued with a military ethos and social solidarity. Ibn Khaldun, the fourteenth-century Muslim philosopher, conceived a three-generational cycle from the corporate and hardened rule of the tribe to the life of ease of the rulers before they gave way to the next conquerors. A possible escape from the cycle, or at least a longer gap between the foundation and the fall, was for dynasties to organise slave armies, on which they eventually became dependent. Indeed, some states were created by slave armies, as in the case of the Ottoman Empire.

The Islamic religion gave the Muslim world a high degree of cultural uniformity, which co-existed with a similarly high degree of political instability. Islamic states tended to have landholding systems that gave little long-term security to landlords and less to peasants, encouraging a predatory

approach with heavy taxation and little encouragement to
strive for agricultural improvement. Towns were for the most
part under military government, and merchants were not able
to create civic governments with specific privileges, while
the development of market economies was greatly impeded
by the absence of secular law.[1] Successive waves of conquerors moving out of central Asia and the crusaders of Western
Christendom failed, however, to displace Islam. The Mongol
threat faded, while the Turks converted.

Islam continued to be a dynamic and expanding entity until
the seventeenth century, and a threat to western Europe:

> Having long abandoned the idea of a universal Muslim cali-
> phate, the separate Islamic sultanates of the early modern
> era dominated an enormous arc of land between the east-
> ern Mediterranean and the Ganges river basin in India. In
> the west the Ottoman Turks ruled over all of Asia Minor,
> North Africa, the Balkan lands, and Arabia; the centre of this
> cultural-religious block was controlled by a Persian Safavid
> state, whose lands included present-day Iran; and the bulk
> of the Indian subcontinent ... was united and subjected by
> the Mughals.[2]

All three of these empires were the creation of nomadic Turks
from the Asian steppes, and all had a military and expansionist
ethos. Neither the West nor Christianity were major threats
to the Islamic world until the late modern period, and wars
between Muslim empires were for long more important and
ferocious than struggles in east-central Europe. Critical fault
lines in the Islamic world divided the Ottomans from the
Shi'ite Safavids of Persia and their successors and the Safavids
from the Mughals of India.

The Mughal dynasty founded by Babur began in 1526 with
his invasion of India. During the reign of Akbar and his immediate successors in the late sixteenth and seventeenth centuries,

the regime was enormously wealthy and powerful. Akbar was unusual in his time for his toleration of religious minorities, and was probably sensible in this, as the regime never succeeded in converting the majority of Hindus or Sikhs. The Empire was fatally weakened by a war with the Persian Empire, during which Nadir Shah defeated the Mughal army and looted Delhi in 1738. Subsequent decades saw incursions from Afghanistan and from mid-century the growing power of the British East India Company, which was to ensure that the Mughal rulers were, at best, puppet emperors until the formal end of the dynasty in 1857.

The Persian Empire was different from other Islamic empires in that Shi'ite rather than Sunni Islam was the established religion. The Safavid dynasty (1502–1736) reached its height during the reign of Shah Abbas II, who reorganised the army and engaged in frequent wars with the Sunni Ottoman Empire. Safavid rule came to an end at the hands, not of the Ottoman, but of its other neighbour, Afghanistan, and there followed a turbulent period in which Afghan rule was succeeded by that of Nadir Shah, a half-century of the Zand dynasty and the establishment by Aga Muhammad Khan of the Qajar dynasty.

Although Qajar rule was to last until the twentieth century, and Persia's prosperity and the grandeur of its court had recovered in the late seventeenth century, the rule of the Qajar emperors was to be paralleled by Persian decline as land was lost to neighbouring countries and the Empire came under pressure from European states. Qajar rulers were beset by many problems: they had to balance the interests of the dynasty, their numerous progeny and their bureaucrats with those of the religious leaders and the landowners and tribal leaders; their realms and autonomy were threatened by two expansionist and rival Western powers, Russia and Britain; and they presided over a minimalist state that had little revenue and no proper army, save for a Cossack brigade with Russian officers and NCOs.

Iranian governments were not expected to do more than provide the conditions in which good Muslims could live as good Muslims. All those economic and social functions that are discharged by modern governments were left to non-governmental agencies; only in the nineteenth century were such basic functions as defence and the conduct of foreign affairs assumed by the central government, and then only imperfectly; in earlier periods they were confused with border problems and left to the appropriate provincial governors.[3]

The spasmodic efforts of the Qajar shahs to reform the Empire met with little success. Islamic leaders regarded innovations, especially those imported from the West, as un-Islamic, while Persia's misfortune was that it was a sphere contested by two imperial powers, Britain and Russia. Thus it thus gained none of the advantages that came to states under the hegemony of a single Western power – assistance with the modernisation of administration, army reforms and financial advice and assistance – and suffered a double dose of the misfortunes and humiliations that came with Western pressure. The absence of a railway system in early twentieth-century Persia was, for instance, due in large part to British opposition to links that might increase Russian influence, and similar Russian opposition to those that might assist the British.

Even capable rulers would have had difficulty in reforming the government and administration of Persia, and neither Nasir al-Din Shah (1848–96) nor his son and successor Muzaffer al-Din Shah (1896–1907) were capable rulers, though the former had a certain ruthless cunning. Both were extravagant with the numerous loans they acquired from Russia or Britain, and were addicted to expensive tours abroad. Nasir al-Din was awarded the Garter by Queen Victoria and was royally entertained by the Prince of Wales. His technique of government was perhaps revealed by the advice he gave to the Prince after they had enjoyed the lavish hospitality of the Duke of Sutherland: 'Too grand for a subject. You'll have to have his head off when you come to the throne.'[4] One of the many late nineteenth-century monarchs to fall victim to an assassin, the Shah was killed by an Islamic extremist in 1896. His successor has been described as 'devoted to religion and cats but ignorant of government and diplomacy'.[5] British decorations and orders of chivalry were highly prized, and Edward VII's reluctance to bestow the Garter on Muzaffer al-Din Shah when he visited Britain led to a period of poor relations between Britain and Persia. These trips to Europe, together with repayment of debts and pensions and gifts to supporters, rapidly used up the numerous foreign loans that the regime secured. Some ministers, like the early twentieth-century Prime Minister, Mirza Ali Asghar, recognised the need for reform, but were unable to curb the Shah's extravagance, raise more money from taxation or convince religious leaders that reform was not intrinsically un-Islamic. His successor, Aya al-Dowla, was acceptable to Islamic opinion because of his opposition to foreign influence, but he fell from power in Persia's rather strange constitutional revolution.

Encouraged by the 1905 revolution in Russia and by Japan's success in the Russo-Japanese War, the 1906 constitutional revolution was a paradoxical affair. Although a number of radicals hoped that there could be reform of government, national unity and democracy within Islam, and that Western ideas could take Islamic forms, far more numerous were those who, opposed to the corruption of the regime, wished to return to a purified Islamic society. The revolution thus embraced conflicting attitudes and ideologies. The panoply of an assembly with elected deputies and with specific rights assigned to shah, ministers and the assembly followed the model of secular Western constitutions, but was accompanied by the declaration that no law could be at variance with the *Sharia*. Just as contradictory was the insistence on reforms but a refusal to agree to the taxation that was necessary to implement them.

Rather than inaugurating a strengthened Persia, the constitutional revolution saw the beginning of a period of even
greater instability. The Shah's authority was weakened, but
no other central authority was found to replace it. Muzaffer
al-Din Shah died shortly after the constitution was promulgated, and his son, Muhammad Ali, though he managed to
crush the assembly in 1908, never managed to fully restore
royal authority and was eventually deposed. The 1907 agreement between Britain and Russia effectively divided Persia
into British and Russian economic spheres. In 1909 the Anglo-
Persian Oil Company was formed. The history of Persia in the
years before the First World War is that of a country virtually
ungovernable from the centre and with considerable provincial autonomy overlaid by British and Russian interests. The
last Qajar ruler, Ahmad Shah, was crowned in July 1914, but
his was not a glorious inheritance.

Persia's experience illustrates in extreme form the experience of all Islamic societies in the face of the expansion of
Western power. Nationalism and religion came together in fury
at the weakness of the government and nation. Resentment
was heightened by centuries in which a consciousness of the
superiority of Islam had been taken for granted. The problem was that to reform state and society so that it could resist
the West involved absorbing Western culture, ideas and institutions. Could Islamic societies reform without becoming
un-Islamic?

The decline of the Islamic empires was rapid. Despite, like
the monarchs of Europe, making war against each other, not-
withstanding, and often because of, common religion, it had
appeared in the early seventeenth century that the Islamic
emperors represented a more dynamic force in the world than
did Christian Europe. In particular, the Ottoman Empire in its
early centuries exhibited powers of organisation and a tough-
ness that contrasted with the softer, more pleasure-loving
aspects of other Islamic civilisations. Converts to Islam, the

Ottoman Turks, it has been claimed, submerged their identity in their faith 'to a greater extent than any other Islamic people', and achieved 'the sense of devotion to duty and of mission, in the best days of the Empire, that is unparalleled in Islamic history'.[6]

The defeat of the Ottoman at the gates of Vienna marked the end of the Turkish Empire's advance into Europe, though in the Middle East the Empire continued to expand. The end of expansion in Europe led not to a period of stability but to losses of territory and to a decline in internal efficiency. All the Islamic empires had drawn their strength from the frontier and from expansion, and the ethos and structure of the state found it impossible to cope with settled, still less shrinking, frontiers. More significant was the major world development, the seemingly ineluctable increase in Western power as Western trade, manufacturing, technology, state organisation and military might began to overshadow all rivals.

The monarchical system must, however, take some of the blame. The difficulties of succession for monarchies where kings or emperors are polygamous and there is no clear system of inheritance have already been mentioned. The Islamic empires shared common problems here with Far Eastern counterparts such as the Chinese and Korean monarchies. Dynasties were royal in the male line only, as those who succeeded might be the offspring of mere slave-girls in the imperial harems. In the Ottoman Empire, a woman who was lucky enough to bear a sultan a son was promoted to the status of *Haseki Sultan*, or Favourite Princess, and should that son succeed to the throne, she became *Valide Sultan*, or Queen Mother. Rivalries over succession encouraged not just perennial suspicion but the assassination and murder of brothers and nephews. The closed worlds of the harem fostered a heated atmosphere of gossip and intrigue and gave great power to chief eunuchs. An upbringing in such environments was, to say the least, not conducive to the production of well-balanced individuals. In the Mughal

Empire sons killed fathers and fathers sons: Emperor Jahangir may have poisoned his father, Akbar, and after Jahangir's son, Khusrau, had plotted against him, he had him blinded and imprisoned for life, while Shah Jahan came to power by way of the murder of most of his relatives.[7]

It was the Ottoman monarchy that had threatened western Europe, and alone among Islamic states it remained, at least nominally, a great power into the twentieth century. Its internal workings and provision for succession demonstrate the weaknesses of Islamic monarchy and the combination of near-absolute power, theocracy and polygamy. The first ten sultans of the House of Osman were capable and intelligent men; the later rulers have been described as an 'astonishing series of incompetents, degenerates and misfits'.[8] Earlier rulers were usually sons of the sultan who had proved themselves as provincial governors or as military leaders and been designated heirs in a Social Darwinist scenario, at least in part because of their abilities. The Law of Fratricide of 1451 allowed a new sultan to kill all his male relatives and their wives and children. In order to ensure secrecy, these murders were carried out by the Court Executioner, assisted by deaf mutes. Ugly practice though it was, this did have the effect of preventing palace coups and ensured that sultans, if not happy and trusting men, were capable and ruthless. When this practice was discontinued in the seventeenth century:

> Sultans devised a more ingenious method of the ridding themselves of all rivals to the throne. The system was adopted of confining the male members of the House of Osman in kafes or cages, where they were consistently debilitated by alcohol, drugs, aphrodisiacs and fornication. The kafes were in fact little huts in a concentration camp in which the princes of the blood were imprisoned for life in darkened rooms, until they lost their reason or died. It

was this habit of family murder that accounts for the almost panic terror in which most Sultans passed their lives.[9]

In among the succession of misfits and incompetents were several sultans who were able, and two who recognised the need for thoroughgoing reform. Selim II (1789–1807) and Mahmud III (1808–39) made determined efforts to catch up with the West. The realisation that the *Tanzimat*, as the reform process became known when it was further pursued under British pressure in the reign of Mahmud's successor, Abdul Majid (1839–61), involved more than simply buying Western weaponry, and hiring military advisers took time to be accepted. Even when accepted, as it was by Sultan Mahmud, who was in some respects Turkey's Peter the Great, utilising his personal power to push reform with an unsympathetic and largely uncomprehending state and society, the problems of the Empire and the lack of a westernised elite to work with ensured only modest success.

The intrinsic problem was that westernisation could not produce a cleansed and invigorated empire without destroying the culture and ethos of the Empire. Modernisation was, in short, incompatible with traditional Islamic society, and opposition to it was religious and cultural. Islam is a much more precisely prescriptive religion than Christianity, and the Koran laid down instructions for almost every aspect of life. Social and cultural change, especially change that was inspired by the West and pointed to a more secular society, was opposed by what was probably the majority of the sultan's Islamic subjects. Top-down westernisation, and there was no other way, was also inevitably autocratic and partial. Western powers, which, throughout the nineteenth century, called upon sultans to embrace greater liberalism, limited democracy and balanced budgets, as well as modern armed forces, missed the point. Sultans could only force reform programmes through by becoming more autocratic and by abolishing the older checks and balances upon their power.

What efforts at reform did was to ensure that the officers of the army became the dedicated modernisers. Having destroyed the janizaries and embarked upon the slow process of giving the Empire a modern army, Mahmud ensured that army officers, frustrated by military setbacks that they blamed upon the slow pace of reform, would form a radical vanguard. Whereas, in the West, army officers with their aristocratic backgrounds tended to be conservative and to reluctantly follow the changes that commerce and technology initiated, in the Islamic world cadres of army officers were a force for change, a radical intelligentsia under arms. They were with sultans who agreed with their agenda, but 'Young Ottomans', and then 'Young Turks', the change in nomenclature is significant, progressively became disillusioned with a sultanate and caliphate that seemed incapable of effective reform. The Young Turks who overthrew the last sultan to exercise real power, Abdul Hamid, in 1908, and then deposed him in 1909 still supported the sultanate and Empire, but were moving towards a secularist and nationalist position that further defeat in war would lead, after the Empire had gone, to the overthrow of sultanate and then caliphate.

It was the Ottoman Empire's slow retreat from its European possessions that gave it the nickname of the 'sick man of Europe'. Faced by revolts by their Christian subjects in the Balkans and the difficulties of putting down such revolts by the time-honoured method of massacre when faced with intervention by the Western powers, the Empire was forced to grant autonomy and then full independence to the successor states of Serbia, Greece, Romania and Bulgaria. At the beginning of the twentieth century, the Ottoman possessions in Europe were, if much diminished, still substantial, including, as they did, Macedonia, Thrace and Albania.

Ottoman control of North Africa and the Middle East had also been eroded by disloyal vassals and European expansion.

Muhammad Ali, Viceroy of Egypt, and his son Ibrahim Pasha had provided the sultan with effective assistance in putting down the puritan and fundamentalist Islamic movement of the Wahabis in Arabia, and then in leading a force of Bashi-bazouks, or Circassian irregulars, to crush a Greek insurrection in the Morea. By this time, however, both father and son had become ambitious, and when the sultan refused to make Ibrahim the governor of Syria, he seized that province and went on to threaten Constantinople. Largely at Britain's insistence, Muhammad Ali was forced to back off and give up Syria, though he remained nominal Viceroy and in reality independent ruler of Egypt. Increasingly the Ottoman Empire survived because the European powers were divided as to what to replace it by, but they proceeded to lop off its extremities. France occupied Algiers in 1830, then moved into the interior and in 1881 took Tunisia. Britain occupied Egypt in 1882, though preserving Muhammad Ali's successors as titular rulers and still recognising the vague suzerainty of the sultan. Only the Ottoman province of Libya and the Sultanate of Morocco, which had never been under Ottoman rule, were not under European control in the southern Mediterranean though the former was soon to come under Italian rule after the Italian-Libyan War 1911–12.

It seemed in the early twentieth century as though there was little to show for the spasmodic attempts at reform instituted by Ottoman sultans. The ruler of this declining Empire in 1900 was Sultan Abdul Hamid. An intelligent and cunning man, he was no blind reactionary, but, in fact, both an autocrat and a reformer. He realised the extent of the Empire's problems, especially the need for an efficient financial and taxation system. He reformed the education system, encouraged railway development and continued military and naval reforms. During his reign, newspapers and journals were published in growing numbers, and the telegraph spread. He genuinely wished to strengthen his empire, but he was no constitutionalist

or democrat, though he could pretend to be when necessary.
A child of the *harem*, born to a lowly mother, lucky enough
to conceive on one of the sultan's rare visits to her bed, who
died when he was young, he learned early to be guarded and
self-effacing amid the plotting and animosities of the imperial
palace. He came to power after his father and half-brother had
been deposed, and his main aim was to avoid their fate. His
methods were technological and administrative westernisation
in the interests of a more efficient absolutism, diplomatic
manoeuvring and a burnishing of his Islamic credentials.

Although previous sultans had revived the title of caliph,
it had become largely symbolic. Abdul Hamid (1876–1909)
attempted to make the Caliphate what it had been in the early
days of Islam, and projected himself as 'The shadow of God
on earth and protector of all the Muslim faithful'. Whether
or not he was particularly religious himself, he was aware that
a movement for Islamic revival was growing in reaction to
European influence. If one reaction to European power was to
seek to learn from it and to westernise, another was to argue
that Islam's misfortunes were due to straying from the paths
laid down by the Prophet. One aspect of the revival was the
growth of fundamentalist and puritan sects such as the Wahabis
in Arabia, and another was pan-Islam, which preached the
need for all Muslim peoples to unite. The revived caliphate
gave Abdul Hamid a potent weapon, for he could appeal not
only to his own subjects but to Muslims everywhere, including those under British and French rule.

Abdul Hamid, therefore, used every tactic in the interests of
survival. He could appear a westernising reformer or a conservative Islamic, a man who was prepared to grant greater
equality to non-Muslim subjects and a proponent of theocracy. Trusting no one, he was the paymaster of a vast army of
informers and skilful in employing the strategy of divide and
rule. In the end, however, his policies were contradictory and
did nothing to improve the position of the Empire.

The aim of reformers for most of the nineteenth century was to reinvigorate the Ottoman Empire, not to replace it. This was probably an impossible task so far as the western parts of the Empire were concerned, because of the rise of nationalism and the fact that most Ottoman reformers were not prepared to concede real equality to non-Muslims. An alternative was to embrace pan-Islam and put the sultan and caliph at the head of it, but even in the Arab provinces of the Empire opposition to Ottoman rule was growing. A new phenomenon at the beginning of the twentieth century was Turkish nationalism. The Turks had submerged their identity in Islam, and the very name 'Turk' was rarely used before the mid-nineteenth century, save as a pejorative term. Among the educated elite, especially army officers, Turkish national feeling was, nevertheless, growing in the early 1900s. 'Young Turks' still professed loyalty to Empire and sultan, but the loss of Christian provinces and the suspect loyalty of Muslim provinces increasingly drew attention to the Turkish homelands.

One of Abdul Hamid's last throws was to seek the support of the dynamic new power in Europe, Germany, and its flamboyant emperor. Here was a chance to find a counterweight to Britain and France. Germany was eager to enter into a close relationship, and German finance and German companies flooded into the Sultan's domains. Kaiser Wilhelm II visited Constantinople twice, in 1898 and 1899, and established a good relationship with the Sultan. A Turkish–German understanding made sense for both sovereigns. It opened the way for German influence in the Middle East and provided Germany with a possible ally against Russia, while for the Ottoman Empire it made sense to become close to the one great power that was uninvolved in the taking of Ottoman territory and had interests at variance with those who had – Britain, Russia and France. After his second visit to Constantinople, the Kaiser went on to Jerusalem and Damascus, where he postured as the friend and protector of Islam and the Sultan-Caliph. In

Damascus he said: 'His Majesty, the Sultan, and the three hundred million Moslems who revere him as the Caliph may rest assured that they will always have a friend in the German Emperor.'

Little went right, however, for Abdul Hamid and his Empire. Victory over Greece in the war of 1897 brought little reward. The Armenians, hitherto a loyal element among the Christian subjects, began to express nationalist sentiments, bringing upon themselves the most savage and brutal reprisals, while even the largely Muslim Albanians became restless. In the summer of 1908 came the moment Abdul Hamid had always expected and feared: open revolt by sections of the army. The army officers who led the revolt were members of the Committee of Union and Progress, founded in 1895. Infuriated by the way the army was starved of new equipment and weaponry, they were not opposed to sultan and Empire but enraged by inefficiency. Their ideals were straightforward: freedom and fatherland, the constitution and the nation; but which fatherland and which nation, the wider Empire or Turkey? Within Union and Progress there were divisions on this, but for the moment they were not visible. Abdul Hamid, after considering repression, gave way and released political prisoners, promised constitutional rule and disbanded his spy network.

Whatever the intentions of the Young Turks, who were now in power, their position was undermined by Austria–Hungary and the Balkan states, which took advantage of the Empire's internal disorder. Austria–Hungary proclaimed the annexation of Bosnia and Herzogovina, still in theory possessions of the Sultan, while Bulgaria declared her independence and Greece incorporated Crete. These blows to Ottoman prestige and the consequent unpopularity of the government encouraged an odd mixture of Islamicists, liberals and the Sultan to oppose the Young Turks, and in 1909 there was a mutiny by pro-Islamic regiments in the capital. The revolt was swiftly put down, and Abdul Hamid was deposed and sent into exile. He was replaced by his brother, Prince Reshad, who became Muhammad V, but was entirely under the control of the Committee of Union and Progress. This to a great extent marked the end of Ottomanism and any notion of an association of different peoples and faiths under the common rule of the sultan.

The First Balkan War of 1912 saw the Turks defeated by the armies of Serbia, Bulgaria, Greece and Montenegro. This was the first time that the Empire had actually been defeated by its erstwhile European subjects, for previous defeats had involved the participation of Russia or pressure from the great powers. The Turks were forced back to a mere pocket-handkerchief section of Thrace as its last remaining part of Europe. These later losses were a particular blow, as Rumelia had always been seen as a heartland of the Empire and the home of the Ottoman elite, while Albania, which eventually emerged as an independent state despite Serb and Greek ambitions, was largely inhabited by Muslims.

Threatened by Russia, which had expanded remorselessly eastwards and along the Caspian and the Black Seas, absorbing Muslim khanates and portions of the Persian as well as the Ottoman Empire, and increasingly pan-Turkish rather than pan-Islamic, the Empire's last desperate throw was to enter the First World War on the side of Germany. Sultan Muhammad V had little to do with this, as political decisions were made by the Young Turkish government, and not by the five-centuries-old sultanate.

SATRAPS, VASSALS AND SATELLITES OF EMPIRE

Empires, it is too easily assumed, always seek to assert the control of their centres over their peripheries by destroying indigenous institutions and establishing a hegemony, which reflects the social, religious and cultural assumptions of the centre. To a great extent this was the Roman model, with considerable standardisation throughout the empire, and it was in large part true of the colonial empire established by France from the early nineteenth century. It was certainly not true of the Chinese Empire, which, outside the Middle Kingdom, was content to allow subsidiary peoples and their rulers on the periphery a degree of cultural and political autonomy, provided the overall authority of the emperor was recognised and tributes were paid. It was, at best, only half true of the British Empire.

European powers, from the beginning of the early modern period onwards, expanded into America, Africa, India, the Far East and the Middle East, largely because they were able to do so. From the beginning the material advantages of territory, precious metals, valuable produce and economic and strategic advantage over other powers, vied with the religious impulse to convert and save the heathen. In areas deemed suitable for settlement, the export of the institutions and mores of the home country was a natural development, though it could be contested in time, as with the British colonies in what became the United States, by the growth of communities with distinctive interests and identities. In populous regions not deemed suitable for settlement by the inhabitants of the imperial power, where the interest was economic or strategic, there were choices as to which institutions and mores of the imperial power should be exported.

The British Empire in the early twentieth century was a very untidy empire. A great part of the map of the world might be painted red, but there was little in the way of a standard structure for the constituent parts. Its major unifying characteristic was that it was ruled over by a king-emperor as opposed to the French 'empire', which after 1870 was a republican empire. French overseas possessions clearly belonged to the state, and indeed the consistent thrust of colonial policy was eventual political and cultural incorporation of colonies into the state. French colonialism was, nevertheless, marked by considerable empiricism and compromise. The expansion of the British Empire, like that of the French, was a haphazard process. If the major determinant was the policies and actions, but also the vacillations and reactions, of governments, there were other factors – the demands of traders, financiers and settlers for the protection of their interests, the victories and defeats of generals and the decisions taken by the 'men on the spot', the governors and pro-consuls. Nineteenth-century British monarchs did not play much of a role in policy when it came to the acquisition of colonies, though Queen Victoria was ever ready to criticise any weakness demonstrated by Gladstone's administrations, but the monarchy played a considerable part in the maintenance of the Empire. It gave the Empire much of its ethos, lent it the charisma that was so important to it, and provided a focus for loyalty that by-passed British governments.

The view that there were essentially two British empires has much to commend it. There was 'One that they [the British] largely populated and worked themselves, and another, as exotic and fast growing as a hothouse plant, where they ruled …'[1] In the former, most obviously in the dominions of Canada, Australia and New Zealand, the monarchy enabled states, which were largely self-governing, though dependent on Britain for defence, to have in the monarch, represented by the governor-general, a sovereign who was at once head of state and head of the Empire. Constitutionally the dominions were multiple kingdoms owing allegiance to the same monarch.

The British Empire was unique in having large settler colonies in which the settlers were in the majority. Canada, Australia and New Zealand formed what late nineteenth-century commentators and politicians thought of as a greater Britain. Made wary by the experience of the American War of Independence, British governments had from the 1840s onwards taken a favourable attitude towards the self-government of the settler colonies, seeking only to retain at Westminster power over matters that concerned defence, foreign affairs and trade. The colonists themselves, eager as they were to look after their own internal affairs, tended often to wish that the home government would take a keener interest in the defence of their frontiers and any problems they had with dissident natives. By 1914, Australia, New Zealand and Canada had virtually complete control over their internal affairs. So too had South Africa after the Boer War, though the situation was different, as white settlers were not only in a minority but fiercely divided between British and Boer. For the rest of the dominions, the crown played a crucial role in that it both symbolised the continued connection with the homeland and could be distinguished from British governments.

If the crown was thus essential to the empire where Britons had settled and moved towards self-government, it was just as important to that other 'exotic' empire where the British 'ruled'. The ways in which the British ruled, and the degree to which they ruled, this empire were, however, many and varied. They ranged from merely appointing advisers to quasi-independent local rulers, as with those Indian states that did not come under the Indian government, working through separate, though essentially subordinate, governments as in the rest of India and in Egypt, to direct rule, as with most African colonies. The resultant patchwork in part reflected the timescale of colonialism and the degree of development of different colonies, together with compromises, which hardened over time into practice, but it also reflected a deep ambivalence in British opinion as to what the empire was for. If one impulse of imperialism was the urge to civilise, to Christianise and to modernise, another was to exert control but at the same time to maintain those institutions and cultures that sections of British opinion found admirable. That Britain was both a monarchy and a hierarchical society with an influential aristocracy ensured support for the latter tendency.

Kings and queens respect the institution of monarchy, even when the monarchies concerned are very different from their own, while aristocracies feel an innate sympathy with hierarchical societies that value land and the ethos of the warrior. Throughout the 'exotic' British Empire, we can discern political and social structures, which, however bizarrely, can be seen as paralleling that of Britain.[2] Provided they were content to accept British suzerainty and become subjects of the British monarch, kings, sultans, maharajahs and tribal chiefs were allowed, indeed encouraged, to maintain their positions, thrones and courts along with varied degrees of autonomous power.

Other colonialist powers did not demonstrate the same enthusiasm for maintaining native rulers and dynasties. The United States brought the Hawaiian monarchy swiftly to an end. King Kalakaua had perhaps foreseen this danger when on a visit to Japan in 1881 he had proposed a league between the countries of Asia against Western dominance. In 1893 Queen Lili'uokalani was overthrown by an insurrection by American residents supported by the US minister in Hawaii, John L. Stevens, and by troops from the USS *Boston*. Although this coup was condemned by President Cleveland, the future of Hawaii was handed over to the US Senate, and in 1898 Hawaiian sovereignty was transferred to the United States. The fate of the Queen of Hawaii can be contrasted with the treatment of King Cakobau of Fiji, whose authority was guaranteed when the British annexed Fiji in 1874.

It can be argued that the great difference between the great variety of colonial governments, which differed between and within empires, was the degree to which rule was direct or indirect. Where it was indirect the empires worked through indigenous rulers, but even when there were governors and district commissioners it was usual to maintain the local institutions in a subordinate role. The French were pragmatic as regards indigenous rulers, ejecting them when possible, as with the overthrow of the Madagascar monarchy, and maintaining them when convenient. In Morocco, which was from 1912 a protectorate, the sultan was maintained, while the complex government of Indo-China included protectorates under local monarchs but also Cochin China, which was considered part of metropolitan France and sent deputies to the French Assembly.

It might have been thought that as the Netherlands was a monarchy, Dutch colonialism would have favoured the maintenance of kingdoms within its Empire. After finding that attempts to rule through native monarchies were unsuccessful, and that the Kingdom of Mararam in particular was always inclined to revolt, the Dutch, from the 1880s, ruled much of Java directly and allowed only the most pliant of sultans to retain the trappings of power in Yogjakarta and Surakarta, monarchies 'kept half-alive as ceremonial camouflage'.[3]

Only the British Empire looked upon indigenous monarchies with positive favour, though when monarchs proved recalcitrant they were removed. The last of the Mughal rulers, Bahadur Shah, was tried for treason after the Indian Mutiny and sent off to a comfortable exile in Rangoon. Nearly thirty years later King Thibaw of Burma made the same journey in the opposite direction. His short reign had begun with the execution of some seventy to eighty members of the royal family, which his queen and her mother had decided to get rid of. He annoyed the British by permitting the ill-treatment of British subjects, refusing to crack down on piracy and refusing to submit a fine of £230,000 imposed on a British company to arbitration. After issuing an ultimatum, the Indian Army invaded and defeated the Burmese forces. The King was made a prisoner and was then packed off to India with his family in 1885. The British soon discovered the disadvantage of discarding the Burmese monarchy; the Buddhist monks had regarded the King as the supreme authority, and bereft of that authority, tended to become politically restless and subversive. On the whole, however, the British preferred to keep the local rulers, and rule above and through them.

The actual political power of the British monarchy decreased in the late nineteenth century, but it became far grander than ever before. It was the Empire that gave it much of its lustre, and the native princes were intrinsic to the projection of imperial majesty. When, after the Indian Mutiny, the British government took over the government of the East India Company's erstwhile possessions, Queen Victoria proclaimed in 1858 that she would 'respect the rights, dignity and honour of native princes as our own'. As David Cannadine has described it, 'The British constructed a system of government that was simultaneously direct and indirect, authoritarian and collaborationist, but that always took for granted the reinforcement and preservation of tradition and hierarchy.'[4] When, at Disraeli's instigation, Queen Victoria took the title of Empress of India, further dignity accrued to the British throne. If this was in part a move to impress British public opinion, and in part a move within the sphere of domestic British politics, it also represented the emergent ethos of British imperialism, which was not to govern directly but to seek to work with the grain of the traditions and the established authorities of the constituent parts of the Empire. The British sovereign at once consciously took over the paramountcy of the defunct Mughal Empire, reinforced the institution of monarchy and pointed to respect for India's past, customs, social structure and culture.

By the late nineteenth century almost the entire African continent was under European control. Ethiopia (then Abyssinia), which could trace its kingship and Christianity back to the Aksumite kingdom of the mid-fourth century, succeeded with difficulty in withstanding Italy's attempts to make it a colony. Within the British Empire, the usual policy of working with local rulers where possible and deposing or exiling them when they proved recalcitrant was followed. Thus, the British in Ghana found staunch allies in the kings and queens of Akyem Abuakwa: Queen Dokua led her army into battle at the side of the British forces against the Ashantis at the battle of Akatamanso in 1826. On the other hand, the kings of the Ashantis proved determined opponents, and one of them was sent into exile in 1876. And in Uganda the head of one of the five kingdoms, Kabalega II of Bunyoro, was also exiled, after a five-year war against the British, in 1899.

If cooperation with, or war against, the British were the two main options open to African chiefs or kings, a third option, that of an appeal to British public opinion, was employed by the major chief in Bechuanaland, Khama, Chief of the Bama-Ngwato. Having used the British as a counter to the threat from the Boer Republic of Transvaal, and cooperated with them in fighting against the Ndebele under Chief Lobengula,

Khama found that his rights and his territories and those of other chiefs were threatened by the tightening control of Cecil Rhodes's British South African Chartered Company. A Christian and teetotaller, Khama journeyed to England in 1895, and his appeals for fair treatment found much support in Nonconformist circles and enabled him to extract more satisfactory terms from the Colonial Secretary, Joseph Chamberlain. That some minor territories and their chiefs and kings in southern Africa managed, like Bechuanaland (Botswana), Basutoland (Lesotho) and Swaziland, to remain outside formal imperial control was, however, largely a matter of luck, circumstance and rivalry between the British and the Boers.

The policy of maintaining the authority of native sovereigns whenever possible had deep roots. It reflected, as David Cannadine has argued, not just pragmatism but the sympathy of the British upper classes, many of whom found new and glittering roles for themselves within the Empire, and themselves at the apex of a hierarchical society, for the institutions of monarchy and aristocracy. It was also highly successful. It enabled the colonies to be governed cheaply with modest cadres of administrators and advisers and without large numbers of British troops. The respectful treatment of kings, sultans, princes, emirs and chiefs, their continued local authority and prestige, the security that British power gave to them and the construction of an elaborate imperial honours system, ensured loyalty to the British crown.

Queen Victoria's Diamond Jubilee first demonstrated the number of glittering satraps that the Empire contained. All those subordinate kings and sultans, maharajahs and emirs made a considerable impact upon the British public and added to the grand theatre of royal pageantry. The effect upon the royal and princely visitors was just as great, impressing upon them in the surroundings of the imperial capital the might of the British monarch and of the Empire of which they were a part.

By the early twentieth century Britain's imperial system was in its heyday. There were a bewildering number and variety of monarchs within the Empire. Within the third of India that consisted of princely states there were maharajahs, rajahs, nawabs and nizams. In Africa there were kings such as the King of the Ashanti and the King (or Okyenhene) of the Akyem Abuakwa in Ghana, the King of Barotseland and the King (or Kabaka) of Buganda, numerous paramount chiefs and chiefs; the Sultan of Zanzibar and the Nigerian emirs. In Malaya there was a galaxy of sultans, while in Sarawak the Brooke family held a unique position as white rajahs. In the south Pacific there were kings of Fiji, of the Solomons and of Tonga. As British power expanded into the Middle East, Britain maintained the khedives of Egypt and patronised their advanced dignity as sultans and then kings, and worked through the region's traditional rulers in the Arabian Peninsula and the Persian Gulf.

There were thus positive advantages for kings, maharajahs, emirs, sultans and chiefs in coming under the umbrella of empires. If independence in foreign affairs was lost, there was enhanced security and little loss of status. Most rulers had been accustomed to paying tribute to more powerful kings or emperors, whether the Mughal or Chinese emperors or simply another monarch with a more formidable army. For the satraps of empire and for the wider ruling elites of subordinate nations there was the lure of becoming part of a global elite with common practices and consumption patterns. Royalty itself became *the* global elite, a fraternity, whose ethos combined reverence for individual traditions and a common acceptance of an international code. It was a fraternity remarkably free from distinctions of race or colour. European and African or Asian royalty did not intermarry but in general held to the notion that royal birth prevailed above race. When the Native American Princess Pocahontas visited England with her English husband in the early seventeenth century, she was given precedence before him; when they dined with James I, she sat on the same level as royalty, while her husband, John Rolfe, who had failed to gain the King's permission to marry a princess, was consigned to the body of the floor. Nearly three hundred years later, the Prince of Wales upset his nephew, the future Kaiser, by insisting that a reigning monarch, King Kalakaua of Hawaii, be given precedence over him. David Cannadine has argued that '... there were at least two visions of empire that were essentially (and elaborately) hierarchical: one centred on colour, the other on class'.[5] Royalty were perhaps a caste rather than a class, but one that transcended colour.

An example of a ruler exerting considerable power and living in great splendour while very consciously acknowledging his role in the British scheme of things was Nripendra Narayan, the Maharajah of Cooch Behar (Koch Binar). His durbars were as imposing and splendid as those of the Viceroy, and at one his eldest son paid homage to his father:

> in a glittering ceremony which simultaneously proclaimed the prince's status, loyalty to the Crown and love of all things British. Outside the palace there were lines of elephants, painted and caparisoned with cloth of gold, and legions of white-coated servants carrying flambeaux. Inside and illuminated by electric light were the maharajah's red-jacketed bodyguard, carrying swords, spears and antique muskets, and his aides who wore British-style white uniforms and pith helmets with spikes. The maharajah was traditionally dressed in a pale blue tunic with a diamond-studded aigrette pinned to his turban. He sat on a gilded

throne behind which was hung his banner, embroidered
with elephants and tigers, a present from Queen Victoria.[6]

By the beginning of the twentieth century many Indian
princes had attended British public schools and had spent
long periods in Britain mixing with upper-class society. Their
lifestyles and mores, their virtues and vices, were an exotic
amalgam of the British and the Indian: elephants and gin and
tonics, palaces and cricket, philanthropy, durbars and chorus
girls. They became part of a trans-national global class while
maintaining their traditional position, privileges and duties in
Indian society. It has been argued that:

> The greatest beneficiaries of the newly constructed colo-
> nial edifices were those members of the ruling elite of the
> respective nations who, through their associations, practices
> and consumption patterns, were also members of a global
> and increasingly cosmopolitan elite.[7]

The admiration of the British upper class for the aristocratic
or the princely ethos countered and to a degree reversed the
earlier impulse of those who, like Macaulay, saw the imperial adventure as an opportunity to export 'progress' and to
modernise and westernise. It was, however, the distant glory
of the British monarchy and, what was at least the half-
truth, the idea that kings, maharajahs and princes were not
yielding to foreign rule but were accepting a vassal position
to a great emperor across the seas, that enabled the British
Empire to be maintained for so long by so few British troops
and administrators.

The British Empire was thus a great force for the maintenance of monarchy, and it can be said conversely that the
British monarchy and the myriad of subordinate monarchies
were a great force for the maintenance of the Empire. The
charisma of monarchy was central to this. That the white

dominions rallied to Britain's aid during the Boer War may have been because of fellow national feeling and an empathy with the *British* Empire, though they did so as subjects of Queen Victoria. Whether Indian or African troops would have fought so fiercely for the Empire in the First World War had it not been that there was the distant but glowing image of the King-Emperor to fight for is debatable.

4

THE EUROPEAN COUSINHOOD

The monarchies of Europe appeared remarkably secure at the beginning of the twentieth century, considering the challenges to their authority from the French Revolution onwards and the pace of social, economic and political change throughout the nineteenth century. They seemed to have survived Jacobinism and to have confounded the predictions of Karl Marx, while they flourished amid urbanisation and the motor car. That year of revolutions, 1848, when so many monarchies had wobbled, appeared to have been aberrant. The Franco-Prussian War of 1870 had resulted in the fall of the Second Empire in France, and the Empire was to prove the last of France's monarchical restorations, but was also followed by the institution of a powerful Second Reich in Germany. The decay of the Ottoman Empire in eastern Europe had resulted not in Balkan republics but in the new monarchies of Romania, Greece, Serbia, Bulgaria and Montenegro.

Europe's monarchies had two somewhat paradoxical characteristics. On the one hand, there was an identification between monarch and nation, for kings were increasingly seen as symbolic of the nation and guardians of its interests. On the other hand, monarchs were interrelated, making up an extended European family, almost a special supra-national caste, which was, nevertheless, overwhelmingly German in origin.

Queen Victoria remarked during a visit to Germany on how odd it was to hear the ordinary people speaking German. It seems clear that she regarded the language as almost peculiar to royalty. The need of the royal families of Europe for endogamous marriages meant a limited choice of marriage partners, further diminished by religion. Catholic monarchies were limited in such choices largely to Habsburgs, Wittelsbachs, Bourbons, Braganzas and the House of Savoy, though there were also some minor German Catholic dynasties. Protestant monarchies, such as those of Britain, the Netherlands and Scandinavia, could marry among themselves or choose from the many Protestant houses of Germany, while Orthodox dynasties and nations were happy to accept Protestant marriage partners. If royal marriages had once been a diplomatic overture, with the assumption that they secured an alliance between the states from which the partners came, by the nineteenth century it was mainly a suitable pedigree that mattered.

One result of this was the ability of families presiding over small dukedoms, that the traveller dozing in his carriage could easily miss, and with royal blood but empty purses, to intermarry with the princes and princesses of great powers. No German house was more successful in the game of upward mobility via marriage than that of Saxe-Coburg-Gotha, which has been described as:

a dukedom possessing just two small blocks of territory in Franconia and Thuringia, a few ramshackle palaces and small homely manor houses, and where the little princes and princesses did their French lessons with patches on their clothes.[1]

Prince Leopold of Saxe-Coburg-Gotha pulled off a great coup when he became engaged to marry the Princess Royal, Princess Charlotte, the only child of George IV. If his hopes of becoming consort to a queen of Great Britain were dashed by the untimely death of Princess Charlotte, the subsequent marriage of his sister to the Duke of Kent and the birth of their daughter, the Princess Victoria, ensured that Saxe-Coburg would mingle with Hanoverian blood. In 1841, Leopold, now monarch of the new Kingdom of the Belgians, had the satisfaction of seeing his long-nurtured aim of a marriage between his nephew, Prince Albert, and Queen Victoria take place. In the early twentieth century, besides ruling over Britain and Belgium, the Saxe-Coburgs were by marriage connected with the royal houses of Russia, Sweden, Spain, Portugal, Austria–Hungary, Italy, Germany, Romania and Bulgaria. A feature of, and a reason for, the success of the ambitious Saxe-Coburgs, was their willingness to be flexible as to religion, remaining Protestant or becoming Roman Catholic or Orthodox as required.

The Battenbergs (or Battenburgs) came behind the Saxe-Coburgs in the dynastic marriage stakes, but nevertheless were remarkably successful, despite the fact that the Battenberg title had been brought out of abeyance to mark a morganatic marriage. Prince Alexander of Hesse had married Countess Julie von Hauke, a lady-in-waiting to Grand Duchess Olga of Russia. Unable to become Princess of Hesse because of her non-royal birth, she was created Countess of Battenberg by the Tsar, and was first an Illustrious Highness, before being elevated to Serene Highness, a rank to which her children were also entitled. Such matters were taken very seriously by the royal families of Europe, and the success of three of the sons of the marriage was therefore no mean achievement. Prince Alexander of Battenberg was elected Prince of Bulgaria, but lost his throne by demonstrating his desire to follow policies independent of Bulgaria's patron, the Tsar of

Russia. His brother, Prince Henry, married Queen Victoria's daughter, Princess Beatrice, but under far from enviable conditions, as the Queen, reluctant to lose her youngest daughter, insisted that the married couple live under her roofs. Prince Henry died of fever contracted during the Ashanti expedition of 1895, which he had volunteered to join. A third brother, Prince Louis, married Princess Victoria of Hesse, whose parents were Grand Duke Louis IV and Princess Alice, daughter of Queen Victoria; he became a British subject and naval officer, and was First Sea Lord in 1914. By the early twentieth century, Battenbergs had married into the royal houses of Greece, Sweden and Spain.

If Queen Victoria was seen as the grandmother of Europe's royalty, with grandchildren including the Emperor of Germany and the wives of the heirs to the Swedish, Greek and Romanian thrones, King Christian IX of Denmark had a claim to be the grandfather. He was, in the early twentieth century, grandfather to Nicholas II of Russia and to the heir to the British throne, the future George V, and then, with Norwegian independence from Sweden, to King Haakon VII, while he was the father of George I of Greece and father-in-law of Edward VII of Britain.

The interrelated nature of Europe's royal families was not an unmixed blessing, and reliance upon a shallow gene pool increased the occurrence of hereditary diseases among Europe's royals. That the Tsarevich Alexie of Russia and Alfonso, Prince of Asturias and heir to the throne of Spain, both had haemophilia, the transmission of which could be traced back to Queen Victoria, has long been well known. Only one of Victoria's children, Prince Leopold, Duke of Albany, suffered from it, but Princesses Alice and Beatrice were carriers and passed it on to their children and grandchildren. More recently, interest in George III's 'madness', combined with increased medical knowledge, has resulted first in a posthumous diagnosis of the King's malady as porphyria and then in an investigation of the transmission of the disease down the royal line. It probably came from the Stuarts, and a double dose came to the Hanoverians and the Hohenzollerns via Elizabeth of Bohemia.[2] Certainly, the amount of mental instability among European royalty seems somewhat higher than the statistical norm among subjects. The Portuguese House of Braganza and the Spanish Bourbons produced some disturbing monarchs, while King Friedrich Wilhelm IV of Prussia and King Ludwig II of Bavaria both went mad. Ludwig was, of course, a Wittelsbach but it would be unfair to describe all that line as necessarily insane, rather than eccentric, over emotional dreamers, artistic and aesthetic, beyond the bounds of their self-interests. Romantics are not best suited to thrones.

It must, of course, be remembered that presidents, premiers and dictators can be unstable, eccentric and megalomaniac, while humble origins do not guarantee mental stability. George Petrovich, 'Kara George', who became Prince of Serbia in 1811, came from a family of peasant farmers; he lived up to the 'kara' (black) part of his name by shooting his father, hanging his brother and forcing a beehive over his mother's head. Nevertheless, there were some very odd blue-blooded monarchs, and interbreeding seems to have played a part in this.

The insistence on impeccable royal genealogy for the marriage partners of princes and princesses continued. One can see why, for it made monarchy a breed apart. Queen Victoria was quite liberal on this question. As we have seen, she was happy to accept Battenbergs, while the marriage of Prince George, the future George V, to Princess Mary of Teck marked a firm defiance of the shibboleths of the *Almanach de Gotha*. Princess Mary was a daughter of the Queen's first cousin and the fiancée of his deceased elder brother, the Duke of Clarence. The Tecks were a junior and relatively impoverished branch of the royal family, but her father, Prince Francis of Teck, was the child of a morganatic marriage. Princess Mary was to become an impeccable if frosty queen consort, but

her relatives proved a bit of an embarrassment. A rare departure from royal endogamy was the marriage of the Queen's
daughter, Princess Louise, to the Marquess of Lorne, a commoner, however aristocratic, though the marriage was not a
great success.[3]

The concept of royalty as an international caste sat oddly
beside the pressure for monarchs to identify with the nations
over which they ruled. As early as the eighteenth century, there
had been a tendency to view George III as the incarnation of
Britain, while Napoleon I projected himself as the personification of the spirit of the French nation, but there was an
inevitable contradiction between a hereditary system which
could give a foreigner the claim to a throne and the notion
of monarchs as the epitomes of nations. Napoleon, of course,
attempted to bridge the concepts by his second marriage,
hoping for an heir that would unite the nationalist charisma of
his name with impeccable royal blood. The Vienna Settlement
at the end of the Napoleonic Wars saw an attempt to reimpose
hereditary kingship and the principle of legitimacy, but French
success and nationalist triumphalism had brought into being
other nationalisms in opposition to it and this soon persuaded
monarchs that it was necessary to mix legitimacy with support
for the nation and its aspirations. The German Empire and the
Kingdom of Italy were, of course, created by kingdoms that
put themselves at the head of what have been called 'imagined
communities' made possible by literacy and new means of
communication.[4] Nationalism was, at first, largely a movement
supported by the middle classes, but gradually the growth of
the power of the state with its national education system and
military conscription brought national self-consciousness to
peasants and industrial workers.[5]

Italian and German unity were forged by the expansion of
indigenous monarchies, those of Piedmont and Prussia, but
even at the high tide of nationalism new states like Bulgaria,
Romania and Greece found it convenient to import their

kings from the multiplicity of German dynasties and from
Denmark. Serbia and Montenegro and, later, Albania, which
made do with home-grown dynasties, were in the minority.
Even the long-established Kingdom of Sweden settled down
happily under a line founded by one of Napoleon's marshals. When Norway, having been part of Denmark and then
become part of Sweden, opted for independence in 1905, it
chose a scion of the Danish house for its monarch. What is
surprising is that many of these transplants took so well.

The incongruity of the nation state ruled over by dynasties
with little or none of the blood of the nation has been insuf-
ficiently remarked upon. It is clearly more understandable in
respect of long-established monarchies, though it is striking
that, while the British monarchy came from the late eighteenth century to be synonymous with Britain and intimately
associated with patriotism, no English or British monarch had
married a commoner (and commoners included aristocrats)
since the reign of Henry VIII.[6] There was just as little Russian
blood in the Romanovs' veins. These were, however, long
established dynasties. That states born or reborn on the basis of
ethnicity should reach for the catalogue of potential monarchs
and consult the *Almanach de Gotha* was remarkable indeed.

To western European eyes, the monarchies and indeed the
states of eastern Europe founded in the wake of the retreating
Ottoman Empire were both remarkable and exotic. Here was
'Ruritania', a world of coups and counter-coups, of peasant
economies and palaces, of rival kingdoms and rival claimants
to thrones. Anthony Hope's novel *The Prisoner of Zenda*
(1884) was loosely based upon the abduction and subsequent
deposition of Prince Alexander of Battenberg of Bulgaria
by his Russian sponsors, and became one of the best-sellers
of its day. Alexander's successor, Ferdinand of Coburg, was a
less romantic figure: ill-mannered and crude, he indulged his
homosexual proclivities with a series of blond chauffeurs and
engine drivers, and was an embarrassment to other monarchs.

He was, nevertheless, cunning and ruthless, as well as vain and ambitious, and was dubbed the 'Balkan Fox'. Like the Bulgarians, the Greeks had to have two goes before finding a dynasty that more or less suited them and would last, with intervals, for a century. Otto of Bavaria, being found unsatisfactory, was replaced by a scion of the House of Schleswig-Holstein-Sonderburg-Glucksberg, the ruling dynasty of Denmark, a dynasty that rivalled the Coburgs in the search for thrones. Romania found a rather respectable king in the person of Charles of Hohenzollern-Sigmaringen, a Catholic branch of the ruling Prussian house. Dutiful, austere and level-headed, he made a sensible, if inappropriate, head of a state that saw itself as Latin rather than Slav, and considered its capital, Bucharest, to be the Paris of the Balkans. His consort, Elizabeth, previously Princess of Wied, was, however, a pure Ruritanian. She was an eccentric and a romantic who surrounded herself with poets and musicians, good and bad (and a lot of them were bad), and herself wrote novels and poems and spent much time in a mock Swiss dairy in the mountainous area of Sinaia. Her eccentricity extended to her political opinions for, bizarrely for a queen, she had republican views.

The rival native dynasties of Serbia, the Obrenovic and the Karageorgevic, were both of peasant stock and did little to give support to theories that humble origins made for better monarchs than long royal pedigrees, managing as they did in a few generations to go from brutal peasants to callous degenerates. The tiny and backward Principality of Montenegro, dominated by its capital, Cetinje, which aspired to be a modern city, was to say the least unusual. The prince-bishops of Montenegro had defied the Turks for centuries, and had had a succession system based, appropriately for celibate rulers, on cousinhood. Secularised as princes with hopes of becoming kings, the Petrovich rulers benefited from their advantageous strategic position betwixt Russian and Austrian spheres, and, their celibacy abandoned, were adept at finding prestigious marriage partners for their offspring. Here was a rather rougher Ruritania, the 'Pontevedro', as Gordon Brook-Shepherd has reminded us, of Franz Lehar's *Merry Widow*.[7] Albania remained part of the Ottoman Empire until 1912, but when this largely Islamic province achieved independence there was a move to attract a king from western Europe. A German prince, Wilhelm von Wied, reigned for a few months in 1914 before, wisely, returning to Germany.

Beneath this western image of 'Ruritania' was a region bereft of a traditional ruling class. There was, except in Romania, no indigenous aristocracy and little in the way of a commercial middle class, save perhaps in Greece and Romania, though in the latter the merchants and middlemen were mainly Jewish. Above the vast majority, the peasantry, were the bureaucracy and the army, with rather too many ambitious men competing for government posts. Newly born national aspirations were fuelled by literary and language revivals, and flourished in an atmosphere where there was everything to play for and new maps to be drawn in an area dominated for so long by the Ottoman Empire. There was still flesh on the moribund Empire, but also gains to be made at the expense of other states, and quarrels with them over the remaining Turkish possessions. Were Macedonians Greeks or conscious or unconscious Bulgarians or Serbs? Were national interests best served by alliance with Russia or Austria–Hungary? The monarchs sat on top of the Balkan powder keg, but – with the exception of the autocratic Nicholas of Montenegro – didn't control the fuses which could ignite it. They had to contend with, live with and sometimes assassinate, or be assassinated by, nationalist politicians and army officers like Stambouloff in Bulgaria and Pasic or, worse still, Apis in Serbia, or the more peaceable Bratianu in Romania. Monarchy in the Balkans had to ride nationalism. It could spur it on like Ferdinand of Bulgaria or try to rein it in like Carol of Romania, but essentially the horses had urges of their own.

On the whole, despite the posturing of the Kaiser, the bravado of Nicholas of Montenegro or the machinations of Foxy Ferdinand, monarchy was probably a restraint, if an ineffective one, on nationalism. The residual influence of the idea of the monarchy as being above nationality was awkwardly combined with the idea of monarchy as representative of the nation and its culture, but resulted in a synthesis with some beneficial results. Multinational empires like Austria–Hungary and Russia could place the emphasis upon the older concept, while in nation states monarchs could emphasise the monarchy as the guardian of national tradition, yet be a break upon 'blood and soil' nationalism and command the support of ethnic minorities. Even Queen Victoria, widely seen as the symbol of British pride and might, objected to the naval education of the sons of the Prince of Wales: 'Will a nautical education not engender and encourage national prejudices and make them think their own country superior to any other?'

Expectations that the complex web of relationships that connected the royal families of Europe would act as a prophylactic to wars or even ameliorate the savagery of war were to be confounded in 1914, but any assessment of the role of monarchical systems in the origins of the First World War requires a consideration of other aspects of early twentieth-century European monarchy, and in particular of the actual power wielded by the emperors and kings.

Historians have long debated the nature of European society in the late nineteenth and early twentieth centuries. A view, heavily influenced by Marxism, is that industrialisation and urbanisation had resulted in a bourgeois capitalist society; one which was in full flower in western Europe and only immanent as one moved eastwards. It was true that kings still reigned and the landed aristocracy retained social prestige, but this was the icing on a cake whose important layers were the middle class and the restless proletariat. The reality was that money, not birth, industry and capital, not land, ruled. An alternative view is that this was not a bourgeois but an *ancien régime* society, one in which not just residual prestige but real power remained vested in monarchs, nobility and landowners. These groups were apprehensive and uneasily aware that they were threatened by socio-economic change, but were far from defeatist; indeed, the years immediately before 1914 witnessed a determined attempt by the old order to strengthen its hold upon power.[8]

The concept of an *ancien régime* Europe is a useful redress of a depiction of pre-1914 Europe, which sees kings and aristocrats as simply the anachronistic veneer on a modern world: crowns, swords, breastplates, plumed helmets and horses against a background of tramcars, railways, mass-circulation newspapers and factories. It is correct to argue that the old order remained vital, but we must not disregard the degree to which it had been forced to adapt to economic change and to mass society, and had accepted a diminution of political power with the growth of representative institutions.

European monarchies had changed considerably in the course of the nineteenth century. The changes were more apparent as one moved from west to east across Europe, with the British monarchy at one extreme and the Tsar of Russia at the other. One of the main features of the adaptation of monarchy to modern conditions has already been discussed – the ever-closer association of kings with the national identity of subjects. Other major changes were the coming to terms with the growth of representative assemblies, the need to project the glamour and symbolism of monarchy to a wider audience and the assertion that monarchs were the leaders of civil society as well as the heads of state.

Almost everywhere, ground had been ceded when it came to direct political power. Constitutional monarchy was the norm, though the powers exercised by sovereigns within the constitutions varied considerably. It was not just the existence of assemblies, however wide or narrow the franchise by which they were elected, or the means by which ministers were appointed, that determined the limits upon royal power, it was the wider audience for government of any kind. Mass literacy, newspapers, photo-journalism and easier physical communications were at once the monarchies' impediments and their opportunity. Monarchs, like governments, needed popular support.

A conventional view of the spectrum of European monarchies at the beginning of the twentieth century is one that sees monarchical systems stretching from the liberal-constitutional model epitomised by the British monarchy to the autocratic model provided by Tsarist Russia. At the one extreme were monarchs who reigned but did not rule, and at the other end those who exercised complete personal power, while in between were multiple gradations of qualified constitutionalism and limited autocracy. In the opinion of liberal contemporaries and of most historians, this spectrum paralleled the modernity of western Europe and the backwardness of eastern Europe. There was little doubt as to which was the progressive model. Monarchies in which kings ruled were either the products of societies that were backward economically and socially or were the result of the anachronistic hold that particular royal houses maintained on government in defiance of the changes that had taken or were taking place in the countries over which they presided. It is, however, worth noting that by 1905 every European monarchy, even that of Russia, was, at least in theory, limited in its powers by some sort of constitution.

A division between eastern and western Europe leaves out the special case of Iberia. The problems of hereditary systems were present in both Portugal and Spain in an acute form. In both instances there were conflicts between rival branches of the royal house, conflicts that became embroiled with tensions between Catholicism and secularism, and conservatism and liberalism, as well as with each other.

With an uncanny similarity, these royal divisions saw young princesses opposed to their uncles. In Portugal, King Pedro had, in 1826, abdicated his Portuguese throne, preferring to continue to be Emperor of Brazil. He abdicated in favour of his daughter Maria, who was engaged to his brother, Dom Miguel. Miguel, however, proclaimed himself king in 1828 and the Queen, who was still a child, took refuge with her father in Brazil. In 1831 Emperor Pedro abdicated his Brazilian throne and came to England, where he set about organising a military expedition with the intention of over-throwing Miguel and re-establishing Maria as Queen of Portugal. In 1832 this expeditionary force landed in Portugal and a civil war began.

The Portuguese civil war became enmeshed with a similar conflict in Spain, where King Ferdinand VII altered the laws of succession to allow his three-year-old daughter to succeed him in place of his brother, Don Carlos, who joined Dom Miguel in Portugal. Britain and France, perceiving the conflicts as between the forces of liberalism and progress and those of reaction, supported the two queens diplomatically and militarily. Dom Miguel was defeated in 1834, but Don Carlos returned to Spain, where a fierce war continued until 1840. The Iberian monarchs were, however, threatened henceforth on two sides; by conservatives and ultra-Catholics, for whom they were too secular and liberal; and in the larger towns by extreme radicals and working-class movements, for whom they were too conservative and too Catholic.

Few of the subsequent monarchs of Portugal were even moderately competent rulers. It was an echo of the Dom Miguel affair that precipitated the end of the Portuguese monarchy when, in the early 1900s, a bill to lift the prohibition that barred his successors from entering Portugal failed to gain the assent of parliament by only four votes. In 1908 King Carlos and his heir, the Duke of Braganza, were assassinated and in 1910 the new monarch, King Manuel, sought refuge in

Britain from a revolution. In 1911 the monarchy was replaced by a republic.

No country was more polarised than Spain, where the politically conscious classes were divided into extreme radicals (*exaltados*) and clerical-monarchists (*apostolicas*). To some extent the Carlist wars of the nineteenth century provided the unifying symbols for those who accepted the need for constitutional reform and the modernisation of Spain and those who felt this was a betrayal of the country's native traditions. Yet the situation was more complex than this: republicans felt that even constitutional monarchy represented too much continuity with control of society by a backward-looking Church and the powerful religious orders, while the separatist demands of Catalans and Basques cut across any simple choice between the ruling monarchs and the die-hard Carlist pretenders. Matters were made much worse by a succession of weak and incompetent monarchs. There can be few better examples of the disadvantages of excessive royal interbreeding than that of Spain's Bourbon line, for which the number of possible marriage partners was limited to the offspring of Europe's Catholic dynasties. Spain's monarchs were classified by one writer as: 'Philip V, mentally unbalanced and sensual; Ferdinand VI, mad and impotent; Charles III, almost normal; Charles IV, imbecile; Ferdinand VII, excessively sensual, cruel and sanguinary; Isobella II, nymphomaniac; Alfonso XII, tubercular'.[9]

That the alliance of dynasties by marriage could still lead to diplomatic ruptures was demonstrated by the 'Spanish Marriages' crisis in the mid-1840s. Whether Queen Isabella should marry a Coburg, an Orleanist or a Bourbon prince embittered Anglo-French relations. Eventually she married the unattractive Duke of Cadiz. Isabella was deposed in 1868, but the repercussions of her deposition led to renewed international friction, this time between France and Prussia. Spain being in want of a monarch, Prince Leopold of Hohenzollern-Sigmaringen, a Catholic branch of the Hohenzollern family, one member of which was already on the Romanian throne, was encouraged by Bismarck to take up an offer to become King of Spain. Leopold first accepted and then withdrew, but the clash between Germany and France had enormous repercussions: the Franco-Prussian War, the end of the second French Empire and the beginning of the second German Empire.

After a brief republic, the Spanish monarchy was restored under Alfonso XII. Under Alfonso XIII, who was born after his father's death in 1885 and came to the throne on his birth, a constitutional monarchy was introduced. His marriage to Princess Ena, daughter of Princess Beatrice and Prince Henry of Battenberg, seemed to be a new departure and to represent a potential widening of the Bourbon gene pool. A strong and healthy crown prince might assist the Spanish house to preside over the modernisation of Spain and heal its sharp divisions. Unfortunately, Queen Victoria's granddaughter Ena was a carrier of haemophilia, which had disastrous consequences both for the marriage and for the Spanish monarchy.

The three great empires of central and eastern Europe have often been lumped together as to a greater or lesser degree autocratic, with Germany the most problematic because of the contrast between an outmoded political-constitutional structure and its modern economic and social structure. There were many differences between these three empires, but perhaps the most important distinction was that while the ethos, style and character of the Russian and Austro-Hungarian monarchies were traditional and dependent upon the spiritual and lineal dimensions of monarchy, the personal rule that Wilhelm II aspired to was a curious hybrid of the traditional and the modern, a monarchy that was charismatic and dynamic. In a sense, the Wilhelmine monarchy sought a 'third way' between traditional and constitutional monarchy, a monarchy entwined with nationalism and one that sought the cheers and adulation of the populace as eagerly as any politician. Wilhelm's style and the image he strove to project were in tune with changes in the nature of nationalism, which was becoming less liberal and more racial in tone, and with neo-Darwinist ideas that pointed to the struggle for the survival of the fittest among nations, in which victory would go to the young, strong and healthy. Carefully disguising his withered arm, he gave the impression of energy and dynamism as, with heroic poses and his moustaches waxed into erection, he sought to epitomise the vigour of the German Empire. The degree to which Kaiser Wilhelm's style of monarchy was popular in Germany, especially at the turn of the century, has been underestimated, and it had also an appeal as a model for other monarchies in eastern Europe and further afield, with the Japanese constitution of 1889 borrowing significantly from the German constitution.

The British monarchy provided the example for the mainstream development in western Europe: a gradual diminution of political power and a move to a position above the struggles and disputes of politics. It was not a deliberately contrived example. British monarchs did not will a cession of political power, and it was as much the accidents of royal lives and the idiosyncrasies of particular monarchs that hastened it. The 'madness' of George III, the age and poor health of George IV and William IV when they came to the throne and the long retirement of Queen Victoria after Albert's death all played their part. By the late nineteenth century, though the Queen herself might not recognise it, the executive power of the British monarch was severely limited. The Queen commanded enormous respect, and insisted upon being consulted, with Lord Salisbury finding her difficult to deal with, but it was the Queen's government, which needed a majority in the House of Commons, rather than the Queen herself, which made political decisions. Things might well have been different if Prince Albert had lived longer, for the Saxe-Coburg theory of constitutional monarchy, implemented by King Leopold I in Belgium, was far more interventionist, and provided for a politically neutral monarch who, nevertheless, exercised power above political parties.

The model of monarchy provided by the German Empire seemed very different. Here was a monarch who ruled, who was in direct command of his armed forces and who determined foreign policy. The irony is that Kaiser Wilhelm II, who attempted to institute a monarchy in which he exercised supreme political power, was the grandson of Queen Victoria and Prince Albert. If a longer life for Prince Albert might have led to a more interventionist British monarchy, a longer life for Kaiser Friedrich III might have led to a less interventionist one in Germany. Friedrich, who was much influenced by his wife, Victoria and Albert's eldest daughter, might, given time, have steered Germany in a liberal and constitutional direction. But Wilhelm, who reacted strongly against his parents and against British and Saxe-Coburg ideas of constitutional monarchy, was determined to rule without interference.

Just how significant Kaiser Wilhelm's contribution to the nature of the German state was prior to 1914, and to what extent we can see him as exercising personal rule, is a matter of debate among historians. German historians have on the whole tended to eschew biography, and have been reluctant to endow either the Kaiser himself or the institution of the imperial monarchy with too much influence, preferring to think in terms of a social and economic order, an imperial system and broad forces such as class development and interest groups. Yet the Kaiser did matter. As John Röhl has argued, it is absurd to suppose that the decision-making process in Germany can be understood 'without paying due attention to the monarch who was in theory and practice the pivot of the whole system of government, to the man who was *summus episcopus*, and had absolute powers of command in the military sphere and total control over all official appointments'.[10] This did not necessarily mean that the Kaiser was the government; it did mean that no government could exist without his support.

German unity, achieved after the defeat of France in 1870, was the work of Bismarck, of Prussia and, only then, of the House of Hohenzollern. It not only altered the balance of power in Europe, bringing into being an industrialised state with an expanding population and great military might, but was a major blow to what had seemed the irresistible march of liberalism in both politics and economics. A federal empire that retained the monarchs and parliaments of its constituent parts under the suzerainty of the Prussian King, now the Emperor, and a parliament, the Reichstag, for all of Germany, it was more federal or less unitary than the USA, where there was only one army, whereas Germany had three. The success of Bismarck in forging German unity from above emasculated German liberalism, bringing National Liberals behind the new regime and imbuing the united Germany with Prussian respect for the power of government, its bureaucracy and the army, while also discrediting liberal economic nostrums such as the free market and free trade. The constitution gave the Emperor considerable, even in theory supreme, power, though until the 1890s this was not exercised; no government could continue without the confidence of the Emperor, but the emperors were usually content to leave quotidian government to ministers and to Bismarck. There was no need for the young Wilhelm to change the constitution – only its practice. Was the so-called 'personal rule' of the Kaiser established after the dismissal of Bismarck fact or fiction? Essentially, Wilhelm II attempted to make the apparent power of the monarchy during the Bismarck years a reality. Some contemporaries appreciated this. The Prussian minister, Botho Eulenburg, wrote:

The King of Prussia has the right to rule autocratically …
If now the Kaiser steps forward as a personal ruler, he has

every right to do so, the only question is whether the consequences can be borne in the long run.[11]

The German Empire might appear to be Prussia writ large,
but as Friedrich von Holstein, a major figure in the German
Foreign Office, commented:

As for ruling with the Conservatives alone, I had thought
we had agreed long ago that the King of Prussia could
perhaps, but the German Kaiser could never, rule on an
exclusively Conservative basis.[12]

To Holstein, the Kaiser instituted 'an operetta regime, but not
one that a European nation at the end of the nineteenth century will put up with'.[13]

Kaiser Wilhelm never established an autocracy, but rather
used the powers he had within the constitution to ensure
that ministers were his ministers and to make frequent and
erratic interventions in state affairs. What he attempted to
establish has been described by John Röhl as a 'personal
monarchy'. The united Germany that Wilhelm II inherited
was a complex entity with its federal monarchies and parliaments, and a Reichstag in which the Social Democrats
became the largest single party. A more patient and cunning
ruler and one with greater consistency might have been able
to create the dynamic, populist, quasi-absolute monarchy
he aimed for. As it was, he was able to use the constitutional position he inherited to create a regime in which
democracy jostled with autocracy and which, while it was
in part a restoration of pre-Bismarckian Prussia, was also in
its populist nationalism very modern. The period in which
the Kaiser exerted the greatest influence on policy started in
1890 with the fall of Bismarck, and lasted until 1908, when
the combination of the scandals involving his close associates and the publication of a rash interview given by the

monarch to the British *Daily Telegraph* rather undermined his authority.

It was Russia that was the state over which the monarch ruled with absolute authority, and that was formally an autocracy. Absolute power has, of course, always been an impossibility, for even the greatest autocrats have found their power limited by distance and the sheer impossibility of controlling every detail of administration personally. Arguably, modern communications were to make personal rule more feasible and would later enable Stalin (Ivan the Terrible with electricity) to keep a closer watch over his subordinates than the mightiest Tsar. Yet the complexity of modern states and their economies pointed to the necessity of entrusting power to subordinates, controlling a vast bureaucracy and coordinating government departments. Hereditary monarchy ensures legitimacy but not necessarily competence. Nicholas was, unfortunately, totally without the ability to rule an empire. As one of his biographers has put it: '... his problem tended to be that he could understand many points of view and wavered between them'.[14]

It was Nicholas II's fate that the Russia he ruled faced a myriad of problems internal and external: pressures for constitutional reform, the tensions of rapid industrialisation, which was essential if Russia was to remain a great power, revolutionary movements, elites that were not prepared to surrender any of their privileges, and the threats and challenges to an Empire stretching from Manchuria to the Balkans. Nicholas had able ministers, but as he felt it necessary to involve himself in everything there was no coordination of government, no real cabinet system. The central problem was the need for the modernisation of the economy, society and the constitution, and the task was to achieve this without engendering such discontent and instability as would lead to revolution. The Tsar was not best fitted for this task, as the Russia he admired, half-imagined and loved was the 'old Russia': 'Unlike the last

German Emperor, Nicholas was consistently old fashioned, not a curious and tension-ridden combination of ancient and modern.'[15]

Russia was perhaps the least modern of European powers, save for her arch enemy, the Ottoman Empire. She was also enormously successful in expanding her frontiers. Indeed, like the Ottoman Empire she was becoming by the early twentieth century more and more an Asiatic power, though in Russia's case by expansion into Asia and in the Ottoman case by loss of European territory. The paradox of Russia is the combination and at times rapid sequence of strength and weakness: a colossus and a laggard, her armies deep into Europe as in 1814 and 1945, and then seemingly torn apart by endemic problems in 1917 or the 1990s. At the beginning of the twentieth century, she was at once pushing at the frontiers of Turkey, Persia and China but facing the enormous problem of achieving modernisation with stability. Nicholas II was no strategic thinker and no war leader, but he was unfortunate to be on the throne at the time when his ministers and generals engaged in war with the one non-European power that had successfully blended its own military traditions with the modern science of warfare. Defeat by Japan not only humiliated Russia but led to unsuccessful revolution and constitutional government that the Tsar was unable to accept or dispense with.

It is, nevertheless, only hindsight from the other side of the First World War and the revolutions of 1917 that has enabled some historians to portray Tsarist Russia as slithering remorselessly towards revolution. Despite all the hesitancy of the reform process and all the procrastination and stupidity of the Tsar, it can be argued that Russia was steadily moving towards a modern economy, would have inevitably achieved a more liberal constitution and would have surmounted the universal tensions that came with early industrialisation had it not been for the First World War. There can be no definite assent or dissent to this proposition, though it can be asserted that both conditions and morale had to be very bad before the long-suffering, but enduring, population lost complete faith in the notion of a paternal Tsar, and that the stubborn and indecisive personality of Nicholas II contributed to the downfall of the Russian monarchy.

As a study of empires has observed, Austria–Hungary and Russia had much in common:

> Both were great land empires covering huge territories and ruling over many different peoples. These were quintessentially continental, military and – in their last centuries – bureaucratic empires. Commerce and the oceans were of secondary importance.[16]

The ubiquity of bureaucracy was the element that gave both countries a claim to modernity, and no country could claim to be better than Austria–Hungary in the number of its civil servants, the careful documentation of its subjects from cradle to grave or the skill with which it exacted taxation and civic duties from its inhabitants. The unsung heroes of Austria–Hungary were its administrators, its judiciary and its functionaries. From the judge or the governor of a crown land to the tax-collector and the policeman, the administrators of the Empire were ever present but on the whole efficient and impartial. This had its downside in a slightly stifling atmosphere of petty bureaucracy; had traffic wardens been invented, the Empire would have had a splendid corps. What moderated the Kafkaesque bureaucratic and police state was a respect for parliaments and the law. Laws might be imperfect, but the servants of the state upheld them. This was less true of Hungary after 1867, when the Hungarians exercised considerable autonomy in the lands they dominated, but it was, nevertheless, the case that the imperial government and its officials provided the Empire with a stability based upon the rule of law, which enabled social, cultural and economic life to thrive despite its lack of national homogeneity.

The Austrian Empire was, in nineteenth-century terms, an accident of history, a cluster of territories and nationalities acquired by a family largely by inheritance and marriage. In 1526 Ferdinand of Austria had become King of Bohemia and of Hungary, two ancient kingdoms with strong traditions. With the ebbing of the tide of Ottoman conquest, the Austrian Empire was further enlarged with mainly Slav territories, while the partition of Poland brought Austria new territory and a frontier with Russia. Like Russia, the Habsburg Empire encompassed many nationalities, but while the Russians who exercised dominion over the other nationalities in their Empire made up some 45 per cent of the overall population, the Germans, the largest national group within the Habsburg Empire, made up only about a quarter of the population in the late nineteenth century. The growing strength of nationalism in the nineteenth century thus presented the Empire with acute problems. On the one hand, Austria aspired to be a German state, even the leading German state, and was a member of the German Confederation, but on the other hand there were eleven major national groups within the boundaries of the Empire, and six of them (Germans, Italians, Poles, Ruthenes, Romanians and Serbs) had more fellow nationals outside the state than within it.

The events of the 'year of revolutions' 1848 demonstrated the weakness of the state in an era of nationalism. Germans were attracted by the idea of a national German state; Italians sought a unified Italy, while Czechs demanded greater autonomy and the Hungarians fought for independence. Franz Josef, who came to the throne in 1848, renewed attempts by his predecessors to centralise rule by Vienna and apply imperial principles throughout the Empire. The defeat of Austria by Prussia in 1866 and the unification of Germany under Prussia in 1871 presented a threat to the Empire's very existence in that Austrian Germans might seek to become part of the new German Reich and forced a reassessment of the policy of centralisation. The agreement with Hungary in 1867 inaugurated the dual monarchy but did little to satisfy Slav aspirations, while it worsened the position of Slav subjects in the Hungarian half of the Empire. There was no good reason for Austria–Hungary to seek territorial expansion. Any expansion to the east would only result in more Slav subjects, and Hungarian opposition ruled out any trialist solution to the Slav problem. The change of dynasty in Serbia in 1903 resulted in a change of diplomatic alignment, with Serbia becoming pro-Russian and anti-Austrian. The Empire's fatal response was a forward policy in the Balkans, resulting in the annexation of Bosnia and Herzegovina, more Slav subjects and more Slav problems.

Despite its problems with its multiplicity of nationalities, Austria–Hungary continued to be a stable state and society. Not only was this imperial state relatively well governed but it commanded widespread support. Positive support came from its aristocracy and bureaucrats; the Hungarian nobility and gentry were satisfied with their newly regained autonomy and saw the Empire as a bulwark against their Russian enemies, while its Catholic German population regarded the united Germany under Protestant Prussia with some antipathy. A more passive support came from the Czechs, who were able to prosper, while if Croats found their traditional rights encroached on by the Hungarians they did not necessarily yearn to be united with Serbia, with its lower standard of living and alien tradition. It was the monarchy and the hard-working if unimaginative Emperor and the imperial administration which kept the cumbersome state together. The very old-fashioned nature of a monarchy in which the emperor did not identify with any section of his subjects and the competing nations under his rule was its strength. A recent study of the Empire has concluded that, far from being the anachronism of caricature, it was an efficiently administered state with a thriving economy and culture in which citizens of differing ethnic groups benefited from, 'shared imperial institutions, administrative practices, and cultural programmes'.[17] Its merits were to be displayed, dramatically, after its demise, by the chaotic and violent histories of the successor states.

Like most of the other monarchs of Europe, Franz Josef, who considered the army the main support of the dynasty, spent most of his time in uniform, though usually a rather dull and plain uniform. A considerable number of his subjects were also uniformed, and this too was true of most of Europe. It was the Kaiser, however, who best personified the close relationship that existed between monarchs and the armed forces. Usually wearing uniform (he had more than four hundred different uniforms) and seen seated on a white charger (he even, somewhat ridiculously, sat on a saddle while working at the desk in his study), he strove to appear the very model of a military monarch. In almost every monarchical state, however, a special relationship between kings and their armed forces existed. This was in part a link with kingly tradition for it embodied the idea of the warrior leader and the notion of leadership in warfare as a royal and aristocratic preserve. Everywhere in Europe, the officer caste was overwhelmingly aristocratic, and this was so even in republican France, where the army was ambivalent about the politicians and the republic it served. Whether or not the special relationship between the monarch and the armed forces was expressly written into the constitution, as it was in most states, it existed in every monarchy.

The small, dumpy figure in widow's black, Queen Victoria, might seem an unlikely icon for soldiers and sailors, but it was to 'Queen and Country' that the British armed forces were committed, not to Mr Gladstone, Lord Salisbury or Mr Balfour and country. Late Victorian soldiers were in a very real sense 'soldiers of the Queen', and these soldiers who were prepared to die for the Queen-Empress included not just British soldiers but African and Indian recruits, to whom the concepts of loyalty to a British Prime Minister or cabinet made little appeal. Perhaps the magic of monarchy has never been so clearly demonstrated in the modern world as by the charismatic appeal of a queen who, without willing it, provided a vital image from the contrast between her elderly, female and non-martial figure and the aura of power that emanated from her. We can distinguish between the appeal to armed men of the male warrior figure, bonded with his followers by his valour and leadership, and that of the anointed female, at once powerful and vulnerable. Which was the more psychologically compelling image; which in the circumstances of a battle, when all seemed lost, rallied the lines? To British rankers, who would have derided any suggestion that they should not be absolute master over their wives in their own house, or to Islamic recruits to the Indian Army, the answer was, against the idioms of normal life, the Queen. This grand and vulnerable queen was more potent than the most resplendent king.

The close relationship of kings with the armed forces was traditional, but it was given an added significance by the militarisation of European societies and the enormous increase in the size of armies. Save in Britain, conscription for a term was almost universal. As well as serving to weld national consciousness, turning peasants into Frenchmen and Italians, a period of service in national armies imbued conscripts with respect for authority and its apex, the sovereign. The introduction of the reserve carried the military hierarchy into civilian life. By and large, the military hierarchy paralleled the civilian one: officers were landowners, or those of less elite regiments businessmen and managers, NCOs were foremen or farmers, while privates were labourers. Yet the relative positions were not just parallel, as the kudos of military rank began to impinge upon the civilian pecking-order.

Germany above all epitomised the society geared for economic and military activity, with the military ethos permeating all strata and uniforms ubiquitous. Only in Germany could an impostor in a hired uniform have taken over a detachment of soldiers and by taking advantage of the immediate respect his uniform demanded 'inspected' the town hall of a Berlin suburb and walked off with 4,000 marks from its treasury under the eyes of the mayor and corporation, as did the 'captain of Kopernick'. Britain was ostensibly very different, having a small army and no conscription, while until the introduction of the territorial army in 1905 there were only the yeomanry, the militia and the volunteers, designed more to check militarism than to assist it, in reserve. Even in Britain, however, where officers never wore uniform when off duty, a military influence was detectable, with military ranks being used in civilian life to a greater degree than in previous periods. If this brought the state more visibly into daily life, it also drew attention to the heads of state and the focus of loyalty in most states, the monarchs.

The other sphere in which crowned heads claimed a special role was foreign policy. They could indeed claim that, despite premiers and governments, it was family business. Edward VII went beyond his intimate though not always friendly relations with the cousins and nephews who sat upon Europe's thrones, and cultivated a special relationship with France. He exercised considerable influence in foreign affairs, and if this amounted not so much to an independent foreign policy as one in tune with his ministers, if sometimes ahead of them, his influence was important. Very much a European in outlook, he had travelled widely on the continent when Prince of Wales, in part to visit his royal relatives but more often to relax at spas and enjoy himself with women and at gaming tables out of sight of his mother. He had, however, acquired considerable knowledge of European affairs and of the people who presided over them. Moreover, Edward had great social skills when he was minded to use them, and he knew how to impress and charm not only kings and politicians but crowds. It would be easy to see Edward's involvement in foreign policy as putting himself and his position at the service of his government, the 'warmer-up' for the diplomats by his visits and crowd pleasing, leaving the real business to the politicians and Foreign Office officials. There was, however, more to his diplomacy than that, and with at least one significant initiative he led and his government followed.

The extended European tour for which Edward set off on the *Victoria and Albert* in the spring and early summer of 1903 was a most unusual breach of the normal protocol that governed relations between the King and the Foreign Minister and Foreign Office. The initial preparations for this tour, which was to begin with Lisbon and then go on to Rome and Paris, were made, not by the Palace or by the Foreign Office, but by the King's great friend the Portuguese Ambassador, the Marquis de Soveral, nicknamed the 'Blue Monkey', who was as much a '*boulevardier*' as the King. As Gordon Brook-Shepherd has put it:

> That … he had declined to tell either his wife or the utterly trustworthy Francis Knollys [his Private Secretary] what he was about to do could be passed off as decisions which, though extraordinary, affected only his own Palace domain. But to launch himself on such a crucial journey at a time when his government stood, still hesitating, at the diplomatic crossroads of Europe, challenged all constitutional practice. To do so without informing any member of the government, from the Prime Minister and foreign secretary downwards, was to drive a coach and horses through that constitution.[18]

The visit to Lisbon was of little importance, but that to Rome was somewhat controversial, given that Italy was a junior member of the Triple Alliance and that Edward met the Pope, Leo XIII, in the Vatican, which was likely to upset Protestant opinion at home and was awkward for King Victor Emmanuel, as the Kingdom of Italy did not recognise the Vatican State. Paris was the important and the difficult leg of the tour. Anglo-French relations, usually edgy, had been brought to the brink of war over rivalries in north Africa, culminating in the Fashoda incident, a confrontation between British and French troops on the banks of the Upper Nile in 1898, a crisis from which the French had to back down in a humiliating manner. The Paris visit saw Edward at his best. Genuinely fond of the city, he wooed its dignitaries and the ordinary inhabitants with his dignified but comfortable figure, expansive charm and excellent French, always finding the right gesture and the apposite phrase.

Did he just prepare the ground for the '*entente*' agreed by politicians and diplomats in the following year? Britain had begun to recognise that her great Empire and her multiple interests had left her position somewhat over extended, and that she needed friends in a dangerous world. Already, in 1902, she had entered into an alliance with Japan. Both government and opposition were gradually moving to an anti-German and pro-French position, which was shared by influential Foreign Office officials. The tactic of compensating France for English predominance in Egypt and control of the Sudan by giving her a free hand in Morocco may have been crucial in securing an Anglo-French understanding. Yet the *rapprochement* between British and French public opinion was not only an essential prerequisite for the *entente*, it was essential for the maintenance of what was never a treaty, and the King had a lot to do with such improved relations. In an age when public opinion was beginning to matter, diplomacy could not be left to the diplomats, and the King was rather more effective in appealing to French opinion than British politicians.

Whereas Edward considered that he had special rights and influence over foreign policy, he recognised the determining influence of his ministers, and was, in any case, usually in general agreement with them. If historians have been on the whole reluctant to accept the degree of influence Edward exercised, his nephew the Kaiser, believing that he himself had the right and duty to make foreign policy, rather overestimated Edward's influence, seeing him as an insidious anti-German, whose hand could be detected in every German reverse. The Kaiser's foreign policy initiatives are usually depicted as rash, impetuous and ill thought out. They were certainly often embarrassing to his ministers, but they were not necessarily stupid. If Germany was not bent on a major war in which she would face both France and Russia, her main problem was the close and firm alliance with Austria–Hungary and the profound enmity between that empire and Russia. Bismarck had, with astute diplomacy, managed to prevent the logic of the alliance with Austria–Hungary becoming too apparent and had maintained an understanding with Russia. Wilhelm, himself, had, in the aftermath of his dismissal of Bismarck, approved the dropping of the 'Reinsurance Treaty' with Russia, with the consequence of the Franco-Russian Alliance of 1894. Wilhelm glorified in Germany's military strength and delighted in the prospect of a big navy as well as a magnificent army, but though he wanted Germany to be great he had no appetite for war itself. As the general staff and ministers increasingly moved towards regarding the fundamental dispositions for a future conflict as set, the Kaiser toyed with ideas of a major diplomatic breakthrough by which, via negotiations with his fellow sovereign, Nicholas II, he could renew cordial relations with Russia.

He found his opportunity in 'yacht diplomacy', when he met his cousin, Nicholas, on board the latter's yacht, *Standart*, in the Gulf of Finland in 1905. The still-born Treaty of Björkö, which provided for a German–Russian alliance if either power were attacked, cut across the policies of both Russian and German ministers and was incompatible with existing alliances. There was, nevertheless, sense in it, for if Germany was prepared to impose restraint upon Austria–Hungary's Balkan ambitions, then Russia had no real need of the French alliance. Things had gone too far, however, and the existing alliances were firmly established. Both the Kaiser and the Tsar, who had been cajoled and browbeaten into signing the agreement, were overruled by their horrified ministers. The incident demonstrates the limits to the authority of two supposedly all-powerful sovereigns, and also the lack of real flexibility in the power politics of the day, for the alliances between Germany and Austria–Hungary and between France and Russia had become so buttressed by financial agreements and most significantly by military planning that their abandonment was almost unthinkable.

Whatever their real power, the splendour of the monarchs of Europe reached new heights at the turn of the centuries. Their capital cities became great stages on which to mount ceremonies and processions. Perhaps the new grandeur of capitals was more an exaltation of state and nation, for it affected republics and monarchies alike. The monarchy that had been the pioneer of this had departed, leaving Haussmann's Paris a great and impressive city for republican rituals, with the Eiffel Tower added for extra *éclat*. Across the Atlantic, Washington was rebuilt in an ostentatiously imperial style, with the Washington Memorial and the Lincoln Monument immortalising the national past, and the grand public buildings surrounding the Capitol underlining, monumentally, national pride and strength. In Rome, ambitious planning saw the transformation of the capital of the newly unified state in the last decades of the nineteenth century and the first of the twentieth culminating in the Victor Emmanuel Monument of 1911. In Vienna, Emperor Franz Josef, in 1857, ordered the construction of the magnificent Ringstrasse, lined with a series of immense buildings, a process which took more than thirty years to complete. Unlike Rome, Vienna and Paris, Berlin had no great cultural or architectural past, but the new Empire needed a capital that would express the triumph of unification, and wide streets, spacious squares, the Reichstag, the Column of Victory and Siegesalle provided such a city. Even little Belgium, its monarch flush with the proceeds of his private fiefdom, the Congo, turned the solid merchant city of Brussels into an imperial capital in miniature. London had never gone in for that sort of thing, with even George IV's inspired creation of the area from Regent's Park to the Mall representing elegance rather than grandeur, but it began to do so in the early twentieth century, with the building of Admiralty Arch and the widening of the Mall providing Buckingham Palace with a more impressive frontage.

The redesigning of capitals was a general trend found in republics as well as monarchies and one that could be seen as reifying the nation, its institutions, and self-image. Republics and monarchies alike could provide gorgeously attired troops for the processions that took place on these national stages, but the theatre of monarchy enabled kings and emperors to, in their person encapsulate, not just the nation of the present, but that of the past, and its achievements and victories. Kings and their consorts made, for the most part, more impressive centrepieces for great ceremonies than politicians in frockcoats. Queens regnant were, by chance, a rarity in the period, with Queen Wilhelmina of the Netherlands, who inaugurated more than a century of female rulers, joining Queen Victoria as the only female European ruler for the last years of the nineteenth century, although, just as the First World War was beginning, Grand Duchess Marie Adelaide succeeded her father as ruler of tiny Luxembourg.

There was a general gilding of the theatre of monarchy, with the production ever more professional and expensive. As the political power of monarchs either dwindled or had to be shared with chambers and ministers, the splendour of royal display amid elaborate ritual increased. This was to a great extent a result of the growth of the audience for monarchy. Cities were more populous, and the crowds that could assemble for a coronation or a royal wedding or to celebrate a national triumph were much larger and were swollen further by the considerable numbers that modern transport systems could bring to the capital for the occasion. Then there was the virtual audience who read of the ceremonial occasions in mass-circulation newspapers and saw photographs or illustrations of it in magazines. Kings, emperors and their advisers also felt the need for an audience to impress, dazzle and win over. As David Cannadine has written:

> In England, as elsewhere in Europe, the unprecedented developments in industry and in social relationships, and the massive expansion of the yellow press, made it both necessary and possible to present the monarch, in all the splendour of his ritual, in this essentially new way, as a symbol of consensus and continuity to which all might defer.[19]

The 'invention' of tradition is perhaps too strong a term for what happened in established monarchies, but there was certainly a lot of refurbishing of ritual and ceremony, and a projection – almost a production – of monarchy. Mass society had a great appetite for display and for 'a show'. Queen Victoria's long period of mourning and her reluctance to appear in public had made her unpopular in the 1860s, and her reluctant agreement to participate in the elaborate celebrations for her Golden Jubilee launched her triumphant last fourteen years on the throne. Edward VII, as Prince of Wales, had realised the necessity for royal occasions to be magnificent and superbly organised, and when he became king he built upon the experience of his mother's jubilees, and his own state and royal occasions were, with the aid of his confidant and adviser, Lord Esher, mounted with pomp and panache. The same tendency was apparent in the way royal funerals, coronations and state visits were organised in Russia, Italy and Germany, while the Habsburg Empire was not to be outdone. None could quite match the exotic nature of the Delhi Durbar held in 1912 to mark George V's accession to the throne of India.

If such magnificence underlined and promoted the role of monarchs as heads of state, other royal activities promoted their position as heads of civil society. One was the development of the tradition that royalty supported charitable endeavours and societies for the improvement and advancement of almost everything. German royalty, especially the females whose families governed small states, had long been noted for their public-spirited activities, involving themselves in schooling and the care of the sick. In Britain monarchs had since Stuart times patronised societies for the advancement of science and the arts and from the reign of George III royal support for charities and organisations dedicated to social and scientific progress became the norm. William IV's consort, Queen Adelaide, increased considerably the number of charities and worthy causes supported by the monarchy. She was particularly attached to charities concerned with providing for children and making provision for maternal care, but supported a wide range of causes. Naval officers' widows, Protestant clergymen in Ireland, infirmaries, schools and lunatic asylums all benefited from her support. Prince Albert was especially concerned to support societies concerned with progress, science and improvement, while Princess, later Queen, Alexandra, combining beauty and compassion, became a national symbol of the generous charitable impulse. By the late nineteenth century almost all European royalty made at least a show of supporting such activities. Wilhelm II founded the Kaiser Wilhelm Society for the Encouragement of Scientific Research, and both shocked and bored his Uncle Edward by pontificating on the relative merits of petrol, diesel and potato spirit as propellants for motor cars while staying

at Sandringham. Such patronage was good for the charities
and societies and for the monarchy. It gained much support
for monarchy from working-class people and among the
more serious and conscientious sections of the middle classes.
Nothing so flattered and endeared the royal family to the supporters of worthy causes as the patronage even of minor royals,
who allowed their names to appear on the society's notepaper,
sent letters of congratulation to assiduous workers and, best
of all, attended as patron the AGM or the annual dinner. To
become the *Royal Society* was the ultimate accolade for most
charities or learned societies.

Then there was the honours system. Peerages and knight-
hoods had, since medieval times, been a means of rewarding
and cementing loyalty. Over time, the number of people who
needed rewarding expanded, and by the late nineteenth century an honour had become a convenient way of gratifying
many echelons of society. On the continent, more and more
of the middle classes received some sort of order or decora-
tion. In Germany there was the Order of the Black Eagle,
the Order of the Red Eagle and the Prussian Order of the
Crown, each divided into classes. It was a practice not confined to monarchies, for the French Republic continued with
the Légion d'honneur created by Napoleon I, and Presidents
inherited the role of Grand Master. There are five grades of
the Légion d'honneur, and, as most *fonctionnaires* received one
of these, few public events or formal occasions were without
a scattering of red ribbons. In monarchies, however, there was
the added thrill that such honours came at least theoretically
from the sovereign, if increasingly at the suggestion of a minister. Mistakes were occasionally made, as when it was suggested
to Edward VII that 'Hardy' deserved an honour; the King was
stronger on sporting activities than novelists, and the honour
went to Mr Hardy, the maker of excellent fishing rods, rather
than to Thomas Hardy, the novelist. Nevertheless, it was an

effective method of honouring service to country and at the same time warming loyalty to sovereign.

It was not just as regal images, the centrepieces of grand ceremonies, that peoples viewed their monarchs. Instead of distant loyalties to abstract figures, literacy and new means of communication resulted in a lively personal interest in kings, queens and entire royal families. They became interested in their individual personalities, how they dressed, spent their leisure time and brought up their children. Newspapers and magazines began to cater for this interest in royalty and to bring news, photographs and illustrations of royal personages into middle-class and then working-class homes in provincial towns and country villages. This absorption in the private lives of royalty was particularly marked among women, and reflected the combined appeal of majesty and domesticity, glamour and common family situations.

One result of this was that royalty began to set the fashion as never before. Of course, courtiers had always followed the tastes of kings, queens and heirs apparent, and fashionable society and even the *demi-mondaine* had been close behind, but this had amounted to a fairly limited sector of the population. Now many more people knew about the interests of royalty, how they dressed, what sort of dogs they kept and which were their favourite spas or holiday retreats. Even as European prosperity increased, there was a vast gulf between the lifestyles of royal families and the bulk of their subjects, but greater disposable income, combined with commercialism and technology, as it narrowed the gap, made the example of the highest in the land ever more fascinating. Quite ordinary women could afford to buy clothes that provincial dressmakers and milliners or the new department stores copied from the dresses and hats designed for queens and princesses. Any clerk could wax his moustaches in imitation of the Kaiser or buy a waistcoat that looked like one worn by King Edward.

In the latter part of the nineteenth century, a number of royal figures became icons of glamour, leaders of fashion, and heroes and heroines of romance. Empress Eugénie, wife of Napoleon III, was perhaps the first royal figure to become widely known, due to mass communications, for her beauty and fashion sense. The relationship between the Empress and the public was a two-way affair, for Eugénie revelled in her assets. Whether her action, when entertaining Queen Victoria at the opera, in turning her back momentarily when moving her seat in her box, thus drawing attention to her well-shaped bottom, was innocent can be doubted. Princess, later Queen, Alexandra was a less self-conscious royal beauty. There was little to her, other than her looks and rather sentimental good nature, but her dresses, hairstyle and collars set the fashion, while as a faithful wife and loving mother, who had to put up with her husband's infidelity, she aroused widespread female sympathy.

An important development was the tendency for royal women to become more important. Reigning queens and empresses had, obviously, always been the central figures, but in the age of photography, illustrated magazines and an expanding fashion industry, interest in consorts and princesses quickened. Queen consorts had always exerted influence on, through and even despite, the sovereign and upon courts and aristocracies. Such influence had sometimes been political and had very often been cultural. Consorts had acted as agents of cultural transmission, bringing music, dances and fashions from their home countries to their new courts, and often inspiring innovations in architecture.[20] That influence was now projected to a wider public. There were difficulties for men in adapting to the new roles required of royalty in constitutional monarchies; symbolic, non-political or less political roles clashed with the concept of the warrior leader, which was deeply embedded in monarchical history, and the mere presiding over politicians and generals could seem emasculating. No such problems confronted queens and princesses.

The royal personalities who most captivate the public are unfortunately not always, or even usually, the most responsible. It is perhaps the contrast between their role and duty and their bids for freedom from it that captivate the public. Beautiful or handsome, but with a hint of vulnerability and dissatisfaction, they shy away from mundane royal duties, are given to romantic airs or causes and are always on the move. Empress Elisabeth, wife to Emperor Franz Josef, was an example. Hauntingly beautiful, and with the Wittelsbach fragile hold on stability, she captivated her Emperor but could not abide the austere formality of the Habsburg court. 'Sisi' roamed Europe like some restless spirit until struck down by an Italian assassin.[21] Romania had the benefit of two romantic queens, the poetic Elizabeth, like Sisi, a Wittelsbach, and the feisty and ever-English Marie.

A downside to the growing public interest in royal private lives was scandal. Royal impropriety – affairs, homosexuality or gambling debts – was nothing new, nor were attacks on it or exposures of it. The difference was the mass audience and the mass media. The mainstream press was constrained and reluctant when it came to royal misbehaviour, but there was also a radical and scandal-sheet press, while, once mere gossip became the stuff of court cases, even the respectable newspapers had to report it.

When made public, mere heterosexual affairs could be shrugged off, as could involvement in gambling, however much they might shock the more puritanically minded. Homosexuality was another matter. Rumours circulated concerning Edward VII's eldest son, the Duke of Clarence, who had, supposedly, been a visitor to a notorious homosexual brothel in Cleveland Street, but these remained mere rumours. The homosexual proclivities of members of the Kaiser's court could not, however, be kept secret when they became the subject of legal actions. There seems no doubt that Count Philipp Eulenburg and other members of the

'Liebenburg Circle', such as Count Kuno Moltke, were homosexuals.[22] After a series of libel actions, Eulenburg, perhaps the Kaiser's closest friend, was declared a practising homosexual by a Munich court. The Chancellor, Bülow, had him arrested and charged with perjury, but he was found to be unfit to plead. The implications of the affair were serious for the Kaiser. It seemed to suggest a certain decadence about a regime that had made so much of its virility. Matters were not helped by the death of the elderly Count Hülsen-Haesler, overcome by his exertions when dancing before his monarch in a ballerina's tutu.

'Mayerling' was a scandal, tragedy and, in the popular imagination, a love story, which struck a serious blow to the Austro-Hungarian Empire and, so it turned out, to the world. Crown Prince Rudolf was found dead in his hunting lodge at Mayerling among the wooded hills to the south-east of Vienna. Beside him lay the body of the beautiful Baroness Marie Vetsera. Rudolf had evidently planned their deaths, and Marie Vetsera's was a willing sacrifice for love. To most of the world it was a romantic tragedy, though some suspected darker plots. Rudolf had inherited the brilliance and the instability of the Wittelsbachs. Out of sympathy with the policies of the government, unhappy in his marriage and affected by a deep melancholy, his death was a futile and despairing gesture against the impasse in which the monarchy found itself and from which Rudolf could see no means of escape. His death meant that the heir to the throne became the ponderous Franz Ferdinand, whose assassination fifteen years later was to precipitate the First World War.

Rather than scandal, the threat of assassination was the main dread of Europe's ruling houses, and, indeed, of presidents and politicians, in the USA as well as Europe. The creed of anarchism, formulated for the most part by angry men in comfortable studies, who conceived of utopias when once the ruling class, the bourgeoisie and government had been destroyed, provided the sanction for angry little men, hungry and embittered, who found revenge in assassination. In 1881, the Russian Populists, or Narodniki, assassinated Tsar Alexander, imagining this would be a signal for a mass rising of Russia's peasantry. From the 1890s there was a succession of victims to the bomb, the bullet or the dagger: President Carnot of France in 1894, Premier Canovas of Spain in 1897, Empress Elisabeth of Austria in 1898, King Humbert of Italy in 1900, President McKinley of the United States in 1901, King Carlos of Portugal in 1908, Premier Canalejas of Spain in 1912 and King George of Greece in 1913. Monarchs, generally conspicuous in their uniforms, adorned with decorations, and driving in open carriages, made obvious targets. There was a price to be paid for the grand theatres of monarchy or presidential office.

Assassination, usually at the hands of a solitary fanatic, was one thing, but what really shocked and horrified the royal houses of Europe was the gruesome murder of a king and queen by their own soldiers. King Alexander and Queen Draga of Serbia were the least prepossessing of European monarchs. Alexander's parents had not been much better, for King Milan was a playboy king with a string of mistresses, who divorced his wife by edict, abdicated and then, financially embarrassed, returned to Serbia demanding money. He and his erstwhile wife, who refused to accept the divorce, had both to be banned from the country. Their son, Alexander, who allowed both his parents back, turned out to be just as deplorable as his father, and he made the enormous mistake of marrying an employee of his mother's, Draga Mashim, a woman of peasant stock, whose father was a lunatic and whose mother was an alcoholic. Once Queen, Draga, who dominated her weakling husband, turned out to be an insane menace to the Obrenovic dynasty and to Serbia. She appears to have planned a fake pregnancy so that a child of her sister could become heir to the throne, she placed her relatives and favourites in high places

and she then began to interfere with army appointments. The
army was one of the few pillars of the Serbian state, and it
responded by assassinating the royal couple. It did not do a
tidy job. Drunken officers invaded the palace in the middle of
the night and shot the King and Queen repeatedly with their
revolvers before hacking their bodies to pieces.[23] So ended the
House of Obrenovic, and on 15 June 1903, some four days
after the assassinations, both houses of the Serbian assembly,
the *Skupstina*, elected Peter Karageorgevic as the new king.

Such was Sultan Abdul Hamid's fear of assassination that the
Turkish press was forbidden to tell the truth about such inci-
dents, and:

> attributed the simultaneous deaths of the king and queen of
> Serbia in 1903 to indigestion. In the same way the Empress
> Elisabeth of Austria died of pneumonia, President Carnot
> died of apoplexy, President McKinley of anthrax.[24]

If monarchs had to live with the fear of assassination, monarchy itself seemed secure in early twentieth-century Europe.
Only real incompetence, a divided royal family and a double
assassination of king and crown prince could result in a republic, as with Portugal in 1911. As we have seen, even such a
conjunction and worse could not shake Serbia's dedication to
a monarchical system. The prime exemplar of republicanism,
France, did not excite many nations to adopt her constitutional
system. The governments of the Third Republic were short-
lived and shaky coalitions, renowned for their corruption, and
France, as the Dreyfus affair demonstrated, remained deeply
divided between republicans and anti-clericals on the one
hand and monarchists and Catholics on the other. Monarchy
seemed the institution that bound a nation together and was
the natural expression of its being.

As we have seen, there was a certain contradiction between
monarchy as aligned with a national ethos and the way in

which the European monarchies formed almost an extended family. To a degree, however, this paralleled the nature of early twentieth-century Europe itself. Nationalism had certainly become a more powerful force during the nineteenth century and had become uglier with the development of mass society. Yet, for those who travelled or sought permanent residence, Europe remained an open continent. Ambassadors and other embassy staff found much that was familiar in the courts and higher social circles of the countries they were accredited to, and upper-class travellers moved freely and, armed with letters of introduction, found a ready welcome in foreign cities. Grand hotels catered for a prosperous tourist trade, and there were numerous foreign residents throughout western Europe. If, for the most part, peasantries and the industrial working classes stayed put or sought to emigrate to America or their states' overseas colonies, there was considerable movement within Europe, with Italian villages sending sons to particular areas of England and Scotland, language teachers finding a living in various countries, and waiters, artists, musicians and entertainers not being constrained by national boundaries. Jews seeking refuge from discrimination in eastern Europe found what was at least a milder prejudice in their new homes, and far better opportunities. The ubiquity of monarchies, for which it was almost axiomatic that consorts were foreign, supported a certain cosmopolitanism.

The great gatherings of royalty for weddings and funerals, occasions made more numerous by the speed of modern travel, and now fixed for posterity by obligatory photographs, epitomised the degree to which European royalty composed an extended, if often squabbling, family. The funerals of Queen Victoria and Edward VII were family as well as national affairs, while, on the brink of war, the wedding of the Kaiser's daughter, Victoria Louise, to Prince Ernst August, son of the Duke of Cumberland, who would have been King of Hanover had not Bismarck abolished that kingdom, brought the Tsar of Russia

and the King-Emperor of Britain, along with a galaxy of
other monarchs and royal persons, to Berlin. Gordon Brook-
Shepherd utilised this splendid occasion to begin his *Royal
Sunset*, contrasting this royal and family occasion with the
opposing military alliances to which so many of the wedding
guests belonged, and commented:

> It is this proximity to Armageddon – still totally obscured
> and out of sight, though now only a hands-breadth away –
> which gave the Potsdam festivities a trance-like air.[25]

The interrelated nature of Europe's monarchies made little difference to the slide towards war in July and August 1914. Was
this the fault of the monarchs or did it merely expose their
lack of real power beneath the splendour of their positions?
The nation, its fears, ambitions and hatreds, prevailed over
the cousinhood of monarchs, but then it prevailed over the
theoretical internationalism of socialism and class and the supposed interest of business in peace.[26] Among the serried ranks
of books dealing with the causes of, and the reasons for, the
outbreak of war in 1914 there are many that scarcely mention
the heads of state, and few that accord them much responsibility for the conflict. What is clear, as we shall see, is that
the last-minute interventions of Wilhelm II, Nicholas II and
George V were feeble and contradictory, while Emperor Franz
Josef appears to have been culpably detached from events.
Soon, Europe's extended royal family was a family at war.

PART TWO

SOME KINGS DEPART

5

EUROPE'S MONARCHIES AND THE FIRST WORLD WAR

The assassination of the heir to the Austro-Hungarian throne, Archduke Franz Ferdinand, on 28 June 1914 lit a slow-burning fuse which led to Austria–Hungary's declaration of war on Serbia on 28 July. The 'Balkan powder keg' proved no mere journalistic cliché and was ready to explode as Austria–Hungary determined to exact revenge for the undoubted Serbian complicity in the Archduke's murder, but it took a month before it was ignited. Thereafter, things moved more swiftly, and by 4 August Germany and Austro-Hungary were at war with Russia, France and Britain. There was a languid air about diplomacy until the end of July. Two of the monarchs, the Kaiser and the Tsar, were literally at sea when they heard the news of the Archduke's death; this was the time of year for holidays, and they were on their yachts. Emperor Franz Josef was at his summer retreat at Bad Ischl. Many of the central figures in the drama that led to war, ministers and generals as well as monarchs, continued with their summer arrangements for much of July. It has been suggested that so far as the Germans and Austrians were concerned this may have been a deception, and that it had been agreed that an Austrian ultimatum, which the Serbs would find unacceptable, would be delivered at the end of the month:

> While all this was plotted behind the scenes, both Vienna and Berlin gave the impression of calm to the outside world, even sending their main decision-makers on holiday to keep up this illusion. It is due to this deception that the other major powers did not play a role in the July Crisis until 23 July, the day when the ultimatum was finally delivered to Belgrade. They were simply unaware of the secret plotting in Vienna and Berlin.[1]

If the personal relations between monarchs mattered, and of course the kings and emperors thought they did, then Emperor Franz Josef's decision that the funeral of Franz Ferdinand should be a low-key affair without royal mourners from abroad was significant. Perhaps a great assembly of monarchs at the funeral would have stiffened these supposed rulers to withstand the reckless demands of ministers and generals and made it more difficult for them to sign ultimatums and declarations of war a month later. The death of the heir to the imperial throne would have normally been followed by an elaborate lying-in-state and a ceremonial funeral attended by the crowned heads of Europe; indeed, several foreign royals had already got ready for the journey. In the opinion of the Court Chamberlain, however, the Archduchess Sophie's relatively humble origins meant that she should not be accorded any such ceremony and, although the two bodies were accorded equal treatment on the journey by trains and battleship to Vienna, the pomp and ceremony ceased with their arrival at the Empire's capital:

> while the coffins were both taken to the Capuchin vault, Franz Ferdinand's was surmounted with his crown, his

helmet, his sabre and all his Orders, but Sophie's stood on a
lower level, and on it rested only a pair of white gloves and a
fan, the marks of a lady-in-waiting. The lying-in-state lasted
just two hours, then the doors were closed and the waiting
crowds were hurried away.[2]

It is difficult to separate the immediate causes of the First
World War from its supposed fundamental causes, and many
have concluded that the German government and general
staff had decided that war was both necessary and inevitable and better sooner than later. Nevertheless, previous crises
had not led to a general war. The weight of historical opinion points to three main reasons for the short-term causes
of the First World War and why the assassination at Sarajevo
led to it: the desire of the Austro-Hungarian general staff
to crush Serbia; the blank cheque of unconditional support
that Germany gave the Austrians; and the difficulty of drawing back from the brink of war once mobilisation orders had
been given. It is nevertheless the case that the moves towards
war required more than nominal royal approval in Berlin,
St Petersburg and Vienna.

Kaiser Wilhelm liked the apparatus of war, the uniforms,
the horses and great military exercises, but whether he was
enthusiastic about war itself is more debatable. It is certainly
questionable whether he was prepared for war with Russia.
Early in July, he was in a 'now or never' mood and sent per-
emptory instructions to the German ambassador in Vienna
as to the necessity of a 'final and fundamental reckoning'. It
is clear, however, that he had every expectation that Russia
would not go to war, and that when Serbia swallowed much
of the stiff Austro-Hungarian ultimatum he was overjoyed and
felt that this was a 'great moral victory for Austria, but with it,
every reason for war falls away'.

He had not reckoned with the enthusiasm for war of
the Austrian Foreign Minister, Count Berchtold, and the

Austrian Chief of Staff, General Conrad von Hortzendorff, nor on the acquiescence in their drive to war of Emperor Franz Josef. At Bad Ischl, and in touch with his ministers only by telegraph and telephone, Franz Josef seems to have been passive throughout the crucial period, a lonely old man, either stoical or unaware of the seriousness of the situation. He seems to have agreed to the Austrian declaration of war without demur. Past wars had proved disastrous to his empire, but he did little to try and arrest the one that would bring it to an end.

The Kaiser had also not realised how determined his own ministers and generals were to support Austria–Hungary in all circumstances. The Chancellor, Bethmann-Hollweg, not only delayed informing Vienna that his sovereign considered war unnecessary and was prepared to mediate for peace, he altered the substance of his views. Bethmann-Hollweg may not have actively sought a general war, but he was prepared for one, and his main concern was that Germany's actions should gain the support of the German population. The Kaiser was not in control of policy. For the moment his minister was, but he was soon to lose control to the general staff.

For much of July, Tsar Nicholas appears to have been more concerned about the health of the Tsarevich and of Rasputin, for the *staret* had been stabbed by a female assailant who believed he was the Anti-Christ, than about the European crisis. George V was upset enough about the assassination of the man he had entertained only seven months earlier to order a week of court mourning and to cancel his attendance at Newmarket Races, but neither he nor his ministers worried that a major European war might follow.

Austria–Hungary's ultimatum to Serbia quickened the pace of diplomatic efforts to avert a general war and spurred monarchs to write to each other. The Kaiser, as ever, was an indefatigable correspondent, and sent a telegram to the Tsar asking 'Nicky' to help him avert war between their two countries. There was not a lot 'Nicky' could do to help 'Willy'. He was concerned to preserve peace, but Russia was bound to come to the assistance of Serbia, and to have stood by while a Slav state was crushed would have resulted in humiliation. In any case, the Tsar had already assured the Crown Prince of Serbia that Russia would stand by his country. Many more telegrams were to pass between the Tsar and the Kaiser, but these two supposed autocrats were powerless to halt the impetus born of ambitions, fears, alliances and military planning that was leading to war.

George V was, in Kenneth Rose's words, 'no more than an anguished and impotent spectator' of the unfolding tragedy.[3] Unlike his father, he had little interest in European affairs, or even in Europe. Would things have been different if Edward VII had still been alive? There can be little doubt that he would have attempted to use his personal influence and connections in the interests of a peaceful outcome. He had a more positive interpretation of his role as a constitutional monarch and would not have simply left things to his ministers. He would have probably been more alert to the danger that a Balkan assassination might lead to a general European war than either his son, who first mentioned the developing crisis in his diary on 25 July, or the government, which was preoccupied with the Ulster crisis. The Kaiser, who had always disliked and misunderstood his uncle, believed that Edward, dead for four years, *was* involved in the crisis, in that Edward had planned the encirclement of Germany: 'Edward VII is stronger after death than I who am still alive.' Wilhelm found his cousin George V more sympathetic, and tried a last tug on the old personal relationship between royal families with a visit to the King from Prince Henry of Prussia, at which George expressed his wish that Britain could remain neutral. The most realistic suggestion for averting war did come from Britain: a proposal that Germany, Italy, France and Britain hold an Ambassadors' Conference during which all military operations should be

suspended. The proposal was promptly turned down by
Germany and Austria.

At this stage military considerations took over. Nicholas II
was prevailed upon to order a partial mobilisation of Russia's
armed forces on 28 July. On 30 July he authorised a general mobilisation, the most significant step towards war. In
between the authorisation of a partial and a general mobilisation there was a protracted struggle by ministers and generals
to get the agreement of the Tsar. Though weak and vacillat-
ing, Nicholas was well meaning, and he hated the prospect of
war. He agonised as his advisers unanimously argued that full
mobilisation was essential if the cumbersome Russian forces
were to be ready for war. He had given his permission for the
ukase declaring general mobilisation, but rescinded it when a
conciliatory telegram arrived from the Kaiser, very different
in tone from the communications received from the German
Chancellor. Cajoled and pestered by the generals, he held out
for twenty-four hours, but eventually gave way. The domi-
noes now fell swiftly: Germany declared war on Russia on
1 August and on France and Belgium two days later; Britain
declared war on Austria–Hungary on 4 August and on Austria
the following day.

The responsibility of the monarchs of Europe for the war
that was to cost so many of them their thrones was varied. The
Kaiser had theatrically played the Warlord, and his operatic
bellicosity and extravagant ambitions for Germany had done
much to destabilise international relations. He had played
a central role in German decision making, but by 1914 he
was no longer the autocrat he felt himself to be. The events
of July and August 1914 demonstrate that his commands
were no longer faithfully obeyed by his Chancellor and that
he was but the nominal head of the military machine he was
so proud of. Having fatally encouraged Austria–Hungary in
its preparations for war with Serbia, he did spasmodically and
ineffectually try to arrest its drive to war. He, who above all

believed in the importance of the brotherhood of monarchs, also made unsuccessful attempts to call in his personal relationship with the Tsar to counter the mobilisation timetables of the generals. In the final days before the European war began, he panicked and vainly strove to pull back Austria and his generals. Even Bethmann-Hollweg performed a volte-face and tried to persuade the Austrians to accept British proposals for an Ambassadors' Conference, but it was too late. As the monarchs had given in to their ministers, the ministers now gave way to the generals and the generals to their war plans.

Kingship and war had a long inter-related history, and European monarchs had for centuries made war on their relatives. Defeat in war had only occasionally meant the overthrow or abdication of a king or queen, and rarely the end of a dynasty. The French Revolutionary and Napoleonic Wars and the Franco-Prussian Wars had intimated that modern warfare could produce different results. The total war that began in 1914 and involved the mobilisation of entire populations and the dedication of whole economies to the war effort, and that required governments to raise the stakes by propaganda to demonise the enemy, was to make defeat and the continuity of the regimes of the defeated incompatible. As most combatants were monarchies, this was to prove disastrous for the near universality of the monarchical principle.

The claim that 'William II, Nicholas II and Francis Josef I led Europe and the wider world into the first of two mass slaughters, which would, in less than thirty years destroy Europe's primacy in global affairs'[4] is, as we have seen, highly questionable. Clearly, the three Emperors must bear some responsibility, but so far as the Emperors of Austria–Hungary and Russia were concerned, their sins were largely those of omission rather than commission. Kaiser Wilhelm did much to create a bellicose atmosphere; he rocked the boat and was unable to return it to equilibrium. The supposed autocrats were not, however, in charge in July and August 1914, and it may be wondered whether either monarchical regimes with more liberal constitutions or republican systems would have managed to avoid war. With Britain, Anglo-French military and naval understandings, of which members of parliament and even many ministers knew little, played as great a part as a commitment to Belgian neutrality in the decision to go to war, while French diplomacy proved no more flexible than that of Russia and the central powers.

That war came because of the remobilisation of the forces of the old order of Europe of which monarchy was an essential and conspicuous part is more plausible. Arno J. Mayer has argued that:

> The inner spring of Europe's general crisis was the over-reaction of old elites to perceived dangers to their privileged positions. In their siege mentality, they exaggerated the pace of capitalist modernisation, the revolt of the plebs, the frailty of the state apparatus, and the breakaway of the industrial and professional bourgeoisie.[5]

Yet if the problems of monarchs, aristocracies and gentries played a part in the drift towards war, the fateful combination of essentially modern developments seems more fundamental. The European balance of power had been upset by the coming of a united Germany. Nationalism and the emergence of the mass societies that embraced it tempted governments of all persuasions to encourage and utilise passions and animosities, only to find that they had aroused expectations that were impossible to fulfil. Finally, the great armies, which monarchs reviewed on white chargers, were at once complex and cumbersome mechanisms, dependent on mobilisation timetables and war plans, and had, almost, minds of their own.

The view of the First and Second World Wars as two separate wars has increasingly been challenged by historians, many of whom now prefer to write of thirty years of European civil war, with the period 1918–39 constituting only an extended armistice. Some would extend this war to cover the Cold War, thus conceiving of almost a century of European conflict, with hot and cold phases. Such a view necessarily casts doubt on the idea that the war's origins are to be found in the failure of Europe's *ancien régime*, and particularly the monarchical and aristocratic government of Germany, to solve internal contradictions. The appeal of war with its potential to unify and to override internal problems undoubtedly influenced German and Austro-Hungarian thinking, but must be seen as only one factor among many, given that the long European civil war was to outlast by so many decades the Europe of monarchs and aristocracies in which it began. What is certain is that, separate war or opening phase of a longer conflict, the First World War was a disaster for the monarchical principle.

Where the Mayer thesis is convincing is in its argument that monarchies overestimated the threats to their position. Monarchies in early twentieth-century Europe faced two direct threats and numerous problems. The most obvious menace was socialism, but the magnitude of this threat has been much exaggerated. Full-blooded revolutionary socialism had several targets, of which monarchy was only one. The very number of those who would find their position in society and their economic well-being destroyed by Marxist socialism, syndicalism or anarchism ensured that, other than in the exceptional circumstances that war was to provide, revolutionary socialism had a decreasing chance of success as societies surmounted the early and harsh dislocations of industrialisation. Democratic, modified, evolutionary or parliamentary socialism continued to pose a threat to those monarchies that were semi- or theoretical autocracies embedded in *ancien régimes*. Yet even the German example demonstrates that a combination of reforms in the sphere of social welfare, and gradual, real improvements in wages and conditions, and concessions on the franchise and parliamentary representation could modify the zeal of much of the working classes for revolutionary change. Austrian social democrats, conscious of the dangerous alternatives, had by the early twentieth century moved to a position of surreptitious support for the monarchy.

The second threat was republicanism. The reputation of republics was not, however, high. The governments of the Third French Republic tended to be short-lived, while its presidents enjoyed little authority and its politics had a reputation for corruption. Nor was the USA seen as a role model, but rather as a state and society where wealth bought power, and senators and congressmen jostled for their shares of the 'pork barrel'. Republicanism had little positive appeal, and was only a threat where, as in Portugal, kings were particularly incompetent.

As well as threats, monarchy faced problems, but had demonstrated considerable ability to adapt in the face of them. The first was nationalism, probably the most potent ideological force in the modern world. As we have seen, monarchs had wherever possible embraced a new identity as the focus of national loyalty. Then there was the coming of mass society with a new ease of physical communication and an increased literacy, which produced a popular press. Again, monarchs and royal families had skilfully projected themselves to subjects at large instead of being distant figures known only to aristocratic elites. Representative democracy was a development that monarchs had, to different degrees and with a general reluctance, come to terms with: adapting scarcely at all in Russia, retaining executive power in uneasy association with parliaments in central and eastern Europe and becoming largely symbolic, if highly influential, figures in Britain.

The debate among historians as to why the First World War began will probably never be over. Once the consensus was that Europe slithered into war, but this was followed by a predominant view that Germany used the crisis to launch a bid for supremacy, an argument then challenged by the thesis that Russian ambitions were largely responsible, while a recent influential study has returned to a Europe, if not 'slithering', then 'sleepwalking' into a disastrous conflict.[6] Two things seem certain: one is that, as Margaret MacMillan has written, 'It was far from inevitable that the assassination at Sarajevo would led to a major European War';[7] the other is that the responses to the crisis of the major monarchs were blameworthy, and their sins were those of omission in that they did nothing to prevent the outbreak of war.

Why was it then that the First World War proved so disastrous for the most powerful monarchies of Europe? One answer that appeals to the liberal view that the development of democracy was not just natural, but resulted in more flexible, popular and more stable regimes, was that the empires that fell were to a greater or lesser degree autocracies, and the monarchies that survived were those that were more constitutional.[8] Another is that the thrones that were overturned belonged to the states that lost the war; it was because they ruled over defeated states that the Tsar of Russia and then the Emperors of Germany and Austria and, eventually, the Ottoman Sultan, rather than the Kings of Britain or Italy were overthrown.

That it is virtually impossible for a government and even a governing system to survive defeat in a modern war is a thesis that has considerable force. The age in which kings and states could go to war and then conclude peace treaties, allotting parcels of territory to the victors, was passing. As Hannah Arendt argued: 'Since the end of the First World War we almost automatically expect that no government or state or form of government, will be strong enough to survive a defeat in war.'[9] Almost inevitably the consequences of defeat mean a revolutionary change in government, either imposed by the victors or as a result of internal revolution.

Just too much is invested in total war for governments who are defeated to survive. Whether or not the Tsarist regime in Russia would have successfully adapted and overcome its massive internal problems without the war, it was when the strains of the conflict and the painful war effort led to military defeats that revolution occurred, while it was the decision to continue the war that led to the October Revolution. The manifold problems of the Austro-Hungarian Empire had for long made its situation 'hopeless but not serious'; military defeat made it serious. George V may have seemed safe enough on the balcony of Buckingham Palace when cheering crowds saluted the Armistice and victory, while Wilhelm II scuttled into exile in Holland, but had the German push of the spring of 1918 succeeded, the positions might well have been reversed.

During the course of the war, the myth of absolutism was revealed. None of the monarchs with pretensions to be in complete command of their governments or their armies had the ability or the training to exercise more than nominal control over states engaged in total war. The Kaiser, the 'Supreme Warlord', had looked impressive enough when reviewing his troops or presiding over military exercises, but he had neither the determination nor the knowledge to exercise control over the complex machinery of war. The view that he became just a 'shadow Kaiser' has, with some justification, been attacked, for he could not be disregarded, but his influence was, for good or ill, increasingly negative. A more decisive and gifted ruler could have used his position to coordinate the military, naval and civilian authorities and orchestrate the war effort, but there was little direction by the Kaiser. He retained, however, that essential component of the 'kingship mechanism', the right to promote and dismiss generals and ministers. This enabled him to protect those whom he approved of, particularly von Falkenhayn and his Chancellor Bethmann-Hollweg, until August 1916 and July 1917, long after the rising stars of the war, Hindenburg and Ludendorff, would have had them removed.[10] He exercised considerable influence over naval decisions and overruled Admiral von Tirpitz, preventing the implementation of his plans to engage the Royal Navy in large-scale battle at the beginning of the war and ignoring his constant demands for unrestricted submarine warfare.[11] The replacement of von Falkenhayn by Hindenburg and Ludendorff in August 1916, the decision to begin unrestricted submarine warfare in January 1917 and Bethmann-Hollweg's resignation in the following July were the major steps in the process by which Wilhelm became only a nominal war leader. Humiliatingly, he was increasingly sidelined by his generals and reduced to a mere figurehead. It was true that he was often close to the front in a château near Spa, but most of the photo-opportunities offered to the press of him inspecting troops in sandbagged trenches were actually arranged at a pretend trench in the grounds of this Belgian château. In the last years of the war, it was clear that it was Generals Ludendorff and Hindenburg who were in command, and not the Kaiser, while at the end of the war the general staff made it clear that they had other priorities than their much trumpeted loyalty to their sovereign. In Russia, Nicholas II attempted to take command of his armed forces by making himself Commander-in-Chief, but with predictably disastrous results.

Even in constitutional monarchies, kings laid claim to special relationships with their armies. War faced kings, even constitutional monarchs, with difficult and poignant choices. The tradition of the 'warrior king', acclaimed by his nobles for his martial qualities, little fitted the recent history of Europe, where no monarch had led his armies into battle since the eighteenth century. Yet kings and emperors had nurtured their special relationships with their armed forces, and served in their youth, in practice or symbolically, with regiments and fleets, and to remain at home in their capitals, flag-waving but essentially emasculated, was invidious. George V had no wish to posture as anything but a titular head of his army and navy, but nevertheless felt it necessary to don uniform and pay visits to the front; one such visit ended badly when he fell from his horse and injured himself seriously. His interpretation of his role was not that he should be able to tell his generals what to do but that he should be able to protect his generals from politicians who wanted to tell them what to do. Asquith rather agreed with his monarch that wars were best left to generals, but in Lloyd George the King was up against a forceful Prime Minister who was determined to be in charge of the prosecution of the war, and when king and Prime Minister clashed over military appointments, it was the Prime Minister who prevailed.

King Albert of the Belgians, hitherto seen as a rather ineffectual figure, was an exception in that when faced with defeat he did take command, led his troops back to the redoubt of Antwerp and then, when the defence of Antwerp proved impossible, to a twenty-square-mile corner of south-western Belgium, where the Belgian army was able to maintain itself as part of the Allied line, and Belgian resistance to Germany could still take place on Belgian soil. Here was a king who was not only in command of strategy but who shared the dangers and deprivations of his army. The cement of Belgium was demonstrably the monarchy, and German attempts to divide Fleming from Walloon foundered because of Albert's example.

Other monarchs also had 'good wars'. The diminutive Victor Emmanuel III of Italy was constantly with his armies, encouraging and comforting Italian soldiers; and if King Peter of Serbia, old and infirm, was not of practical help to the Serbian army, he was almost an icon to it; with his soldiers when they briefly recaptured Belgrade, he was carried by them over the mountain passes, along with coffins containing the remains of previous Serbian rulers, when the army retreated to the Adriatic coast.

Crown princes faced similar difficulties and frustrations. Most had received a military or naval education and served on ship or with regiment, but could a government allow a crown prince to be killed, or worse, captured? The Prince of Wales, like his late-eighteenth-century predecessor, felt that it was bogus and humiliating to be in uniform and be allowed to visit the western front, but be prohibited from taking part in the fighting, and then then be awarded the Military Cross.

The fortunes of empresses and queens were mixed. Tsarina Alexandra was unjustly accused of being pro-German, but otherwise her misfortunes were of her own making. Her naïve interpretation of the character of the Russian population led her to believe that all her decent but weak husband had to do was to play the autocrat and all would be well. Besotted by Rasputin, the *staret*, a charismatic priest of the people, who combined visions with a priapic sexuality and alone seemed to have the ability to help her haemophiliac son, the Tsarevich, to recover from his frequent bleedings, she became the wicked witch of the regime to much of the Russian population, and gave her husband the worst of advice. The Kaiser's consort, Empress Augusta, seems to have quickly lost patience with her mercurial and unstable husband and allied herself with her son, Crown Prince Wilhelm, who had all his father's faults without his hesitations, and the most warlike generals. Other queens, by contrast, served their countries well and enjoyed considerable popularity.

In many ways reigning queens have found it easier to adapt to constitutional monarchy, and to reigning rather than ruling, than kings, while queen consorts have had to change their roles least of all. There were by chance no reigning female monarchs involved in the First World War, though one hereditary ruler Grand Duchess Marie Adelaide of Luxembourg confined her defence of the duchy to driving to the frontier to order the invading Germans out, an order they ignored. Queen consorts, however, played a variety of roles. There were, as we have seen, examples of consorts who, as most spectacularly with the Tsarina, were seen as exerting a malign and unpopular influence, but there were two positive roles for queen consorts, both hallowed expressions of femininity: the encapsulation of the spirit of the nation in female form, and the nurturing angel. The one spurred on the soldier, for how could he let down the queen and woman in whose bosom patriotism burned so brightly; the other comforted the wounded and the bereaved.

Queen Mary wasn't particularly cut out for either role. Too formal and too subordinate to her husband for the former, she did her best to fulfil the latter as, stiff-backed and buttoned-up, she made the rounds of hospital wards and convalescent homes. Her keen interest in hospital management didn't quite make up for her lack of bedside manner, and contrasted with Queen Alexandra's ability, lame and deaf though she was, to impart her almost overwhelming sympathy. Queen Mary's little parcels to the soldiers were, however, well chosen; containing, as they did, cigarettes in an embossed metal box, they contrasted with the equivalent parcels from the purblind and insensitive Tsarina, which contained bibles.

Two queens were magnificent in responding to the challenge of war. Queen Marie of Romania was a fitting successor to Queen Elizabeth as queen consort. Like 'Carmen Sylvia', this granddaughter of Queen Victoria was theatrical and bohemian. Well aware of her beauty, her dress and the elaborate gold rooms in which she posed were designed to enhance and display it. Her husband King Ferdinand had succeeded King Carol I, who had no direct heir, in 1914 and, fiercely in favour of Romania's alliance with the *entente* powers, she became an ardent Romanian patriot. In Theo Aronson's words: 'in her snowy nurse's uniform, with its vivid red cross on the armband ... was jolted along muddy roads to work in squalid hospitals and to bring solace to wounded men'.[12] It was well for her that Romania entered the war on the side of Britain, for her Romanian patriotism co-existed with an equal fervour for her native Britain. As she wrote to her cousin George V: 'I can only tell you dear George that I held firm as only a born Englishwoman can.' Another queen with artistic and bohemian inclinations, Queen Elisabeth of the Belgians, rose to the challenge of war and became a national heroine. Based with her husband on the last strip of Belgian soil, she too devoted herself to nursing the wounded and becoming a saintly figure to Belgian soldiers. She was, however, a Wittelsbach, and amid the discomfort of her villa on the North Sea shore entertained poets and artists in a small pavilion, where the decor and conversation reflected the interest of the art world in Eastern art and religion.

There was, inevitably, an ambiguity and a conflict of loyalties for the royal families of Europe in the context of a European war. The cousinhood of monarchy had to take sides against the ties of family. This was no new dilemma in the *longue durée* of the history of monarchy, but this was not a war where eventual peace could result in an exchange of territory with rulers still secure upon thrones, for it became a war for national survival, a 'war for civilisation' against the 'barbaric' other side, and a war which involved economies and whole societies.

The rather recent and somewhat optimistic idea that royal family ties were a barrier to war was no longer tenable after August 1914. Rather than an asset, the relationship between the royal families became at the least an embarrassment. Some saw no reason for heart searching. Queen Alexandra had hated the Germans ever since Prussia's war with her native Denmark in 1864, while Kaiser Wilhelm subdued his ambivalent attitude towards his mother's homeland and blamed Britain and especially his Uncle Edward for the war. For most others, loyalty to nation was tempered by regret that cousins and even brothers and sisters were on the other side.

The nature of the war made it difficult to preserve older notions of honourable enemies as national feelings became feverish. The British royal family was placed in a particularly invidious position. George V's naval upbringing had produced a very British monarch, with no great enthusiasm for European connections, but he did belong to the European caste of royalty, and Germanophobia presented him with embarrassing problems. His belief in 'fair play' was

affronted by the hounding by super-patriots of such diverse
individuals as Prince Louis of Battenberg, Lord Haldane and
the members of Gottlieb's German band, all of whom suffered in one way or another because of German origins or
connections. He was reluctant to give in to demands that he
should deprive enemy emperors, kings and princes of their
honorary commands of British regiments and of the orders
of chivalry that had been bestowed upon them, but gave
way reluctantly under pressure from his mother and from
Asquith. Things were easier for the British officers and diplomats who had proudly worn with full dress or at formal
dinners the insignia of the orders presented to them by the
Kaiser or the Austro-Hungarian Emperor; these handsome
trinkets were put away.

As the war dragged on, the King deeply resented and became
worried by innuendoes that he could not be whole-heartedly
behind the war effort because of his German ancestry. In the
spring of 1917 there was what seems to have been a concerted
campaign against the King and the royal family, with a spate of
letters arriving at 10 Downing Street asking how the war could
be won when the King, himself, was German. H.G. Wells's call
for the abolition of 'an alien and uninspiring court' touched a
raw nerve. 'I may be uninspiring, but I'll be damned if I'm an
alien', protested the King. The February Revolution in Russia
and the knowledge that the Tsarina's alleged pro-German
attitude had played a part in the unpopularity of the regime
galvanised George into action. He decided that a grand public
gesture was necessary to impress upon the nation the British
nature of the dynasty: the names of the royal family had to
be anglicised. Lord Stamfordham, the King's secretary, came
up with the inspired choice of Windsor, redolent of British
history, as the new name for the royal house, and other members of the royal family were told they had also to change
their names, with Battenbergs becoming Mountbattens and
Tecks Cambridges. The Kaiser made the rather good joke that

he was off to the theatre 'to see the Merry Wives of Saxe-Coburg-Gotha'.

As the war continued, more and more of the monarchies of Europe were drawn into it. If the initial combatants went to war either in the face of aggression or in the context of longstanding alliances, later entrants to the conflict were motivated by fine judgements as to which side was likely to win and which could offer the best rewards. Despite treaty obligations to Germany and Austria, King Victor Emmanuel III and his government surveyed the war's progress before opting for the side that could promise more in the way of furthering Italy's territorial ambitions, and in 1915 Italy declared war first on Austria–Hungary and then on Germany. The 'Balkan Fox', Ferdinand of Bulgaria, saw the opportunity of retrieving the losses of the Balkan Wars and joined the central powers in September 1915. In east-central Europe, it was almost impossible for any state to keep out of the conflict. King Ferdinand of Romania was a Hohenzollern and was bound to Germany by family ties, but his country's main territorial ambition was to take Transylvania from Hungary, and after much bargaining with the *entente* powers, Romania entered the war on their side in 1916. Just how difficult it was to remain neutral is demonstrated by the case of Greece. King Constantine desperately clung to neutrality, while his Prime Minister, Eleftherios Venizelos, encouraged the western Allies to land troops in Salonika. Slandered by British and French propaganda, and with Athens blockaded and bombarded by an allied fleet, Constantine was forced into exile in 1917.

If the monarchs of Europe cannot be accused of starting the war, they had at least presided over its outbreak, and they continued to at least ostensibly lead their nations at war. As the full horrors of this total war became evident, so did the threat to a dislocated European civilisation and its traditional order, of which monarchy was such a prominent part. If the interlinked nature of the monarchies of Europe had presented little obstacle to a European war, could it halt the war? Communications either direct or indirect remained open between royal relatives on opposing sides, and the neutral monarchs of Scandinavia, Spain and Holland were available as intermediaries. As early as November 1914, King Christian of Denmark attempted to initiate talks between the Kaiser and the Tsar; in the spring of 1916, the Grand Duke of Hesse, the Tsarina's brother, made a secret visit to Russia and had discussions with the Tsar; and, overtly, in December 1916 the Kaiser approved a rather vague German Peace Note. Against national passions, hardened by the sacrifices of war, the loosening control of kings over governments and generals and the shifting fortunes of the combatant powers, royal diplomacy failed.

The most serious effort was made by Emperor Karl of Austria–Hungary, who succeeded on the death of Emperor Franz Josef in November 1916. The Empire was not an inheritance to be envied. The dynasty still exerted a charismatic influence, and the armies had proved loyal and tenacious, granted that Slavonic troops had to be restricted to the Italian front, but the national rivalries of its subjects were exacerbated by the strain of war. Was there still a chance of saving the Empire? Karl and his consort, Zita, were attractive, youthful and well intentioned. He favoured a constitutional monarchy and some sort of federal solution to the Empire's problems, and he realised that peace was essential and time was short. If the main obstacle to a new federal structure was Hungarian intransigence, the main obstacle to peace was the German alliance, more and more simply a German hegemony. Karl's peace overtures, at first conducted clandestinely via royal networks but then taken seriously by the British and French governments, foundered on Italy's territorial ambitions and on the fact that, even if he had been able to take the Kaiser into his confidence, it was the German High Command and not the Supreme Warlord who now made Germany's decisions. Probably Wilhelm II himself would have been horrified if he had known that his royal ally was prepared to see Alsace-Lorraine returned to France, a fact the French government was to make known in the early months of 1918.

That the true cost of the war was to be high for the monarchies of Europe was made apparent by the deposition of the Tsar in the February Revolution of 1917. By then the monarchs were no longer in control of their states or of their own fates. Once monarchs might have survived defeat in war, dynasties might have survived by judicious abdications or alternative dynasties might have been enthroned. Even at this stage, however, the full enormity of the situation had not dawned upon the royal families of Europe. As Germany consolidated its victory in eastern Europe, there was excited talk of new thrones that might be created in the wake of the Treaty of Brest-Litovsk: perhaps a new King of Poland – the Archduke Charles Stephen might be the right candidate; the crumbling Russian Empire provided opportunities for ambitious and optimistic princes (kings of Lithuania, Latvia, Finland or even Ukraine?). Finland, erstwhile Grand Duchy of the Russian Empire, did briefly become a kingdom, and in October 1918 Friedrich, Elector of Hesse, was offered the throne, though in the circumstances of Germany's defeat he withdrew a month later; for almost a year the country remained a monarchy under regents, but with no satisfactory king being found, it became a republic in July 1919. For the really rash prince in search of a throne, Albania had been in need of a monarch for some time.

Count Czernin, the Austrian Foreign Minister, introduced a note of realism. When the Kaiser proposed that his relative, Ferdinand of Romania, should be relieved of his throne for having been on the Allied side, Czernin opposed him, later recalling:

At this time there was a certain decline in the value of kings on the European market, and I was afraid that it might develop into a panic, if we put more kings off their thrones.[13]

When thrones were at a discount, the desire of monarchs to hold on to their own triumphed over a natural sympathy with the troubled positions of relatives. George V looked very much like his cousin, Tsar Nicholas II; 'exactly like a skinny Duke of York', as one of Queen Victoria's ladies had described the Tsar in 1896. Close family ties, the memories of pre-war visits and years of correspondence might have been expected to imbue George with a ready sympathy and a desire to assist his fellow monarch in distress. Few suspected that the overthrow of the Tsar would result in the massacre of the royal family at Ekaterinburg in July 1918, but since the 1790s kings had had to live with the prospect that revolutions did not necessarily end with a comfortable exile. Britain seemed the obvious place for the Tsar and his family to come to, and the British ambassador requested that he be authorised to offer asylum to the Tsar. Lloyd George and the cabinet were willing to accede to this request, but the stumbling block was Nicholas's cousin, George V. It seems clear that George and his secretary, Lord Stamfordham, were convinced that left-wing opinion was much prejudiced against the Tsar, and at a time when they were fearful of arousing anti-monarchist feeling, they cold-bloodedly decided that to give the Russian royal family sanctuary might compromise the British monarchy. Cousin Nicky was abandoned. The King later wrote after the murders at Ekaterinburg, 'It was a foul murder. I was devoted to Nicky, who was the kindest of men and a thorough gentleman: loved his country and people.'[14] The ties of blood and friendship were not, however, allowed to come between a monarch and his first love, his throne.

The entry of the United States into the war had ominous implications for monarchies, especially in central Europe. The 'Fourteen Points', President Wilson's list of principles on

which a peace would be concluded, did not specifically mention the German monarchy, but it is clear that for Wilson its
overthrow was a precondition for peace. Wilson's naïve belief
that democracy and national self-determination would result
in governments dedicated to cooperation and amity between
states went hand in hand with the view that monarchy was an
obstacle to a better world. Even European republicans were
not enthusiastic about Wilson's ambitions to remodel Europe
on the lines of democracy and national self-determination.
'Fourteen points,' exclaimed the French Prime Minister,
Clemenceau, 'it's a bit much. The Good Lord had only ten.'
Wilson's desire to do away with the German monarchy was,
however, not contentious; the Kaiserdom, even without the
particular Kaiser, had few supporters among the Allies.

Wilson's 'Fourteen Points' of January 1918 had the effect
of weakening the Kaiser's position. They provided an opportunity for the German general staff to conclude an Armistice
in the expectation that the sacrifice of the monarchy might
bring more generous terms. In January 1918, of course,
Hindenberg and Ludendorff still hoped to win, but when,
after the failure of the spring offensive, victory no longer
appeared possible, an Armistice on the basis of the 'Fourteen
Points' *and* regime change seemed the best of the bad options.
The Wilsonian obsession with national self-determination
presented little threat to the continued existence of Germany,
and in fact countered French plans for its dismemberment. It
pointed, however, to the dissolution of the Austro-Hungarian
Empire, and even if there was little personal animosity towards
Emperor Karl, Wilson's anti-monarchist attitude was a further blow to dwindling hopes of a Habsburg leadership of
a possible confederation of successor states. The consequent
turbulent history of central Europe was to demonstrate how
necessary the Empire had been.

Could the monarchies of Germany and Austria–Hungary
have survived if the Emperors had been more astute, or, in

Wilhelm's case, more unselfish? They had different problems, for in Karl's case the problem was the state over which he ruled and Wilson's dislike of monarchy and support for the principle of national self-determination, while in Wilhelm's case it was the ruler himself. Karl was well intentioned and popular, but the prospects of the dual monarchy surviving in its existent form were unlikely. His attempts to promote a separate peace were thwarted by Germany, while moves towards a confederate empire allowing Slavs autonomy were by 1917 belated and still opposed by Hungary. Wilhelm could perhaps have saved the Hohenzollern dynasty by a spectacular and suicidal decision to lead a cavalry charge on the western front, or less dramatically by abdication in the late summer of 1918 in favour of his grandson, the twelve-year-old Prince Wilhelm. After all, Ferdinand of Bulgaria managed to save the monarchy by an astute abdication. Neither option was acceptable to the Kaiser.

The spectacle of King George V and Queen Mary receiving the acclaim of the jubilant crowds from the balcony of Buckingham Palace on 11 November 1918 was in marked contrast to the situation of many of his relatives. Sharing the universal joy of his countrymen that a dreadful war was over and the sacrifices had not been in vain, the King was nevertheless shaken by the appalling fate of the Russian royal family, and could not be sanguine at the end of the monarchies of Germany and Austria–Hungary. As Asquith had remarked to him a fortnight before the Armistice, the war had brought 'a slump in Emperors … Russia murdered, Austria a fugitive and Germany on the edge of abdication'.[15] The humiliation of monarchs did not please him. He might consider the Kaiser 'the greatest criminal known', but he was annoyed when he heard that the wife of the British minister had jeered at the Kaiser on his arrival in Holland, and entirely lost his temper when he learned of Lloyd George's proposal to have the Kaiser extradited and put on trial in England, a proposal that luckily foundered upon the Dutch government's refusal to agree to such an extradition. He arranged for a British officer to be assigned as guard to Emperor Karl and Empress Zita until they were safely in Switzerland.

With the German Empire went all the subsidiary German kingdoms and duchies, which had for so long provided brides and grooms for the royal houses of Europe. George V could congratulate himself on having symbolically broken his ties with these minor German dynasties. Although gradually relations were discreetly renewed between defeated and victorious royal families, the age of the extended royal family was over. Those photographs of the royal families of Europe gathered together for funerals and weddings that were a feature of pre-war Europe were less ubiquitous after 1918, when the remaining monarchs preferred to stress their links with the nations they governed rather than their commonality with each other. When such photographs were taken there were more ex-monarchs, and the ranks were thinned by animosities that excluded many potential guests.

The institution of monarchy survived in Britain, the Netherlands, Belgium, Luxembourg, Norway, Sweden, Denmark, Italy, Romania, Bulgaria and the greater Serbia that was Yugoslavia. It spluttered spasmodically in Greece and lasted for a while in Spain. Albania even produced a new monarchy with the enthronement of King Zog. In Europe, however, monarchy was no longer the norm, and where it survived it had lost confidence and for the most part sought to shed or disguise its remaining powers and take on a purely symbolic role.

A recent study of the First World War has categorised it as 'the greatest error of modern history', and the replacement of monarchies by republics as 'one of the least intended consequences of the war'.[16] The kings and emperors had not on the whole sought war and had tried to pull back from the brink in July and August 1914. The residual internationalism and cosmopolitanism of monarchy had jostled with the necessity of monarchs gaining popular and democratic acclaim from subjects all too ready to embrace nationalism, but it had provided something of a brake on national animosities, if in the end an inadequate one. The redrawn geopolitical map of Europe that emerged from the Versailles Settlement and, in eastern Europe, from confused and fierce warfare did not fulfil the impractical dreams of Woodrow Wilson, nor the less idealistic ambitions of the European victors. The kings departed not because they were autocratic, undemocratic, militaristic or despotic but because they were not ruthless, unscrupulous or populist enough. They had flirted with populism and nationalism, but total war had toughened these forces, which now demanded harder men and real autocrats.

EUROPE: THE SURVIVORS

The early years of the twentieth century had seen the end of the Portuguese and Korean monarchies, and, most importantly, of the imperial system that had ruled China, the world's most populous state, for thousands of years. It was the events of 1917/18, however, which signalled the demise of monarchy as the normal and natural system of government. The end of the three imperial monarchies of Russia, Germany and Austria–Hungary was a colossal blow to the monarchical principle. Of the world's great powers only two, Britain and Japan, or perhaps three, if Italy was included as a great power, remained monarchies.

The fall of the imperial thrones in Europe occurred in 1917/18, but was the long-term result of the outbreak of war in 1914, the year in which the die was cast. The enormity of the consequences of July and August 1914, not just for Europe's monarchies but for European society as a whole, has inevitably led to counterfactual historical questions. *What if* war had not broken out? *What if* Britain had stood aside and the central powers had won a reasonably swift victory?

Though stern historians will tell us that counterfactual mus-
ings have no place in the historical discipline and that only
what happened matters, great turning points in history ineluctably suggest alternative scenarios.

One possible counterfactual alternative has Britain staying out of the war, a rapid victory for the central powers and
the emergence of a European union under German leadership, leaving Britain to concentrate on her Empire.[1] Other
scenarios include victory for the central powers after a long
and bloody war; had the German government refrained from
launching unrestricted submarine warfare only months before
the first Russian revolution, then without American intervention and with a disintegrating Russia a victory for the central
powers would have been probable.[2] Another possibility is that
Tsarist Russia might have managed to stave off revolution
until an eventual Allied victory removed many of the causes
of discontent.

At the least, such imagined histories do pose the question
as to how stable the empires were in 1914, and the degree to
which it was exclusively the war that led to their fall. The same
question may well be asked with reference to the entire social
and political structure of pre-war Europe. It is quite possible
by a judicious selection of sources to portray either a placid
and stable Europe stumbling into war or a feverish Europe
beset by problems, animosities and divisions.[3] No state or society is without its problems and discontents, but there seems
little reason to believe that Europe in 1914 was on the brink
of succumbing to revolution. What is more imponderable is
whether the considerable challenges to stability could have
been withstood, and problems solved or at least ameliorated.
There is much truth in the observation that it wasn't the problems of early twentieth-century Europe that led to disaster but
the solutions to them,[4] and it was the impact of the First World
War that provided more fertile soil for drastic solutions, whose
proponents were prepared to wade through blood in the name
of supposed Utopias.

That it was defeat in war that led to the fall of the Emperors of Russia, Germany and Austria–Hungary suggests that victory would have led to their continued rule. Further counterfactual musing, however, suggests that, once the war had lasted more than a few months, it is unlikely that these monarchies could have survived in their old form. Long before their overthrow, the stress of war had exposed the hollowness of the pretensions of the supposed autocrats. Had the Tsarist regime contrived to keep revolution at bay until an eventual Allied victory in 1918 removed many of the causes of discontent, it is unlikely that the failings of the Tsar as a leader in war or the Tsarina's indulgence of Rasputin would have been forgotten. The Kaiser, as we have seen, had neither the professional knowledge nor the consistent determination for his ostensible position as Supreme Warlord once real warfare succeeded exercises and reviews, and by the end of the war he was regarded as at best a nuisance and at worst a joke by the German general staff. Emperor Franz Josef had, by the time of his death in November 1916, long ceased to exercise control over either military or civilian affairs, even though he worked earnestly at his desk in the Schönbrunn Palace reading and signing documents. Eventual victory might have enabled the imperial regimes to survive, but in drastically modified forms.

That the monarchs of central and eastern Europe did not live up to the carefully cultivated image of leadership is not surprising. It was some time since princes had done a more than nominal service in armies or been permitted to risk their lives in battle. Even in matters of government and politics, the growth of government and of bureaucracy had distanced a cosseted and ceremonial kingship from the realities of administration. An increasingly nominal autocracy had come to seem more a brake on dynamic government than its epitome.

By the end of the First World War the context of government had changed. It was not just that some states had lost and others won, though this was of enormous importance, but that total war had meant the mobilisation of entire economies and societies, with profound consequences. War had proved a great disruption, shattering pre-war social norms, arousing expectations and hatreds and challenging the social hierarchy. Even in victorious states the post-war years saw instability in the form of strikes, demonstrations and fear of revolution. There could be no return to pre-war 'normality'. Niall Ferguson has argued that:

> Ultimately, the position of the monarchs was bound to be threatened by a war which mobilised millions of men: at root the First World War was democratic.[5]

The war's effects were certainly not democratic in the sense that there was to be more democracy after the war – rather the contrary – but the war had certainly the effect of a diminished respect for social superiors and hierarchy. A strident and vulgar populism gained ground. Aristocracy and gentry, as well as royalty, lost much of their influence.

It was not just that three monarchies had fallen but that they had been three of Europe's great monarchies. Smaller saplings had withstood the storm, even those which has been on the losing side while great oaks fell. Those minor monarchies that had been on the winning side were safe enough, though King Nicholas of Montenegro, rather unluckily, lost his throne to the Serbian royal house when his tiny kingdom was absorbed by the new monarchy of the Kingdom of the Serbs, Croats and Slovenes, while the Romanian monarchy found its prestige enhanced by its territorial gains, even if those gains were too great to be digested. The judicious abdication of King Ferdinand preserved the Bulgarian monarchy, while the neutral monarchies maintained their kings and queens on their thrones. Of the great monarchies, only the British monarchy survived.

Active political monarchy had failed the test of war, and it was significant that in western Europe it was those monarchies that claimed to rule rather than merely reign that were discredited. The remaining great monarchy of Europe, the British monarchy, not only presided over a victorious power but had become 'constitutional', not in the older sense of working within a framework in which the sovereign respected law and took advice from elected governments, but in the newer sense of advising and warning governments while accepting their decisions outside a diminishing number of areas in which the royal prerogative was supposedly retained. The position of the British monarchy was, nevertheless, greatly enhanced, and its particular charisma and special features came to appear the model for modern monarchy, if indeed monarchy was to have a future.

One feature of the British monarchy was that it had become more ceremonial as it had become less politically powerful. It has usually been considered that royal ceremonies take place to buttress royal power, though, as we have seen, it has been argued that in Bali the reason for the monarchy's very existence was to be the centrepiece, projecting the state itself and the head of state by ever more elaborate public ceremonies and spectacles. British public ceremonial is, however, particularly interesting because it came to concentrate upon the 'dignified' part of the constitution rather than upon the practical. In the early nineteenth century the British monarchy, which retained considerable political power, had been maintained on a relatively modest scale, and its ceremonies were often low-key affairs. By the early twentieth century the lifestyle of the king and royal family had been elevated far above that of even the richer aristocrats, while coronations, funerals and weddings, even the celebration of the sovereign's official birthday, had become grand, carefully orchestrated theatre. By contrast, Prime Ministers were lodged in the modest house in Downing Street and had minor walk-on parts in national celebrations.

Other facets of the British monarchy included its unchallenged position as the head of society, whether in the narrower sense of elite society or society as a whole. The *Season* of fashionable society depended greatly upon royal patronage, but so did national societies for science and the arts and the major charities, while a new town hall or hospital in a provincial town usually started its formal existence with an opening or the laying of a foundation-stone by a member of the royal family. A fascinated but for the moment respectful press regaled its readers with accounts of the details of royalty, tastes in furniture and clothes, fondness for particular pets and sporting activities.

King George V had both consciously and unconsciously remodelled the style of the monarchy. The grand ceremony of his father's reign was maintained and even further embellished, as with the investiture of his eldest son as Prince of Wales. The King's predilection for a quiet family life and his fidelity to his queen contrasted with his father's habits, however, and was in keeping with the opinions and prejudices of the respectable majority of his subjects. If the concept of the royal 'soap opera', a nation ceaselessly entertained by the evolving family that ruled it, had yet to be thought of, the gruff, rather old-fashioned king, his rather stiff but statuesque consort and the fashionable, daring and dashing Prince of Wales provided figures which old and young could identify with.

Above all, the change of the family name to Windsor had made the royal family appear a much more British family, and the King himself could have scarcely been more British in his outlook and tastes. In the aftermath of the war and at a time when the Empire had never seemed so important, the association of king and country was crucial. Before 1914 the European royal houses had tried to combine the links of blood that made them an extended European caste with an identification with the countries over which they ruled. After the war, this was no longer possible. European links were downplayed and German relatives were not welcome guests. The marriage of the King's second son, the Duke of York, to Lady Elizabeth Bowes-Lyon, the daughter of a Scottish earl, was universally popular because she was attractive and charming, but most of all because she was British. George's sister, the Princess Royal, was also married to a Scottish landowner, while, if another sister had married a foreign monarch, her husband was, fortuitously, King of Norway, a state that had been neutral during the war.

Any analysis of the *British* monarchy as of Britain itself in this period is incomplete and misleading unless it places emphasis upon the Empire and upon the self-governing dominions referred to increasingly from the time of the Imperial Conference of 1926 as the 'British Commonwealth of Nations'. The influence of the Empire was constant in almost every aspect of British life, from the celebration of Empire Day to literature and cinema and to the goods on sale in the shops. Public opinion well understood that Britain's great-power status rested not on the economic and military power of Britain alone but on the strength of the Empire. As we have seen, the monarchy and the Empire were closely entwined. George V was Emperor of India and the King of the individual dominions. If the Empire was a recurring theme in British life, so the influence of the 'home country' was ubiquitous in the Empire, and particularly in the white dominions. Distinctive national characteristics and interests had long been apparent, and there was often an ambivalence in the relationship with Britain, but the influence of British culture and customs remained strong and was even increased by the development of broadcasting. Loyalty to the monarchy, with a stress upon it as a link that transcended the connections with the British government, was crucial to the position of the self-governing states in the emergent Commonwealth.

Most of the remaining monarchies of western Europe had already, like the British monarchy, to a greater or lesser degree conceded much of their political power. As heads of state, monarchs retained a role of more than symbolic importance, for, being outside politics, they could be seen as above politics and the enduring focus of national loyalties. Many had, again on the British model, seen social position and influence actually increase as political power declined. There were, however, differences. The Scandinavian states had gone further in divesting monarchy of its power to govern; the new state of Norway had from its beginning in 1905 a constitution that strictly limited the monarch's political power. Denmark had moved towards a position where the king could advise and warn. In Sweden there was greater conflict between a monarchy determined to hold on to much of its power and the demands of elected assemblies. The constitution of 1809, which gave considerable power to the monarchy, was to last in a modified form until 1974, but from the mid-nineteenth century ministers had moved from being servants of the king to being responsible to parliament. The crunch came in February 1914, when King Gustav V appealed to the people over the head of parliament in his famous 'courtyard speech' and failed to win the day; a rather low-key, even nominal, monarchy was to be the result. In Belgium, the Netherlands and Luxembourg the sovereigns retained considerably more power than their Scandinavian counterparts, and rather more than the King-Emperor in Britain.

In the majority of these constitutional monarchies, sovereigns and their families found new roles as the heads of civil society, entwining the adjective royal with charities, learned societies, opera houses and even with national industrial and commercial enterprises. Kings and queens might no longer govern states, but monarchy and nation could be made synonymous. In the Netherlands and Scandinavia, this marked just an acceleration of traditional royal bounty, and in Belgium and Luxembourg the Catholic Church and monarchy were able to cooperate in charitable work. Even on the stony ground of Spain, Queen Ena tried to sow the British tradition of royal charitable work, an innovation which was greatly resented by the Church, which regarded charity as its own fiefdom.

The cult of royal personalities was not confined to Britain, either. King Albert and his consort, the romantic Queen

Elisabeth, were enormously popular in post-war Belgium because of their leadership when most of their country was occupied by German forces, and because they were happily married. Albert's predecessors, Leopold I and II had both scandalised Belgian Catholic society, not so much because of their mistresses, but by the flagrant manner in which they flaunted them. Crown Prince Leopold's marriage to Princess Astrid of Sweden was also a love match. Even though she came from a Lutheran family, the Princess established herself as a central figure in Belgian life, beautiful, fashionable and at the same time caring, involving herself in charitable work as the effects of the Depression were felt in Belgium. The death of King Albert in a mountaineering accident in 1934 brought Leopold to the throne. Little more than a year later, Queen Astrid was killed when the car the King was driving plunged down a slope in Switzerland. The conjunction of a royal beauty and a violent death is a potent one. Empress Elisabeth of Austria–Hungary was, as we have seen, assassinated, but it was the motor car that was to claim the lives of three twentieth-century charismatic royal women: Queen Astrid, Princess Grace of Monaco and Princess Diana. Belgium possessed, as it still does, a press that was restrained in its treatment of the royal family, but Astrid's death was followed by an emotional reaction from ordinary Belgians, who had admired and identified with her. Two million attended her funeral, and if the formal response of the Belgian government was merely a commemorative postage stamp, cities and provinces made their feelings plain by striking medals and mounting ceremonies, while a plethora of books in French and Flemish bore witness to the national grief.

Constitutional monarchy seemed best suited to northern Europe, or perhaps it was simply that this form of monarchy is best suited to relatively cohesive and prosperous societies, and Britain, Scandinavia and what was later to be known as Benelux experienced more benign conditions and less fratricidal tensions in the inter-war period. Elsewhere in western Europe there were to be monarchical casualties.

Only a most remarkable ruler could have presided with success over Spain in the 1920s. Alfonso XIII, though brave in the face of attempts to assassinate him, was faced with challenges he had neither the judgement nor the skill to deal with. Spain had acute problems: the combination of its poverty and deep divisions, religious, political and separatist, would have confounded the wisest of men. Alfonso XIII reigned until 1923 over a constitutional monarchy that was nominally a democracy, although the votes were delivered by local political power-brokers, and the system ensured a rotation of moderately liberal and conservative governments. Bereft of the remains of its once-great Empire after the loss of Cuba, Puerto Rico and the Philippines, Spain found itself bogged down in increasingly bloody wars in Morocco. The Church retained enormous power and wealth, but had stimulated a fierce anti-clericalism. Uniquely, anarchism was a potent force. Alfonso possessed guile but little direction, and sought to play off faction against faction in what was almost a dysfunctional nation. A disaster for the Spanish army in Morocco endangered the monarchy, which was saved for the moment by the dictatorship of Primo de Rivera (1923–30). Alfonso, by this time derided as 'Alfonso the sixth and a half', neither stood firm for constitutional government nor stood by his well-meaning dictator once de Rivera's popularity declined. The coming of a republic in 1931 aroused fierce passions, but even monarchists found it difficult to regret the passing of Alfonso himself. His reign might have done little to solve his country's problems, but his overthrow merely exacerbated them.

Victory in war is supposed to be good for rulers, but victory in 1918 was a triumph neither for Victor Emmanuel III nor for Italy. The King had earned considerable popularity during the war, but the Peace Settlement brought only minor rewards for three years of struggle. Disappointed nationalist expectations, post-war hardships, political and geographic divisions, together with widespread cynicism as to the capacity of government, brought Mussolini to power. It was a characteristic of Italy's fascist regime that, although it theoretically aimed for a state totally controlled by party and Duce, it lived with its and Italy's inheritance; the monarchy remained, and the 1929 *Concordat* gave the Church and the Vatican their place. The House of Savoy retained its titular position and its palaces, but the little King was at best a cipher, while Mussolini had the reins of power. When the position of the Duce weakened, however, the retention of the monarchy proved to be significant. The King might have been, as it were, put in a cupboard, but as the man who still embodied legitimate government, especially for the armed forces, he was brought out of the cupboard again in 1943 and was a key figure in the overthrow of Mussolini.

The fall of the three great Empires left much of central and eastern Europe a monarchy-free area, for none of the new states that arose in the wake of the Empires chose monarchical systems, unless we include the enlarged Karageorgevic realm (the Kingdom of the Serbs, Croats and Slovenes; from 1929 Yugoslavia) and the nominal monarchy of Hungary. The Soviet Union was, of course, *sui generis*, a state formally dedicated to the cause of international revolution, but it is significant that republican systems were adopted in the new states of Finland, Latvia, Estonia, Lithuania, Czechoslovakia and Poland. A few decades earlier, the new states that emerged with the retreat of the Ottoman Empire had universally become monarchies.

The change was due in part to the weakened appeal and charisma of monarchy after the First World War, and to the influence of the anti-royalist Woodrow Wilson in the shaping of post-war Europe. It was also a result of the social revolution that affected many of these states. Monarchy had almost everywhere been entwined with aristocracy, the other great victim of the war. Not only was the number of aristocrats killed in battle relatively higher than for other social groups, but almost everywhere aristocracy lost influence after the war, and great landowners experienced a loss of wealth as agricultural prices and therefore rents declined after 1918. The very existence of the nobility in great swaths of east-central Europe was in danger. Here many aristocratic landowners had been of a different nationality from their peasantries, and with the creation of new national estates they lost their land and position. In Latvia and Estonia, for instance, the landowners were German, while in Lithuania they were Polish. Land reform in east and central Europe resulted in the redistribution of millions of acres from great estates to the peasants, and in general the confiscation was highest where the nationality was not of the nationality of the new state.

It was not surprising that Czechoslovakia, where Bohemia had lost much of its native aristocracy three centuries earlier and the great magnates who remained had been intimately associated with the Austrian Empire, while most landowners in Slovakia had been Magyar, emerged as a state with little taste for either aristocratic or monarchist traditions. The position in Poland and Hungary, where there were influential native nobilities and a monarchist tradition, was more complex.

The Polish monarchy that ended with King Stanislaw Augustus the Last and the third partition of Poland in 1795 had been unusual, to say the least. Poland had been a commonwealth reigned over by an elected monarch. The new independent Poland, which arose after the defeat of the empires between which it had been divided and which had by 1921 defeated the Soviet Union, had lost its monarchist tradition, and there was no pretender. The constitution of March 1921 was based on that of the French Republic, not perhaps the happiest of models. More than a century of foreign rule, where the only national politics were the politics of opposition, produced a state in which a fractured party system resulted in power passing first to Marshal Pilsudski and then to an army oligarchy. The suggestion that the Duke of Kent was interested in plans to revive the Polish monarchy and was in 1941 offered the Polish throne by General Sikorski would indicate, however, that the appeal of monarchy was not entirely dead.

Hungary, after the fall of Bela Kun's brief communist dictatorship, became a monarchy again, but a monarchy without a king. A restoration of the monarchy under a regent, Admiral Horthy, was declared. The Regent, however, seemed more than happy to continue to rule, and showed little inclination to fulfil his promise to restore the throne to the exiled ex-Emperor Karl. Two attempts were made by Karl to reclaim his throne by arriving in Hungary and appealing to the people. In the last attempt, Horthy had the ex-Emperor and Empress expelled by force. The last Habsburg Emperor died the following year on the island of Madeira, and Hungary continued to be a kingdom without a king ruled over by an admiral without a navy, or, indeed a seacoast.

If constitutional monarchy and a withdrawal from political leadership seemed the answer to many of the surviving monarchies of northern Europe, this was a luxury not available in east-central Europe. There was an alternative view as to the lessons to be learned from the fall of the three Empires. Perhaps the Emperors had not been sufficiently autocratic and had not held firmly enough onto the levers of power. In eastern Europe the option of comfortably reigning over democratically elected governments, while personifying the state, leading civil society and wielding enormous social influence, was not on offer. Democracy worked, at best, erratically and spasmodically, and society was fractured. Peasant parties, communist parties and parties representing the small urban elites could reach little agreement as to even the most basic rules of democratic government, a form of government that demands that those who lose have to, at least in the short term, accept the legitimacy of the victors. Armies whose soldiers

were drawn from the peasantry and whose officers came from
the urban elites were unreliable; whereas in western Europe
army officers tended to be conservative, loyal to crowns and
dedicated to the preservation of order, in eastern Europe they
could be dangerously radical and shrilly nationalistic. In the
face of coups, disorder and unstable governments, as agrarian
nations suffered from low prices for agricultural produce, the
appeal of strong men and dictators grew.

It was in the Balkans that monarchy survived, and it was
there that social, economic and national problems were acute.
One effect of the war had been the emergence of the peasantry as a self-conscious class, and the entry of the peasantry
into politics was a marked feature of post-war politics. Peasant
parties often saw their interests as diametrically opposed to
those of the urban elites, but equally opposed to those of
socialist and communist parties; events in the Soviet Union
demonstrated the way the needs of the countryside could
be ignored for the sake of industrialisation. In most Balkan
states there was a multiplicity of parties, which made stable
elected government difficult, and even peasant parties could
be fractured by nationalism. Despite the parlous economic
and social conditions of the states, it was foreign policy that
largely dictated the political agenda. The territorial ambitions
of ethnic groups and states were incompatible, and the effects
of the post-war peace settlement had exacerbated rivalries
between states that had gained territory, those that had lost it
and those that felt that what had been gained was insufficient.
For the most part the Balkan kings sought to rein in those
who favoured expansionist foreign policies, but the force
of nationalist opinion was too strong for them not to give
it at least lip service. Above all, the Balkan kingdoms were
not to be allowed to work out their disputes and rivalries
by themselves, but were subject to the ambitions of mighty
neighbours, the Soviet Union, Germany and Italy. It was in
these circumstances that the Balkan kings turned towards

royal dictatorship. If democratic government meant perpetual crisis and the alternative was being a cipher while an upstart dictator ruled, then why not be the dictator yourself?

Developments in Greece were a warning to other Balkan monarchies as to the dangers of Prime Ministers with overweening ambitions. During the First World War, Greece had had, in 1916/17, two governments, the one based in Salonica and led by Eleftherios Venizelos, and the other based in Athens and led by King Constantine I. Venizelos was determined that Greece should join the *entente* powers, with the expectation that their victory would result in great territorial gains for Greece at the expense of the Ottoman Empire and Bulgaria. King Constantine wanted Greece to remain neutral. With British and French forces in Salonika, the *entente* powers became increasingly impatient with Constantine's neutralist policy, a policy which could be presented as pro-German, especially as the King's consort, Queen Sophie, was the Kaiser's sister. After an abortive landing by British and French troops under French command at Piraeus, which was repulsed by the King's forces, Anglo-French pressure continued with bombardments and a blockade, until in 1917 the King was forced to abdicate in favour of his son, Alexander, and go into exile.

This 'national schism', the deep divide between royalists and the supporters of Venizelos, was to have far-reaching repercussions for Greek politics, which would be influenced by it for decades.[6] The army had already been involved in politics, but the purge of royalist officers by Venizelos set an ominous precedent. Henceforth every coup would be followed by a purge of officers loyal to the previous regime, and the army's role in political life increased.

Venizelos's pursuit of the dream of a greater Greece, a 'Byzantium reborn', led to the Greek invasion of Anatolia in 1919. It was already apparent that the Greek army faced an arduous task for which it was little prepared when the combination of the death of King Alexander from blood poisoning, following a bite from a pet monkey, and a general election resulted in the return of King Constantine and the retirement of Venizelos from politics. Churchill's comment that 'It is perhaps no exaggeration to remark that a quarter of a million persons died from this monkey bite' was based on his belief that the defeat of the Greek forces and the 'ethnic cleansing' by which the Greek citizens of the Turkish coastal towns were either massacred or forced to leave, was due to the return of Constantine and the now obligatory replacement of the generals and colonels loyal to the previous regime by less experienced royalists. The strategy that led to disaster had, however, already been determined by Venizelos, and the atrocities committed by Greeks on Turks provided a precedent for the subsequent massacres of Greeks. Constantine's great mistake was not to extricate Greece from its ill-fated campaign. He paid the price for Greece's defeat by Turkey in the war of 1921–2 and the subsequent expulsion of Greeks from Anatolia in 1923. Less than two years from his triumphal return to Athens he was on his way to exile again. The great divide in Greek political life had not run its course. Constantine's successor, King George II, had an interrupted reign (1922–4, 1935–47). A republic was declared by the resurgent Venizelists in 1924, but a referendum in 1935 brought the so-called 'King of Claridges', after the hotel in which he had spent much of his exile, back in triumph to rule until the Second World War in conjunction with Greece's dictator, the tough, but not entirely ruthless, General Metaxos. He who would be King of Greece, it has been said, 'should keep his bags packed'.[7]

After the catastrophe of 1923, Greece abandoned, for the moment, any ambitions for a greater Greece, but territorial ambitions or the desire to hold on to territorial acquisitions, together with competing nationalisms, dominated the politics of the other Balkan states. The interests and fates of the monarchies were intimately bound up with foreign policy and nationalisms. Considering the massive problems of Balkan societies, rural poverty, the divide between town and country, politicised armies and the desperation of pockets of a proletariat, the centrality of national divisions and ambitions may seem irrational. Yet, whether a sublimation of economic and social problems in the emotion of national rivalry, or a recognition that ethnicity and culture are in the end more important than economics and class, nationalism was the dominant force.

In the Kingdom of the Serbs, Croats and Slovenes, which was later renamed Yugoslavia, nationalism could be alternatively a unifying or a divisive force. From one point of view, Serbia had played a role comparable to that of Piedmont or Prussia, which had led Italy and Germany towards unification, in providing the leadership that had resulted in a union of the south Slavs. The alternative view was that the new state was simply an expanded Serbia, in which the Serbs exercised a hegemony over the peoples the Serbian Kingdom had incorporated. The problems facing the new state were considerable. Slovenes had on the whole been comfortable with Austrian rule, while Croats, though deeply resenting Hungarian rule, had remained loyal to the Habsburg dynasty until the final days of the Empire; Bosnian Muslims had rioted in Sarajevo against Serbs after the assassination of Archduke Franz Ferdinand; Macedonians and Montenegrins were ambivalent about a new order in which they were assumed to be Serbs. King Alexander I, who succeeded his father in 1921, inherited a fractious kingdom, divided by ethnicity, religion and alphabets. The refusal of the main Croatian party, Stefan Radic's Croat Republican Peasant Party, to appear in parliament during the first years of the new kingdom resulted in the ignoring of Croatian grievances by the Serb-dominated central government and deepening of Croatian discontent. In fact, Radic's aim was greater Croatian autonomy within the kingdom.

King Alexander was torn between a loyalty to Serbia, whose armies had fought so bravely and doggedly during the wars, and a recognition that it was necessary to restrain Serbian ambitions in the interests of balance and unity. He managed to do without a coronation, realising that a ceremony with Orthodox rites would be an affront to Catholic and Muslim subjects. In 1925, he came up with a bold initiative, and approaching Radic, who was in prison, through an intermediary, managed to achieve agreement between the Croats and Serbian radicals under Nikola Pasic. A firm start to Croat–Serb *rapprochement* seemed to have been made, with the Croats accepting not only the state but the monarchy. The hatreds of the previous years were not, however, to be so easily stilled, and in 1928 Radic and four of his party's deputies were gunned down during a debate in the Assembly. With their leader dead the Croats withdrew all cooperation with the government, and parliamentary government was seen to have failed. The King acted decisively in January 1929 and embarked upon personal rule, suspending the constitution and transforming the Kingdom of the Serbs, Croats and Slovenes into the Kingdom of Yugoslavia. A royal dictatorship had begun.

Alexander was a well-meaning dictator who saw the problems of his country clearly enough, and if he was less clear as to solutions then he was in good company. His personal rule was widely accepted, as was his claim that he had taken over reluctantly, faced with the obvious failure of the democratic system. Whether, if Yugoslavia had been left alone, Alexander would have succeeded in improving Serbian–Croat relations under a relatively benign if firm autocracy, and perhaps gradually restored a democratic system, can only be guessed at. There can be little doubt, however, that the intervention of first Italy and then Germany exacerbated Yugoslavia's internal tensions. Mussolini, fired with ambitions in the Adriatic, began to nurture and support the Croatian fascist party, the Ustase. To Mussolini Yugoslavia was a 'heterogeneous conglomerate' that would soon fall apart. The Ustase's campaign of terrorism led to the Yugoslavian regime adopting harshly repressive measures. Alexander, realising that he could best deal with Croatian terrorism by coming to an agreement with the Italian dictator, opened negotiations with him, only to discover an Italian-backed plot to assassinate him when he visited Zagreb in 1933. The following year he was assassinated in Marseilles while on a state visit to France. Alexander's eleven-year-old son was now King, but power was in the hands of a regency council headed by Alexander's brother, Prince Paul.

Whether or not Mussolini had been behind Alexander's assassination, Italy with its support for Croatian independence was clearly a major threat to Yugoslavia, but there was a counterweight to Italy in the offing, Germany. The new German government, with Hitler as Chancellor, which came to power in January 1933, was both eager to advance German influence in the Balkans and concerned at the defensive alliance, the 'Little *Entente*', agreed between Czechoslovakia, Yugoslavia and Romania in February 1933. Hitler's aim was to improve relations with Romania and Yugoslavia and to make their economies dependent on trade with Germany. Yugoslavia had little option but to respond positively. It is easy for those who loftily expect small countries to sacrifice themselves for a common good they perceive with hindsight to criticise Prince Paul for Yugoslavia's ever-closer relations with Nazi Germany, but his alternatives are far from apparent. It would, indeed, be difficult to argue that the 1941 Belgrade uprising, which removed him after he had agreed that his country could be used as a base for Germany's invasion of Greece, did Yugoslavia much good.

The Kingdoms of Romania and Bulgaria after the First World War can be regarded as opposites, a winner and a loser, the one stuffed with the fruits of victory, the other exhausted by defeat and bereft not just of grandiose hopes of expansion but of hard-won territory. These gains and losses were dependent not on the fortunes of the countries' own armies but of those of the great powers with which they had been allied.

The greatly enlarged Romania was to find that the acquisition of territories with non-Romanian majorities and greedy
neighbours was not an unmixed blessing but for the moment
her position was symbolised by Queen Marie, who paraded
Paris from her twenty-room suite at the Ritz, impressing
the press and the fashionable world with her grand style, her
dresses and her hats. Romania differed from her Slav neighbours in seeing herself as a Latin state and in having a native
aristocracy, the boyars. Bucharest was a fashionable city, justi-
fying its claim to be the Paris of eastern Europe by its good
food, chic lifestyle and beautiful women. Its successive glamorous and poetic queens, Elizabeth and Marie, seemed to
emphasise this. The higher social classes added a touch of decadence to the luxury in which they lived, though there were
limits, and no officer under the rank of major was allowed to
wear make-up.

Both King Ferdinand and Queen Marie had hearty sexual
appetites, which they satisfied promiscuously, but they did so
within certain bounds of discretion, which maintained royal
dignity. The King for instance recognised all six of his wife's
children as legitimate, though there is evidence that their
fathers varied. Their son Carol, however, had no notion of discretion. Before ascending the throne in 1930 he had twice
renounced his claim to it. On the first occasion, he astounded
his family and subjects by deserting his regiment in 1918 and
eloping to Odessa with a dancer, 'Zizi' Lambrino, and declared
that he wished to renounce the throne in perpetuity. He was
persuaded to annul the marriage and retract his renunciation,
and in 1921 he was married to Princess Helena of Greece, by
whom he had his son and heir, Prince Michael. The marriage
proved to be only a brief brush with convention for Carol,
who in 1926 ran off again, this time with the voluptuous
Elena, or 'Magda', Lupescu. The age of a popular press with an
obsessive interest in the lives of the rich and famous, and especially royalty, was dawning, and journalists and photographers

tracked the errant couple to Milan and encamped outside their hotel. They eventually settled in a Paris suburb, and Carol once more renounced the throne in order to be able to live with his mistress.

On the death of King Ferdinand in 1927, he was succeeded by Carol's young son, King Michael, who reigned with a regency council. Carol was, however, not finished with Romania yet. After an abortive attempt to return in 1928, he reached an agreement with the royal family by which he could become king provided he broke with Lupescu and lived once more with Queen Helena. Carol returned and the nine-year-old King Michael's first reign came to an end. There was no happy outcome, however, for Queen Helena refused to return to her ex-husband, and Carol, king once more, soon had Elena Lupescu installed in a villa in his capital. In a manner reminiscent of Queen Draga of Serbia, though even Carol did not dare to make his mistress queen, she dispensed patronage to her family and aspired to an alternative court.

The backdrop to this exotic soap opera was a country with grave economic difficulties, a pitifully low standard of living for the majority and ethnic animosities. Unusually for an eastern state, Romania had a tradition of strong and cohesive political parties – the Liberal Party, which had usually managed elections so as to ensure its monopoly of government, and the National Peasant Party. King Carol exhibited considerable cunning in dividing and manipulating party leaderships in the interests of greater power for himself. One party or movement he found he could not influence was the Iron Guard, or the Legion of the Archangel St Michael. Romania was one of the few countries to produce a fascist movement that was original, indeed idiosyncratic. The Romanian peasant was to the Guards' leader, Cornelius Codreanu, the ideal figure, for in him rested the soul of the nation; ultra-nationalist and xenophobic, the Guard had a fascination with death, and Codreanu's assassination seemed only to increase the dead leader's appeal. King Carol probably shared Codreanu's belief in the corrupt and rotten nature of Romania's ostensibly democratic system, but he knew him for an enemy and he could act decisively and toughly when he had to. In 1938 he not only dealt with the Guard but banned all political activity and became a royal dictator. Unlike other monarchs who dispensed with political parties, he formed his own movement, the Front for the Rebirth of the Nation. With its blue tunics and special salute, it looked suspiciously like the movements of many commoner dictators.

Probably no one could have done better than Carol, faced with Romania's dangerous position in the late 1930s and early 1940s. Romania just had too much. Hungary wanted Transylvania back, the Soviet Union wanted Bessarabia and northern Bukovina, while Bulgaria hungered after the southern Dobruja. Both Germany and the Soviet Union eyed Romania's oil fields. King Carol realised the dangers of German economic penetration, and until 1936 backed his able Foreign Minister, Titulescu, who limited German influence and was careful to prevent German firms gaining any share in the oil industry. The confused politics of Bucharest as war came closer and the social life of the capital continued has been best described by Olivia Manning's *Balkan Trilogy*, as the 'playboy prince' turned dictatorial king struggled to keep his country out of the approaching war. By the late thirties, however, Romania's and Carol's options were very limited.

King Boris of Bulgaria was perhaps the most well-meaning and intelligent of the royal dictators. He had little inclination to emulate the 'Balkan Fox', his father King Ferdinand, although the latter attempted to interfere from his long exile; he didn't die until 1948. Bulgarian government was dominated in the immediate post-war years by Alexander Stamboliski, the leader of the peasant party, the Bulgarian Agrarian National Union, and King Boris got on well enough with this blunt and burly figure. He sympathised with Stamboliski's anti-revisionism and desire to address Bulgaria's internal problems rather than concentrating on regaining Macedonia from the Kingdom of the Serbs, Croats and Slovenes. Stamboliski, who had grown increasingly dictatorial, managed to alienate nearly every other political party and social section in the country but his own agrarian followers. His most deadly enemies were the officer corps and IMRO (the Internal Macedonian Revolutionary Organisation); the Treaty of Neuilly, signed by Stamboliski, had both drastically reduced the size of the army and signed away Macedonia. In June 1923 Stamboliski was overthrown by a coup, and although he escaped from Sofia, he was captured and killed by IMRO, and his head was sent back to the capital in a tin. The Communists who had sat on the sidelines during the coup against Stamboliski then tried their own insurrection in September, which was easily put down and followed by killings and reprisals organised by the new strongman, General Vulkov.

The King distanced himself from these bloody events and seemed an ineffectual figure, at best a cipher, at worst a monarch prepared to preside over repressive regimes. Yet he could be a man of action, as was shown in 1925:

> As the royal car negotiated a mountain defile a hail of bullets killed a passenger and immobilised the chauffeur. Seizing the steering wheel, King Boris ground the gears into reverse and backed off at speed down a narrow dusty road. Then when the car rode up the stay cable of a telegraph pole, he flung himself into the roadside ditch. Round the bend came a post office bus. As the King ran into the road there was another burst of firing; but while the driver and passengers ran for cover, the King commandeered the bus, drove to the next township where he ordered the telegraph wires to Sofia to be cut and hurried on to the capital before news of the attempt could spread.[8]

In the same year, a state funeral was arranged for an assassinated general in the St Nedelya Cathedral, and just as the Archbishop finished intoning the promise of everlasting life a massive bomb went off, killing 160 people and wounding hundreds more. Boris had providentially been delayed, and by luck no member of the government was among those killed.

It was not until the 1930s that Boris intervened decisively. The 'man in the fedora [hat]', a withdrawn, rather intellectual figure with a mild manner, decided that the confusion and lack of stable government caused by the multiplicity of political parties and the violence caused by the rivalry between IMRO and Zveno (the Link), a republican organisation with close allies in the illegal Military League, could not be allowed to continue. In 1933, encouraged by the new Nazi German government, he made a move to improve Bulgarian–Yugoslavian relations by contriving a meeting with King Alexander at Belgrade railway station. Perhaps royal cousinhood could do something to ease tensions over Macedonia. This was a risky venture and one that was likely to enrage IMRO. Boris was, however, able to take advantage of his country's internal animosities. A coup by Zveno in 1934 was followed by the extermination of much of IMRO's leadership and then by a falling out between Zveno and its erstwhile ally the Military League. King Boris saw his opportunity and took control of the state. The rule of an unostentatious and well-meaning royal dictator began.

Albania provides us with the sole instance of a new monarchy established in inter-war Europe. Not surprisingly, since the majority of its inhabitants were Muslims, Albania remained loyal to the Ottoman Empire long after the Christian subjects of the Empire had risen in revolt. Albanian irregulars had indeed been very useful to the Ottoman regime in putting down Christian revolts with considerable ferocity. By 1909, however, the Albanians, finding that Turkish rule provided little protection for them against the newly independent states of Serbia, Montenegro, Greece and Bulgaria, and that the Young Turks had little respect for their national ambitions, themselves rose in revolt, and by 1911 this had turned into a full-scale rebellion. Although the 1913 Treaty of London, which ended the second Balkan War, recognised the sovereignty of an Albanian state, against the wishes of Serbia and Greece, the frontiers of the new state left large numbers of ethnic Albanians within the borders of the neighbouring Balkan states. The new state was to be a monarchy, but who was to be king? The first candidate, as we have seen, didn't last long, for Prince Wilhelm von Wied, confronted by the anarchic conditions within his new realm, left the country. Possible candidates for the throne of Albania became an international joke and included C.B. Fry and Aubrey Herbert.

Whether Albania was likely to survive as a state, even an unstable state, seemed unlikely in the early 1920s. The acquisition of Albania had been proffered to Italy as a reward for her support of the *entente* powers during the First World War, while Greek and Yugoslav territorial ambitions were also a threat. The country also lacked internal cohesion: the divide between the tribal Ghegs in the north and the semi-feudally organised southern Tosks was only the most obvious division, for the northern tribes had little love for each other and the blood feud was perhaps the country's major social characteristic.

Ahmet Bey Zogulli, or Zogu, and finally King Zog, as he was consecutively known, was the son of a prominent tribal leader and first rose to power in the context of the assertion of Albanian sovereignty against Italian ambitions to turn the country into a protectorate. Ousted by a coup in 1924, he secured Yugoslav support and returned to power as President, and on 1 September 1928 he proclaimed himself king. Albania can thus be seen, along with Serbia and the now defunct Montenegro, as having found an alternative to the Balkan habit of importing foreign princes as rulers by finding its royal houses among its own population.

As president and then king, Zog did his best to turn Albania into a centralised state and to maintain its independence. These were not easy tasks, and Zog's was an uneasy crown. If he had not such good reasons to fear for his life, he could be described as paranoid, rarely leaving his room in the royal palace in Tirana, and only eating meals prepared by his mother. Misha Glenny has given a vivid account of his extraordinary routine:

> On those rare occasions when he could not avoid venturing onto the open street, his mother would act as his chaperone. According to the strict role of the gjakmarrje, the blood feud, a marked man could not be killed if accompanied in public by a woman.[9]

King Zog had hundreds of blood feuds on his hands, for he had not gained power, nor did he hold on to it, delicately. He did, nevertheless, attempt to modernise his backward country, and he gave it some temporary stability and a very modest amount of law and order, while he attempted to keep it intact by playing off his neighbours Italy and Yugoslavia against each other. The price he had to pay for survival was the sacrifice of any expansionist ambition. Albanians in Kosovo, Macedonia or Montenegro received no encouragement in their aspirations to become part of a greater Albania. Albania's and Zog's greatest weakness was poverty. The tax base didn't produce the income for an army, a police force, an education programme or modern buildings for its capital, Tirana. The solution was to borrow money, and the lender was Italy, with the result that the country eventually became an economic dependency of Italy. This cost the Italian economy dear, but meant that, as military control followed economic control, Albania was virtually an Italian protectorate long before Mussolini invaded in 1939. In the meantime, Albania enjoyed a brief period of comparative stability, and King Zog brought a whiff of Ruritania to his mountainous kingdom. His engagement and wedding to Countess Geraldine Apponyi, the daughter of a Hungarian count and an American heiress, in 1938 were events to delight the world's glossy magazines, with their combination of an exotic setting, a forty-carat engagement ring, a wedding dress by Worth and a Hungarian gypsy band. One of the witnesses was Count Ciano, Mussolini's son-in-law. A year later King Zog and Queen Geraldine had to leave Albania in a hurry as Italian troops took over.

None of the Balkan kings of the inter-war period was able to provide his country with a prosperous economy, none presided over a stable parliamentary system and none was able to avoid disastrous involvements in the Second World War. They can scarcely be blamed for any of this. The twenties and thirties were harsh times for predominantly agricultural economies; parliamentary democracy survived hardly anywhere but parts of western Europe, the USA and Britain's white dominions, while the Balkan monarchies pursued their foreign policies within much circumscribed limits. On the whole, all the monarchs, even the louche King Carol, pursued policies that, within the pressures of their time, were in their countries' interests. There was little practical support forthcoming from Britain and France, the Soviet Union was the enemy of everything they stood for, Italy was a predator and, if German hegemony was unwelcome, it appeared to most Balkan states to represent the better bargain and one that, in any case, could not be resisted.

The royal dictators of the Balkans seemed to belong to another age in comparison to the monarchies of western and northern Europe, where monarchy had in general stepped back from the political fray and become a placid institution, a force for national unity and social consensus. In Benelux, it is true, monarchy continued to play an important political role. In Holland, the monarchy, well into a century of matriarchy, did not merely reign over premiers, cabinets and assemblies but was an integral part of constitutional government. In Belgium the monarchy was a major force for the unity of a state in which divisions between Flemings and Walloons threatened to break up the hundred-year-old kingdom, and King Leopold played a major role in foreign policy; Belgium's return to neutrality in 1937 was largely the doing of Leopold, and was guided as much by domestic pressures as a hard-headed view of the previous alliance with France.

The dominant image of monarchy in western Europe was, nevertheless, one of a traditional institution that had come to terms with democracy and exerted a beneficent, somewhat conservative influence that blunted the sharper edges of social and political divides. No monarchy seemed better at doing this than the British monarchy, and George V's Jubilee in 1935 revealed to his own surprise the enormous affection with which the great majority of his subjects regarded this gruff, rather irascible, but well-meaning sovereign. Equally popular was his very different son, David, the Prince of Wales. If the father stood for traditional ways and values, the son seemed to epitomise the hopes and fashions of the younger generation. Above all, he had glamour. As we have seen, there had been glamorous and beautiful queens who had been fashionable icons to previous generations, but David, Prince of Wales, was the first male royal figure since the invention of the camera to be seen by the general public as the epitome of good looks and the leader of fashion. He was not only the first royal 'superstar' but one of the great superstars of the twentieth century. The camera adored and flattered him, and he had the ability to project himself to large audiences on his royal tours at home and abroad. He had a charisma that was almost entirely physical. It was not just that his movements and gestures were graceful, that he was young and fashionable in a post-war world that valued youth and fashion, or that he could, when he wished, exude empathy and sympathy. The key to his attraction was the boyishness which lasted well into middle age, and the combination of poise and vulnerability and in the hints of moodiness that alternated with his smiles. Similar characteristics would be found in future superstars, James Dean and Princess Diana. His liking for fashionable clothes, jazz, night clubs and all things American tuned in with the tastes of the post-war generation. He was not 'stuffy' and seemed to many to be likely to become an innovative monarch who would remodel a rather formal monarchy. His father thought differently, and towards the end of his reign, George V said to Stanley Baldwin, 'After I am dead the boy will ruin himself within twelve months.' It was an astonishingly accurate prophecy.

The drama of Britain's abdication crisis was a foretaste of what was to be the major problem of monarchies in the late twentieth and early twenty-first centuries: the degree to which the personal, the sexual and the marital lives of royalty should or could accord with the prevailing social mores or should be more circumspect and exemplary. George V had provided the nation with an almost middle-class model of propriety, but the Prince of Wales and his brother the Duke of Kent had enjoyed sex lives that could be seen as alternatively echoing those led by previous generations of royal princes or as in tune with the faster set of contemporary high society. That David had, from his early manhood, had mistresses was scarcely surprising; even that paragon, his father, had kept girls in Southsea and the mistress suburb, St John's Wood, while his brother Bertie, later George VI, had affairs with the actress Phyllis Monkman and Sheila, Lady Loughborough. The problem with the Prince of Wales was that he settled into a prolonged bachelorhood marked by relationships with often older and usually married women. By 1934, however, the future King was madly in love with Wallis Simpson, a twice-married American, and, what was more of a problem, it was soon apparent that he was determined to marry her.

The abdication crisis was more a clash between two cultures than two moralities. To much of more traditional British opinion, the Prince of Wales, though dashing and handsome,

seemed too associated with a rather flimsy modernity: a trans-
atlantic world of golf, ocean liners, aeroplanes, night clubs,
cocktails and divorcees. The moral arguments were indeed a
little mixed. The court and respectable society, high and low,
would, no doubt, have infinitely preferred a king both married and faithful, but had been prepared to put up with a
king married if discreetly unfaithful and even, perhaps, would
have endured an unmarried king with a mistress. To the more
overtly modern sections of society, divorce and remarriage
were acceptable, as were Americans.

There was also a political dimension. King Edward, as he
became in January 1936, had the affection of a broad swath
of British society to whom he had been for long the nation's
Prince Charming. He nevertheless aroused deep misgivings
at court and among politicians. George V seemed to have
imprinted a definitive image of constitutional monarchy
as solemn, ceremonial and deferred to, but save at awkward
moments when the remaining prerogatives called for it to
descend from the clouds, inherently passive. Edward was not
solemn, and was ambiguous as to ceremony, while he had an
alarming, if fitful, desire to rule as well as reign. If his lack
of respect for tradition and ceremony irritated courtiers, his
impulsive trespasses into the political sphere and their popularity alarmed politicians. His enthusiastic reception in South
Wales, where he visited the most depressed areas and, in
implicit criticism of the government, declared that 'something
must be done', was not appreciated by ministers nor by the
leaders of the opposition. The opportunity to get rid of a king
who was refusing to play the role written for him may have
been welcomed by the establishment.

For the majority of the British public the crisis was concentrated into a week in early December 1936. The enormous
discretion of the British press and the BBC had kept the news
of the King's relationship with Mrs Simpson and its implications from the public domain. As the gossip column writer

'Chips' Channon recorded in his diary entry for 3 December: 'The country and the Empire now know that their Monarch, their young King-Emperor, their adored Apollo, is in love with an American twice divorced, whom they believe to be an adventuress.'[10] A week later, Edward had abdicated and was on a destroyer bound for exile.

King Edward's overseas subjects were as taken aback as his British subjects by the rapidity with which a problem of which they had been unaware turned into a crisis, which resulted in the abdication of their King or Emperor. The implications for the dominions in particular and the importance of the agreement of their Prime Ministers were recognised by the care with which Baldwin took to consult Commonwealth opinion.

Could things have turned out differently? The attenuated nature of the crisis played into the hands of the Prime Minister, Stanley Baldwin, who had decided that the marriage of the King and Wallis Simpson, even a morganatic marriage, ruled out the King remaining on the throne. The nation got the news, the problem and the solution in a week. The King was easily outmanoeuvred and was rushed into abdicating, ignoring the advice of his supporter, Winston Churchill. Which side the British people and the King's overseas subjects would, given time, have come down on can never be known, though the thousands of letters that Edward received just before he gave up the throne cast doubt on the received view that marriage to Mrs Simpson was unacceptable to the great majority of his subjects.[11]

The maverick King departed, but fortunately there was an almost perfect successor with a perfect family to hand. Albert, Duke of York, was dutiful and prepared as George VI to reign in the pattern woven by his father, even if his stammer and frail health made this an arduous task. Most importantly, he had a strong-willed wife, who would make a charismatic queen consort, and two attractive daughters. Court, government and media strove mightily to put the royal show back on the road, to obliterate memories of Edward's short reign and, as far as possible, of Edward himself, though, like some unwanted ex-star, he kept on trying to get back into the picture, and to relaunch the family on the throne.

Monarchy suited Britain, a nation more or less at peace with itself, and was an important force in binding together the British Empire, that amalgam of self-governing dominions and colonies. There was also a consensus in favour of monarchy in those other countries of western Europe that had neither massive internal problems nor aggressive demands on their neighbours. It remained a vital institution in the Balkans, where it was, on the whole, a restraint on nationalist aspirations and modestly paternalist in the context of economic inertia and internal divisions. In Italy, it was almost supernumerary in the context of the Fascist state, yet like the Catholic Church, it was still there, an exception to Mussolini's unitary control. It can't be pretended that monarchy was a dynamic force in the Europe of the 1930s, but nor was liberal democracy or democratic republicanism. The dynamic forces promising glorious futures were socialism and fascism, both posited on contrary appeals to modernity, to violent change and a break with the links to the past represented by monarchy.

This coronation photograph by Cecil Beaton of Queen Elizabeth II in Westminster Abbey illustrates two parallel themes: the youth and sincerity of the Queen represent the optimism and hope felt at the beginning of a new reign, while the continuity of monarchy (as opposed to the ephemeral nature of individual monarchs) is expressed by the Abbey setting and the symbols of legitimacy, the crown, orb and spectre. (© Cecil Beaton/Victoria and Albert Museum, London)

Dowager Empress Cixi, the effective ruler of China from 1861 to 1908. The photograph was taken c. 1900. This 'wicked empress' has been seen as presiding over the last years of the Chinese Empire and maintaining her opposition to reform by the murder of relatives and anyone else who stood in her way.

The Meiji Emperor, Emperor Mutsuhito, who reigned 1867–1912, in Western-style uniform. The Meiji Restoration was, in part, a reaction against the Western powers and their influence, which had humiliated Japan, but it became the means to Japan's modernisation and acceptance by the West as a great power.

The King of Siam and the Royal Family (*c*. 1890s). Here is an oriental monarchy modelling itself upon European depictions of royalty. It shows a nuclear family of king, queen and five sons. King Chulalongkorn (Rama V) had, in fact, many wives and seventy-six children.

Abdul Hamid, Ottoman Sultan. The last sultan to exercise real power, he ruled from 1876 until he was deposed in 1909. Adept as well as ruthless, he played alternately the roles of moderniser and protector of Islamic tradition.

Nasir al-Din Shah. The Persian monarch (1848–96) was assassinated by an Islamic extremist. He looks and was a ruthless ruler, but he faced enormous problems in holding Persia together.

The Queen's Diamond Juiblee, 1897 by A.C. Gow depicts the arrival of Queen Victoria at St Paul's. Much of the power of the picture derives from the contrast between the simply dressed and elderly queen and the uniforms of her soldiers.

The British and Russian royal families in 1909. Queen Alexandra and the Empress Marie of Russia were sisters and the photograph shows how physically alike were their sons, the Prince of Wales and Tsar Nicholas II.

Empress Eugénie of France at Biarritz in 1858. Portrait by E. Defonds. The Empress was one of the great royal beauties, and this portrait shows her in a romantic setting as she sits in a pensive pose with her dog on a beach on a cloudy day. (Photo © RMN-Grand Palais (area of Compiègne)/Jean-Gilles Berizzi)

Empress Elisabeth of Austria and Queen of Hungary photographed with her dog in 1868. 'Sisi', daughter of Duke Maximilian of Bavaria, was beautiful but restless. Almost the archetype of the romantic royal rebel, she disliked the atmosphere of the Habsburg court and travelled around Europe. She was assassinated in Italy in 1898.

Portrait of Queen Alexandra, when Princess of Wales, with her dog, Facey, by Luke Fildes. A placid royal beauty, sentimental, charitable and family oriented, she was tolerant of her husband's infidelity and was an icon of fashion for late Victorian women.

King Nicholas of Montenegro with family in 1911. The realm he inherited from his prince-bishop ancestors was poor and mountainous, but Nicholas was adept as a match-maker and his daughters married members of the royal houses of Europe, one becoming Queen of Italy. (Library of Congress)

Kaiser Wilhelm II. With moustaches erect and withered arm concealed, the Kaiser's pose suggests authority and dynamism. (Library of Congress)

Crown Prince Rudolf of Austria–Hungary and Baroness Marie Vetsera. The joint suicide of the Crown Prince and his seventeen-year-old mistress at the shooting lodge at Mayerling could be seen as a scandal, a tragedy or a love story. It was one of the great sensations of the late nineteenth century.

King George V addressing the nation on Christmas Day 1934. Not noted for his sympathy with modern ways, George proved an adept communicator on the radio and the monarch's address remains a central part of the British Christmas.

Edward VIII while Prince of Wales. Despite his youth, the photograph demonstrates the essence of his glamour and future appeal. He is fashionably dressed and there is a hint of vulnerability and moodiness. (Library of Congress)

King Zog, the self-made King of Albania. The uniform adds a touch of late Ruritania.

Emperor Hirohito, the Showa Emperor, mounted on a white horse in Tokyo, 1937. Portrayed here as a martial figure, the Emperor followed, rather than led, his generals and ministers.

King Michael of Romania. The handsome young king reigned from 1927 to 1930 and again from 1940 until his forced abdication in 1947.

King Ibn Saud (Abdul Aziz), founder of the Saudi Arabian Kingdom, seated between his sons, Prince Faisal on the left and Prince Saud ibn Abdul Aziz, later King Saud ibn Abdul Aziz (1953–64), on the right.

King Hussein of Jordan. Few in the 1950s would have prophesied a long reign for the king, but bravery, good judgement and some luck enabled him to survive wars, coups and attempts at assassination until his death in 1998. (Library of Congress)

Coronation of the last Shah (King) of Iran, Mohammed Reza Pahlavi, in 1967. The Shah's attempt to modernise his kingdom ended in failure when the combination of economic depression and Islamic fundamentalism led to his overthrow in 1979.

Film star Grace Kelly bidding farewell to her home country before her marriage to Prince Rainier, ruler of the tiny principality of Monaco, in 1956. The fairy-tale wedding that followed seemed a realisation of a Hollywood script. The Princess died in a car crash in 1982. (Library of Congress)

Princess Diana in 1985. This photograph of Diana epitomises the conjunction of celebrity and royalty. The fashion sense, the slightly upturned eyes and the vulnerability beneath the boldness recall the other royal 'superstar', Edward VIII.

Proclamation of Juan Carlos of Spain as king in 1975. Brought up under the aegis of General Franco, he ascended the throne after the Caudillo's death and successfully steered his kingdom towards constitutional democracy.

Wedding photograph of Prince Akihito and Princess Michiko in April 1959. The Crown Prince, now Emperor, and his bride pose in traditional Japanese wedding attire before putting on western clothes to parade through Tokyo.

The Thai royal family in 1966 with King Bhumibol (Rama IX) on the left and Vajiralongkorn, the future Rama X, on the right. The Thai monarchy is seen as an essential expression of national identity.

The funeral of Diana, Princess of Wales, in September 1997, following her tragic death in a car crash in Paris, was marked by an unprecedented outpouring of public grief. An estimated 3 million people came out on to the streets of London to mourn the Princess while a further 2.5 billion people watched the worldwide television coverage. (Paddy Briggs)

Prince William, the Duke of Cambridge, and Catherine, the Duchess of Cambridge, on their visit to Ottawa during Canada Day festivities, 1 July 2011. (Flickr/Tsaiproject)

HM The Queen and Prince Philip on the Balcony of Buckingham Palace, 16 June 2012. (Wikimedia Commons/Carfax2)

The carriage procession through the streets of Windsor following the wedding of Prince Harry and Meghan Markle, 19 May 2018. (Wikimedia Commons/Londisland)

Royal procession through the streets of Bangkok following the Coronation of King Maha Vajiralongkorn (King Rama X), 5 May 2019. (Wikimedia Commons/Tris_T7)

Emperor Naruhito and Empress Masako at the Ceremony of Enthronement of His Majesty the Emperor of Japan, 22 October 2019.

Morten Morland's cover image for *The Spectator* on 24 August 2019, depicting the Duke and Duchess of Sussex as part of a parodic coat of arms with the motto '*Wokes Populi*'. (Courtesy of *The Spectator*; illustration by Morten Morland)

THE SUCCESSORS TO THE OTTOMAN EMPIRE: THE NEW MONARCHIES OF THE MIDDLE EAST

The long-anticipated end of the Ottoman Empire was a direct consequence of the Empire's decision to enter the First World War on Germany's side. Like the Austro-Hungarian and Russian Empires, but not the German Empire, it had structural weaknesses that called into question the very state, not just the regime, and it had long been seen as in decline. Whether the disintegration of what remained of the Empire, largely Turkey and its Middle Eastern possessions, could have been prevented without defeat in the war is open to conjecture.

There were three possible solutions to the Empire's problems: to promote an imperial patriotism, which meant treating all the inhabitants of the Empire as equal citizens; to emphasise Islam as the unifying force for an Empire that had lost most of its non-Islamic territory; or to turn to the emergent force of Turkish nationalism and transform the Empire into a greater Turkey. Especially from the viewpoint of Constantinople, a great cosmopolitan city where, as late as the mid-nineteenth century, Muslims made up less than half the population, the first solution had its attractions and was hesitantly and intermittently pursued for much of the nineteenth century; but equality of citizenship for believers and infidels went against core Islamic beliefs, while as Christian provinces were lost the Empire became more cohesively Muslim. The second course was the one largely pursued by Abdul Hamid; it involved emphasising his role as Caliph and therefore the leader of all Islam. This was in the end no solution to the Empire's problems, for though a return to Islamic purity might bring about unity, it would militate against the modernisation, which even the Sultan saw as essential. In the long run Turkish nationalism and the existing Empire ruled each other out, as Turkish rule was bound to be incompatible with Arab interests, though many of the Young Turks hoped that Turks under foreign rule, especially those in the Crimea and Caucasus, could be reunited with the homeland. Thus, if the attempt to reinvigorate the caliphate went along with the main reaction of most Muslims in the Islamic world to the preponderance of Europe with its superior economies, technology and military and civil organisation, the overthrow of Abdul Hamid by the Young Turks represented the reaction of an alternative elite of radical army officers, who embraced nationalism and rejected both Western liberalism and Islamic conservatism.

By 1914, Turkish nationalism had already brought about widespread unrest in the Arab world. Ottoman rule had always been a matter of vague suzerainty rather than direct government in Arabia, and had been much diminished from the mid-nineteenth century by the intervention of Britain via its bases and clients on the periphery, while France had established a special position as the protector of the Maronite Christians in the Lebanon. In the early twentieth century Turkish attempts to impose direct control in Arabia had been repulsed.

It is easy enough with the benefit of hindsight to see the Ottoman Empire's intervention in the world war as a disaster, but it made sense enough on the assumption that the central powers would win the war. Arab revolts backed by Britain and France could easily have been put down or their achievements reversed in the circumstances of such a victory, while there would have been rich pickings at the expense of a defeated Russia. As it was, the combination of the imperial designs of Britain and France, an aroused Arab nationalism and an aggravated Turkish nationalism, responding to the disaffection of other nationalities, Armenian and Kurdish, and the desire of Greece and Italy for Turkish territory, resulted in the loss of the Arab territories, the end of the sultanate and then the caliphate, and the establishment of a Turkish republic. The new Turkey could hold its head high, having alone among the defeated powers of the First World War successfully resisted the provisions of the Paris Peace Settlement and also repelled the incursions of Greece and Italy, but the Empire was no more.

Even if British and French power had not moved into the vacuum left by Ottoman demise, fundamental problems would have remained for the Arabs. Their varied ambitions in the wake of the Empire and in the face of Western military and economic superiority were not unlike a mirror image of the possible solutions to the problems of the Ottoman Empire. There was the model of the new Turkey, which pointed towards secularist, nationalist republicanism, and there was the alternative of a return to traditional Islamic values and ways. There was no single vision. Pan-Arabism and Islam had always made for overlapping identities, but they were not synonymous. A minority of Arabs were not Muslims, while Islam extended beyond the Arab world. Was Egypt Arab, even if it was largely Islamic? Where did Persia fit in? How important were the sub-divisions of the 'Arab world', the distinctions between the urban, the agricultural and the nomadic, between tribes, nations and Arabism or between Sunni or Shi'ite? Several major cities, such as Beirut, Baghdad and Alexandria, had mixed populations with no overall Arab or even Islamic majority.

That monarchies of differing types reigning over states with varying degrees of independence became the predominant form of government in the post-Ottoman Middle East can be explained by a combination of the interaction of the interests of

Britain and France with those of Arab leaders, and the intrinsic appeal of the concept of monarchy to Islamic and tribal cultures.

British strategy during the war, although it held to what was seen as the priority of the western front, was tempted by the opportunities proffered by attacking the Ottoman Empire; not only might victories against the Turks assist in defeating the central powers, but they held out the opportunity of furthering traditional British ambitions with respect to the Straits and control of the Mediterranean and the expansion of the Empire in the Middle East. If the Gallipoli campaign was a conspicuous failure, the conjunction of General Allenby's army advancing through Palestine and the Arab revolts encouraged by the British brought about victories culminating in the taking of Damascus.

It was Sherif Hussein ibn Ali, a direct descendant of the Prophet, and a member of the Hashemite dynasty that had ruled Mecca for centuries, who proclaimed the Arab revolt in June 1916, and it was Captain T.E. Lawrence who persuaded the British government that what the revolt needed was not the assistance of a British army but gold and armaments. It was the consequent guerrilla war that opened the road to Damascus. Sherif Hussein appeared in a strong position to become leader of the Arabs. His aim was a theocratic kingdom, with himself as king and caliph, which would encompass Mesopotamia, Syria, Palestine and the Arabian Peninsula. After the capture of Damascus by British and Arab forces, Hussein's son Feisal, supported by the British, established a new Arab government there, a possible basis for a pan-Arab kingdom.

The hopes of the Hashemites were, however, to be dashed. The demise of the Ottoman Empire left Britain with the problem of reconciling her own interests in the Middle East with the claims of France and with the pan-Arab nationalism she had encouraged. The secret Sykes–Picot Agreement of 1916 had provided for a division of the Ottoman territories between Britain, France, Italy and Russia. Discovered by the Bolsheviks after the October Revolution, the agreement was published, to the embarrassment of the remaining *entente* powers. So far as the Arab lands were concerned it provided for a division of spheres of interest between Britain and France that could only uneasily be reconciled with the letter of British promises to the Arab leaders, and it certainly contradicted the spirit of the Arab revolt.

There were two further problems. In November 1917 the British government issued the Balfour Declaration, which favoured a national home for the Jewish people in Palestine. Considering the main strategy of British policy, a dominance of the Middle East by a mixture of direct rule and a partially independent Arab state, this was a bizarre and fateful initiative. Interestingly, it was opposed by the only Jew in the British cabinet, Edwin Montagu, and it was to bedevil British–Arab relations, significantly weakening the British position in the region. The second complication was the defeat of Britain's principal protégé, Sherif Hussein, the Grand Sherif of Mecca, by Abdul Aziz, also known as Ibn Saud.

The League of Nations confirmed the essence of the Sykes–Picot Agreement by giving the French a mandate over greater Syria and Britain a mandate over Palestine and Iraq. The French government was not prepared to see its mandate ruled by a British ally, and Feisal was asked to retire. Despite the fact that a Syrian Congress, called in March 1920, demanded independence under Feisal, the French persisted in demanding that he give up the throne and divided the short-lived state into Syria and Lebanon.

British decisions as to the future of the Middle East were tardy and hesitant, as the victorious great power was torn between the desire to seize great prizes and an uncertain resolution born of economic weakness, social problems at home and a waning of its imperial spirit. The aim was to placate the French, reward Arab allies, safeguard British interests and do something for the Jews. As Robert Lacey has described the confusion:

the Arab world remained a jumble of military administrations and local rulers swirling in the vacuum left by the defeated Turk; and into this formless ether stepped Mr Winston Churchill ...[1]

A conference at Cairo in March 1921, chaired by Churchill, then Colonial Secretary, drew a geopolitical map, much of which has endured.

The pan-Arab state dreamed of by Sherif Hussein was ruled out by the necessity of accommodating French and Jewish interests, but it was still felt necessary to reward the Hashemites. The Sherif himself was left with a Kingdom of the Hejaz. His son Feisal's bid for Syria having been ruled out, not by the Syrians, with whom he was popular, but by the French, a throne was found for him in Iraq, hitherto Mesopotamia, and then under British rule; he was elected in August 1921 with a majority that would have befitted that future ruler of the country, Saddam Hussein. Palestine was made a British mandate and Britain undertook the thankless task of reconciling Jewish and Arab aspirations. A new Emirate of Transjordan was carved out of an area between Iraq, Palestine and Syria and given to another son of the Sherif, Abdullah.

What Gertrude Bell called 'creating kings' was a happy pastime for the British. It was in tune with the general preference for princes, maharajahs and emirs who stood for tradition and stability, together with a touch of romance. British Arabists, of whom the Foreign Office was alleged to possess a camel corps, tended to favour the Arabs of the desert rather than of the towns, and sheikhs rather than middle-class politicians, and indirect rule via friendly potentates guided by British advisers. Royal princes were educated in England and, it was assumed, developed loyalty to Britain and acquired an outlook which combined the traditions of the Arab world with those of the British upper class.

The fact that erstwhile emirs became kings reflected the desire for equality with European heads of state. 'King' was not a title revered by Islamic or Arab tradition and had tended to be used to describe infidel rulers. There remained, however, interesting differences between Middle Eastern monarchies and their Western counterparts. The notion of the monarch ruling by right of birth was eschewed, for, although kings, like emirs before them, came from a ruling family, the theory was one of consensual agreement between ruler and ruled with some similarities to the acclamation of monarchs by lords in medieval Europe with principal subjects and tribal leaders giving oaths of allegiance. Succession was only loosely hereditary, with crown princes being as often the brother or even the cousin of a reigning monarch, while such heirs apparent were often changed during a king's lifetime and did not always succeed to the throne. Both the Saudi and Hashemite dynasties were to continue this practice. Such a process reflected the extended family nature of Arab monarchies, and the practice of family counsels deciding who was best fitted to succeed, but also the difficulties of succession, already noted, where rulers had several wives and harems. That traditionalist, Ibn Saud, is estimated to have had some three hundred wives altogether, although never more than four at a time, and about forty sons. King Abdullah's grandson, King Hussein of Jordan, adopted the more modern practice of consecutive monogamy.

British interests and preferences were not, however, the sole reasons for the dominance of the institution of monarchy in the Middle East. Monarchy had indigenous roots. The concept of the ruler as the leader of the Islamic community with a duty to promote conditions in which subjects can live as good Muslims is fundamental to Islam. In theory there should be a single Islamic community under one leader, but even under the earliest caliphates such a unified leadership was rarely realised, for if religion made for unity, the great distances between cities and fertile areas separated by desert made for local interests, cultures and loyalties. Monarchies were able to assert the ideal of the benevolent ruler, paternalistic but firm, who was the nexus of a host of personal and tribal loyalties as well as the guarantor of Islamic rule.

The example of what became the Kingdom of Saudi Arabia demonstrates that a monarchy could emerge that was far from a Western creation. An unexpected disruption to the nation-making and map-drawing of Britain came in the shape of Abdul Aziz, the ruler of the Nejd. A scion of the Saud family that had in the early nineteenth century defeated the Hashemites and ruled over most of the Arabian Peninsula, Abdul Aziz had revived his family's fortunes by judicious marriages, conquests and support for militant religion. He had been the greatest proponent of Arab autonomy prior to the First World War and ruled over an area of central Arabia in which the Turks found it very difficult to enforce their rule or put down revolts. The family of Saud were the standard bearers of a strict and puritanical Islamic sect known to others, but not to its followers, as 'the Wahabis', after Muhammed ibn Abdul Wahhab, an eighteenth-century teacher who preached a return to the fundamentals of Islam, including government and justice in accordance with the *Sharia* and the duty of conversion if possible, *jihad* if necessary. Abdul Aziz was the hereditary imam of the sect.

Before 1914, the British government was ambivalent in its attitude towards Abdul Aziz, giving him modest support when it suited it, but then switching to a policy of accommodating the Young Turk government in Constantinople.[2] The Saudis were the first to take the field against the Turks in the First World War, but they did not receive a great deal of British assistance, and the defeat of Emir Abdul Aziz and his forces at the battle of Jarrab in January 1915 seemed to mark the end of the Saudi ambition to lead the Arab world.

By the early 1920s Abdul Aziz had, however, recovered from his set-back at Jarrab by enlisting the support of the Bedouin tribesmen of central Arabia, who had been enthused by the Ikhwan movement, a twentieth-century revival of the Wahabi. The fundamentalist puritanism of the desert and tribesmen, who considered the telegraph and the motor car the inventions of the devil but happily accepted the rifle, thus made an important contribution to twentieth-century history. The ruler of the Nejd, with his capital at Riyadh, was ultimately able to defeat the Hashemite Sherif of Mecca and to unite the Nejd and Hejaz. Only a footnote to the protocol of Churchill's Cairo Conference, Abdul Aziz had, by the late 1920s, established himself as the ruler of most of the Arabian Peninsula. His victory was religious as well as political. Sherif Hussein had overreached himself when, on the abolition of the Ottoman Caliphate in 1924, he had attempted to succeed it by calling himself 'Prince of the Faithful and Successor to the Prophet'. Widely considered presumptuous in the Islamic world, this declaration inflamed the Wahabi tribes, who considered the Sherif a lax Muslim, and Abdul Aziz unleashed them on the Hejaz. The Sherif's armies, commanded by his less than capable son, Ali, were defeated, and in 1926, Abdul Aziz, now usually known in the West as Ibn Saud, was proclaimed King of the Hejaz.

In 1927, the new map of the Middle East, with its three new kingdoms of Iraq, Transjordan and the Hejaz, which was soon to become Saudi Arabia, was formally recognised by the Treaty of Jedda, which also recognised the Persian Gulf kingdoms under British protection.

What had emerged from the Ottoman Empire in the Middle East was predominantly an Anglo-French hegemony with a range of relationships between the imperial powers and the states under their influence. As with the Ottoman Empire, it was the most economically and socially advanced areas that were most firmly under outside control, while the most backward areas achieved the greatest independence. Differences between British and French imperial aims were also important. It was no accident that within the British sphere of influence monarchies with varying degrees of autonomy predominated: the Egyptian monarchy, elevated to a kingdom in 1922, which had exchanged Ottoman suzerainty for British in the course of the nineteenth century, the sheikhdoms of the Gulf and the new Anglo-Arab monarchies. The British preferred to work through monarchs to whom they were prepared to extend considerable autonomy, provided British strategic and economic interests were protected. The French interpreted League of Nations mandates as a thin cover for straightforward colonialism and an opportunity to export French institutions and culture. Syria and the Lebanon became republics, with the French retaining control of security and foreign affairs. In North Africa, unaffected by the end of the Ottoman Empire or the Arab revolt in the East, a policy of inculcating French culture and encouraging French settlers continued, although Morocco, despite being under French and Spanish rule, was allowed greater autonomy than Algeria or Tunisia, and retained its Alawite Sultan, who could trace his ancestry back to the Prophet.

Outside the lands of the old Ottoman Empire, where Sunni Muslims had predominated, lay the Persian Empire with its largely Shi'ite population. Subject to Russian and British informal imperialism, attacked by the Ottoman Empire in the First World War and faced with opposition from tribal chiefs, religious leaders and radical reformists, the once proud Qajar dynasty exercised an increasingly nominal control over most of its territory and staggered towards an ignominious demise. Reza Khan, a soldier trained in the Russian Cossack brigade, was in many ways Persia's Ataturk. He seized power in 1921 and set about attempting to turn Persia into a modern, westernised and secular state. Unlike Ataturk, he was not content to be the leader of a republic, but was proclaimed Shah of Iran in 1926. Like Ataturk, he introduced secular education, enforced the adoption of Western dress, outlawed the wearing of the veil by women and placed great faith in a modern army. He did little to develop democratic institutions, though this was probably only a mistake in Anglo-American eyes. Even a semi-democratic Iran would have resulted in greater opposition to his westernising programme than did his autocratic rule. The problem he faced, and that eventually brought his successor down, was the resolute opposition of a majority of the population to a secular society. In Iran, the opposition of Islam to westernisation was exacerbated by the development of a religious hierarchy. Islam, it is always said, has no church, but the Shi'ite *ulema* of Iran had become, since the foundation of the Safavid dynasty in the early sixteenth century, rather more than individual scholars, and they exerted an influence, especially in rural areas, that penetrated every aspect of Iranian life.

In general, the analysis of Middle East history and of the Islamic world since the First World War by historians and writers on politics has been, at any rate until recently, marred by an assumption that events would follow a pattern set by Western history, and that an ineluctable secularisation of society would be part of that pattern. The real struggle was between traditional social and political norms and 'progressive' developments, which included democracy, economic development and secular nationalism. The establishment of new monarchies and Western support for old ones ran against the tide of modern development. 'History', the *bien-pensant* considered was on the side of urbanisation, emergent middle classes, political parties, westernisation and republics, and monarchies were either native, as with Saudi Arabia, or imposed, as with the Hashemite kingdoms, reactionary anachronisms. Very little credit was given to religion as a dynamic force. That analysis appeared to be confirmed in the mid-twentieth century, when with the weakening of Anglo-French power several thrones were removed. King Farouk of Egypt was overthrown in 1952 and left to while away his last years on the French Riviera; in 1958 King Feisal II and his able minister, Nuri Said, were murdered, along with the Crown Prince, in a coup led by army officers; and the removal of King Idris of Libya in 1969 from a throne established only in 1951 seemed to confirm the trend. Arabs, it seemed, when faced with a choice between monarchies or nationalistic republics led by strong leaders, opted for the latter.

Such a sweeping and determinist analysis concentrates too much on the notion of a choice between institutions of government, and ignores the impact of major historical developments, the Second World War, the establishment of the state of Israel, and the extent and importance of the region's oil fields. It is, also, most importantly, an implicitly secular analysis.

Given the continuing determination and ability of Britain and France to enforce the broad parameters of the post-First World War settlement in the Middle East, the region enjoyed no less, and probably more, stability than had been the case under the Ottoman Empire. States and their regimes were maintained in being by the ability, charisma or ruthlessness of governors and monarchs, and by a web of tribal loyalties and interests, which were constantly subject to disruption by rivalries, feuds and revolts. The traditional duties of providing a context of basic living standards and modest prosperity, of rewarding the fidelity of supporters and enforcing the tenets of Islamic law, continued to be incumbent on rulers. The periodic raids upon dissidents by the RAF in Iraq can be compared to the forays of Ottoman garrisons. That British imperial power lay behind the monarchs of Egypt, Transjordan and Iraq was obvious, as were the demands of its economic interests, but British policy was, within limits, to put more and more power into local hands and to encourage the development of representative institutions. By the late thirties, it still seemed possible that, despite impatience with Anglo-French paramountcy and periodic revolts, the post-First World War settlement with its Anglo-Arab kingdoms and Franco-Arab republics might develop as increasingly autonomous entities still closely associated with their patrons.

The Second World War transformed the situation. It saw the Middle East become a major theatre of war, encouraged nationalist elements opposed to Britain and what were seen as its client monarchies to see Germany as a possible ally, and forced the British in Egypt and Iraq to revert to a more overt control. British intervention in Iraq in 1941 to restore the Hashemite monarchy after the coup by the pro-Axis Rashid Ali was successful, but it exposed the degree to which the monarchy depended on the British.

THE FAR EAST
BETWEEN THE WARS

Alone among the monarchies of Asia, the Japanese monarchy emerged from the First World War with its strength and prestige enhanced. Not only had Japan's position in the world risen, but as emperors represented the essence of the nation, their reputation and charisma rose with the nation's.

Though not required to do so by the terms of the Anglo-Japanese Alliance, Japan had promptly declared war on Germany in August 1914, and Japanese naval support was valuable to Britain in the Pacific and even in the Mediterranean. Involvement in the war enabled Japan to occupy German colonies in the Pacific and on the Chinese coast and to put pressure on the Chinese to extend Japanese privileges in Manchuria and elsewhere.

Japan thus rightly took its place at the Paris Peace Conference as a victorious and a great power. Even so, strains in Japanese–American relations were already discernible in 1919. Woodrow Wilson was opposed to concessions that the Japanese had gained from China, and only gave way in return for Japanese membership of the League of Nations, while the

Japanese resented the refusal of the British, Australians and the Americans to include a clause in the League of Nations Charter banning racial discrimination.

The fundamental problem was Japanese ambitions in Manchuria and China. Britain was uneasy at the incursions of her ally but was pragmatic and essentially concerned with protecting her own overstretched positions in the Far East. The USA was equally concerned for her own position, but had also a strong sentimental attachment to China; important sections of American opinion had adopted China as a country that, spared formal inclusion in Western empires, could be reformed on an American pattern. Britain worried that enmity between America and Japan might lead to a conflict that could embroil Britain via her alliance with Japan, and agreed to the Washington Conference of 1921 by which the Anglo-Japanese Alliance was replaced by a rather nebulous four-power pact between the USA, Britain, Japan and France, and an agreement as to the size of navies.

Many of the factors that would lead to Japan's continued expansion, her attempt at Asian hegemony and war with Britain and the United States were now in place. A question that historians continue to debate is what responsibility for the forward policy in China and for the war launched by the attack on Pearl Harbor can be attributed to the emperor system and Emperor Hirohito.

As we have seen, the Japanese constitution of 1889 was ambiguous as to the practical powers of the Emperor, incorporating as it did the ideas of both absolute and constitutional monarchy. The Emperor's traditional religious authority was reclaimed and formed the basis of his new-found secular authority. The Emperor was 'the sacred pillar of the *kokutai* or "national polity"',[1] and he was to exercise important prerogatives and to enjoy supreme command of the armed forces, a command that bypassed the cabinet. The concept of the Meiji restoration as bringing about an emperor who ruled was, however, something of myth, for the constitution invested considerable authority in the National Diet and the cabinet placed checks and qualifications upon the exercise of imperial authority. In practice the Meiji Emperor himself complied with the concept of limited monarchy, exercising his prerogatives 'only on the advice and consent of the heads of the various state organs and of the elder statesmen'.[2] As it turned out, the Japanese constitution and its practice were a dangerous combination: there was an emperor whom the majority of subjects believed to be a 'living God', who ruled, while in reality he left decisions to ministers or to generals; decisions not made by the emperor, and perhaps even disapproved of by him, were thereby invested with the full force of the 'imperial will' and his Godlike authority. This is not to say that Emperor Meiji was a passive monarch, for he did seek to influence his ministers and would question their policies, but rather that the British constitutionalist theorist, Walter Bagehot, would have approved of him in that he insisted on his rights 'to be consulted, to encourage and to warn', but did not overrule his ministers.

The Emperor Meiji died in 1912, and his successor, the Emperor Taisho, son of one of his father's concubines, being both mentally and physically unfit to govern, had little option but to be a passive figurehead, who deferred to the advice of his ministers. In 1921 he withdrew from active rule, and the twenty-year-old Crown Prince Hirohito was appointed Regent.

Most writers on Hirohito agree that the young prince desired to be a constitutional monarch on the British model. He was indeed much impressed by George V and the Prince of Wales on his visit to Europe in 1921. The gruff King had treated the young Prince in an avuncular manner, which surprised and delighted him:

Hirohito was amazed that the King of England should wander the corridors of his palace unescorted, tieless, and clap him on the shoulder like an old friend. 'I hope, me boy, that everyone is giving you everything you need,' said the King. 'I'll never forget how your grandfather treated me and me brother when we were in Yokohama. No geishas here, though, Her Majesty wouldn't allow it.'[3]

He was equally impressed by the fashionable and informal Prince of Wales, whom he entertained in Japan the following year, and envied the freedom he enjoyed, a freedom that contrasted with his own life in Tokyo, where tradition and convention circumscribed his every move and he had to take the leading part in elaborate religious rituals.

Along with a yearning for greater personal freedom, the Regent derived from his visit to Britain an understanding of and admiration for the concepts of constitutional monarchy. The problem was how to follow British constitutional practice in Japanese circumstances. The British monarchs had Prime Ministers and cabinets who carried on the business of government subject to the retention of parliamentary majorities and exercised relatively clear lines of command via the civil service over the machinery of the state, including the armed forces. Monarchs retained their aura of authority, which gave them influence, and their limited prerogatives. In Japan the lines of command were far from clear: they were different when it came to civilian and army matters; the *genro*, or elder statesmen, exercised an influence that was accepted but not mentioned in the constitution; while the court officials constrained the wishes of the Emperor rather than facilitated them. Hirohito came to the throne in 1928, a far from fortunate time to choose the name Showa, or 'enlightenment and peace', for the name of his reign.

Was Japan an honorary Western power content to trade in an international market and take her place with the USA and Britain in the prevailing Anglo-American order, or was she rather a radical 'have not' power, which could lead Asia in the establishment of a new post-colonial order? Essentially, the inter-war period saw Japan move from the former to the latter position, a move that interacted with internal changes in Japanese politics. The 1889 Constitution had seen her hovering between the attractions of constitutional monarchy and the autocracy of the German Empire, while the 1930s proffered the new attraction of the example of Nazi Germany and made militaristic nationalism seem to many the way forward. The world economic recession, which hit Japan hard, made the concept of economic autarchy within a Japanese economic sphere attractive.

It is tempting to see some grand plan behind the successive steps by which Japan expanded: the Sino-Japanese War of 1894–5; the Russo-Japanese War of 1904–5; the annexation of Korea in 1909; the twenty-one demands on China of 1915; the further expansion into Manchuria from 1931; the beginning of the war with China in 1937; and the attack on Pearl Harbor in 1941. Yet what seems to have happened is that as Japan grew stronger, the military gained more influence, while patriotic societies poured out xenophobic propaganda. Japan's economic development made it a power dedicated to growth, whether by trade or conquest, for its modest raw material resources were insufficient to maintain its rising population. Military factions and particular generals made aggressive moves, and civilian governments found it impossible to disavow them.

A combination of economic problems and quarrels with the League of Nations and with the USA and Britain over China tended to discredit the policies hitherto favoured of close understandings with the Western powers, the pursuit of free trade and liberal economics and parliamentary government. Emperor Hirohito came to the throne at a time when there was a strong reaction against such policies.

Studies of Emperor Hirohito have disagreed as to the extent of his responsibility for Japanese policies in the thirties and for the outbreak of war in the Pacific in 1941. He has been depicted by Edward Behr[4] and Herbert Bix[5] as the man who rode the tiger of militarism, and by Stephen Large[6] as an all-too-exemplary constitutional ruler. Herbert P. Bix argues that the British constitutional model could not be applied under the Meiji constitution because the imperial house was 'the one effective force for integrating state and nation, civil government and military affairs'. This was certainly theo-retically possible, and the real charge against Hirohito is that whatever the policies he favoured, good relations with Britain and the USA or the forward policy in China and alliance with Germany and Italy, he failed to coordinate state and govern-ment and to ensure that decisions and strategies were rational and calculated. He allowed Japan to drift, headless, divided and overstretched towards a war it couldn't win. But it would have taken a very strong personality to have purposefully exercised imperial power. There was little traditional basis for such rule, and the Emperor's education and training had not prepared him for the exercise of executive authority.

Hirohito seems to have interpreted his constitutional role as supporting his ministers and generals rather than choosing between them or their policies. The Imperial Court's main aim was to ensure that he was not put in positions where he had to make a decision. A dedicated but passive constitutional-ist, he was nominally in charge but rarely in control, involved in decisions but rarely making them. The crucial period was the late 1920s and early 1930s, when elements of the Kwantung army in Manchuria moved out of control and were backed by senior officers and nationalist elements in Tokyo. Hirohito disapproved but failed to exert his authority to curb the army's mutinous spirit and rein in its headstrong factions. He sought to use his influence, but he was ever reluctant to offend the military.

The regime he headed has been described as fascist, but though it was nationalist and militarist this is a misnomer.

There was no charismatic leader and no dynamic political party. What made the Japanese militarist state such a strange entity was the lack of strong leadership. Japan moved slowly and ineluctably towards a new internal order and a radical expansionist position on foreign affairs with an establishment riven by faction and with no clear mechanism for decision making.

If the Emperor was not in control of Japan's government nor of the military nor of the expansionist policies, he was crucial to the ethos of inter-war Japan. The half-revived, half-invented state Shintoism portrayed the Emperor as the Godlike repository of all authority and the incarnation of the national character. Even the most mutinous army officers claimed to act in the name of the Emperor, even as they disobeyed his wishes. Most Japanese, however, saw him as the absolute ruler he was not.

Since the demise of the Chinese Empire, the Japanese Emperor was by far the most powerful Asian monarch. It is interesting, however, that rather than simply incorporating Manchuria into Japan, the Japanese thought there was still enough residual appeal in the deposed Qing dynasty to make the last Qing Emperor, Puyi, now styled Emperor Kangde, monarch of the puppet state of Manchukuo. On a visit to Japan in 1935 he was treated almost as an equal by Hirohito, and the two Emperors, seated rather unsteadily on horseback, reviewed troops together.

Japan may have been by far the most powerful Asian monarchy, but until 1932 the King of Thailand was the monarch who wielded greater personal power than any other monarch in the world. King Mongkut, or Rama IV, had adapted skilfully to the dominant position of the Western powers in South-East Asia. Rather than opposing British demands for trading rights, he accepted them and began a programme of modernisation at the same time. It was largely because of these timely moves that Thailand was never formally colonised and can congratulate itself on its unbroken independence. It was subject, however, to a degree of informal imperialism, with the British maintaining an influence not far short of indirect rule, while they and other Western powers acquired extra-territorial rights and were able to try their own nationals in consular courts. Mongkut's successor, King Chulalongkorn, or Rama V (1868–1910), retained his country's independence, but at the cost of the loss of much territory; territory on the frontier with Burma went to the British, as did four Malay states over which Siam had long claimed suzerainty, and in the face of a considerable threat from France, the King was forced to concede Siam's Laotian territories.

Monarchies attempting to modernise their countries and maintain independence in the face of Western pressure have, as we have seen, faced tasks of enormous difficulty. They have to comply with Western demands and yet at the same time maintain their integrity and charisma in the eyes of their people. They have to build up their military power and institute economic reforms without bringing into being new social formations that may well become anti-monarchist, while retaining the loyalty of conservative forces, such as the aristocracy and the peasantry. At the same time they are faced with demands from the West for constitutional reform, and internal economic and social change can lead to similar demands.

What the Siamese kings sought was a state in which a modern administration and a popular nationalism could develop within the context of absolute monarchy; monarchy and national identity would become synonymous. Like many a state, Siam declared war against Germany in the First World War mainly as an expression of status and in the hope of gaining acceptance of that status from Britain and France. One problem for the monarchy was the army. As we have seen, the army officer corps in developing states poses particular problems. Monarch and state need an efficient army, but the officer corps ineluctably becomes the home of those who desire radical change and nationalist policies. National humiliations can lead to a further radicalisation, which can easily become anti-monarchist. The necessary concession of territory to Britain and France had made for the development of an anti-royalist nationalism within the Siamese officer corps. Another problem was the introduction of Western education for the children of the administrative and commercial elite, necessary to promote efficiency and further development, but dangerous, as it introduced notions that challenged absolute monarchy. That such a brew of problems would have necessarily led to the end of the absolute monarchy can be challenged, for we must take into account the effects of the worldwide economic depression between the two world wars, as the Depression hit the country with considerable force. As Roger Kershaw has argued: 'It was the consequent cuts in the military budget that brought military opposition to the boil.'[7]

The end of the absolute monarchy in 1932 might well have been the end of the monarchy, for the 'Young Turks' who made what was effectively a revolution felt no need for the institution and would have been content to allow military strongmen to rule alone. But the enormous loyalty of the mass of the population to the throne and the way that the Chakris had successfully blended monarchy and national identity quickly persuaded the generals and their technocrat allies that they needed the monarchy and its charisma. Having deposed King Prajadhipok (1925–35), the generals then reinstated him and begged his forgiveness. The King, himself a cause of the coup, because he was indecisive and had been neither an efficient absolute ruler nor a confident instigator of a more democratic constitution, lingered as monarch for another three years, though he was clearly sympathetic to a royalist revolt in 1933. He abdicated in 1935, leaving the throne to a boy king, his nephew, King Ananda. Thailand, as it was now known, remained a monarchy, though this was increasingly an ornamental canopy for the military dictatorship of Marshal

Phibul. The military-nationalist dictatorship with imported fascist trimmings became increasingly a Japanese ally or satellite, which enabled it to acquire territory during the Second World War, when it was essentially a Japanese base. There was an irony in the fact that the overthrow of its own absolute monarchy subordinated Thailand to an Asian rather than a Western imperialism, and to the Emperor in Tokyo in place of the King-Emperor in London or the President in Paris.

For the most part the other monarchs of the Far East enjoyed only modest degrees of autonomy within the empires of the Western powers. They performed their largely honorific roles in the dangerous gap between the demands of their colonial overlords and the nationalistic aspirations of their middle classes.

PART THREE

A FURTHER
THINNING OF
THE RANKS

MONARCHIES AND THE SECOND WORLD WAR

Europe's monarchs were caught up in the Second World War. No monarch pressed for war or played a significant part in its causation. Once it had begun, monarchs had to play their and, where they held them, their nations' cards as best they could. Not surprisingly, no monarchs were enthusiasts for war; after all, the last war had been disastrous for the cause of monarchy. In this the monarchs of western Europe were at one with the great majority of their subjects. There was no enthusiasm for a war against Germany, Nazism or Fascism in any of the democracies of western Europe, nor much evidence of enthusiasm for war for Fascism among the subjects of the King of Italy, while Hitler despaired of the German people's lack of enthusiasm for armed struggle. Among the populations of the monarchies of eastern Europe, there were sections who saw possibilities for national aggrandisement in a great war, but the majority viewed the approaching maelstrom with the same apprehension as their monarchs. There is, of course, little evidence of an appetite for war among the populations of any country in 1939, apart from a minority of political fanatics, so the monarchs were on the popular side.

In Britain the attitudes of George VI towards the worsening diplomatic situation of the late 1930s were broadly in line with those of his Prime Minister from 1937, Neville Chamberlain. He appreciated the military and economic weakness of Britain in the circumstances of its overstretched commitments to the defence of the Empire and the likelihood that a major war could lead to a decline from great-power status. He shared the feelings of the majority of his nation that every effort must be made to avoid a war with Germany, and those of a substantial section of influential society that the Soviet Union constituted a greater threat than Germany. The exceptional privilege the King accorded to Chamberlain, whom he invited to appear with him and the Queen on the balcony of Buckingham Palace on his return to Britain after the signing of the Munich Agreement in 1938, demonstrated his personal support of his Prime Minister's policies. If a rather incautious gesture, this was in tune with popular feeling at the time.

George VI was an impeccably constitutional monarch who was prepared to exercise his prerogatives but knew their limitations. He was also, even more than his father, a very British monarch, somewhat removed from the intimate web of royal relationships that had once bound the royalty of Europe so closely together. That web and the cousinhood of monarchs still existed, however, if much weakened by the divisions of the First World War. Kings and queens and princes and princesses retained a common interest in the preservation of the remaining monarchies and had channels of information separate from those of chancelleries and intelligence services. Edward VII had made much use of these intimate lines of communication in his quasi-diplomatic initiatives in the early years of the century. George VI was restrained in his use of them, and his main diplomatic role was orchestrated by his government and involved cementing relationships with France and the USA via his and his queen's successful visits to both countries. Other members of his family were more proactive in utilising their connections with Britain's potential enemies.

In this respect, the once, and, sometimes in his imagination, future king, the Duke of Windsor, proved, as in much else, an embarrassment. Having, rather lackadaisically, given up his throne 'for love', he found that love did not quite make up for the withdrawal of position, influence and automatic respect. He hankered after recognition for himself and his wife, and after a short reign in which neglect of his red boxes had alternated with impetuous, sentimental, but sometimes insightful forays into politics, he welcomed any opportunity to become a player on the world's political stage. He was, in short, a rather dangerous 'loose cannon' from the viewpoint of both his brother, George VI, and the British government. His views seem contradictory to posterity, involving as they did an admiration for the USA, golf, jazz and international capitalism, a very genuine sympathy with the unemployed and particularly with ex-servicemen and a belief that Fascism and National Socialism were dynamic and necessary forces to guard Europe from the threat of Communist Socialism. In the context of the time, such views were not unusual, and so long as Hitler's and Mussolini's ambitions were containable, they had an uneasy coherence. Windsor and his opinions, plus his wish to seem important, provided Hitler and his accolites with opportunities to open up a gap between the policies of the British government and the considerable section of the British public that still admired the Duke of Windsor.

The relationship between the Duke and Hitler's regime both before and during the war has been the subject of many books. There can be no doubt that the Duke was opposed to war between Britain and Germany, that he believed it could have been avoided if he had remained king, that he was defeatist and hoped for peace in 1940–41 and that he was foolish and indiscreet. There is, however, no firm evidence that he was actually disloyal. Perhaps he occasionally toyed with the idea that he might become king again after a peace between Britain and Germany, but he seems to have done nothing that could help provide such an outcome. The Duchess may have considered such a scenario more consistently. His sojourns in Spain and Portugal after the fall of France occasioned Nazi attempts to win him over and worried the British government, but the only agreement he came to with the Germans was, typically, to gain permission for a maid to proceed to Paris to collect his possessions. He would have preferred to return to Britain and take up a post there, but having offered to serve his country anywhere in the Empire, he was despatched to one of its minor outposts as Governor of the Bahamas. Even there he continued to be an embarrassment due to his friendship with the Swedish industrialist, Axel Wenner-Gren, who had extensive business interests in Germany, and because of an indiscreet interview he gave to an American journalist, predicting that there would be no real victor in the war. The weight of the evidence points not to a traitor but to a man who, having given up his exalted destiny, found the consequences disagreeable; he shared the views of many of his contemporaries as to the undesirability of war with Germany but retained them long after it was prudent to do so.

Another member of the royal family, Prince George, Duke of Kent, presents a more intriguing instance of royal involvement in European politics. He was an attractive if wild young man, and easily the most intelligent member of his family. Bisexual and fond of fast society, George had been rescued from his cocaine addiction by his elder brother, the Prince of Wales, who had, responsibly, taken him into his care. His marriage to the glamorous Princess Marina of Greece was, it is usually stated, the making of him, though the attractive and fashionable princess managed to combine a lofty conception of the importance of royal lineage, even, supposedly, denigrating Queen Elizabeth and the Duchess of Gloucester for their mere Scottish aristocratic origins, with a taste akin to her husband's for the fashionable set. She was beautiful and chic; effortlessly fashionable whereas the Duchess of Windsor was relentlessly so, and neither Queen Elizabeth nor the Duchess of Gloucester was particularly fashionable at all.

It may well have been due to his wife's influence that the Duke of Kent became interested in European politics. As a princess of the Greek royal house, itself a branch of the Danish royal house of Schleswig-Holstein-Sonderburg-Glucksberg, Princess Marina had close connections with a number of members of European royalty. The Duke seems to have become an unofficial source of information to his brother the King on European affairs and had good contacts in Germany and eastern Europe. It has been suggested that there were plans, supported by Lord Mountbatten, for him to become King of Poland. In normal circumstances a revival of the Polish monarchy with a British prince as king would have appeared a most hare-brained scheme, though Kent appears to have worked quite hard at burnishing his reputation as a friend of Poland, but from the time of the British Guarantee to Poland of March 1939, Britain was seen by many Poles as the main defender of its independence. It may well be that in the unusual circumstances of 1941 he was formally offered the Polish crown by the government in exile.[1] Kent was killed in 1942 when the RAF plane he was travelling in crashed in Scotland. He was supposedly bound for Iceland, but some mystery surrounds the destination and, indeed, the circumstances of his death.

Too much can be made of the significance of the royal network. The remaining monarchs did have common interests and maintained useful, though sometimes embarrassing, contacts with deposed relatives, such as the brothers Prince Philip and Prince Christopher of Hesse-Cassel, who still retained some influence in Germany, but the network operated on the whole on the margins of the gathering storm in Europe. There were very likely papers and correspondence that the royal family wished to be kept from the public domain at Schloss Friedrichshof, the home of Philip of Hesse-Cassel, probably concerning Windsor's indiscreet contacts with German agents when he was in Portugal. Anthony Blunt, who was to become Surveyor of the Queen's Pictures, and who worked for MI5 and also, as was revealed later, for the Soviet Union, was dispatched along with Owen Morshead, the Royal Archivist, to Friedrichshof and other castles in Germany immediately after the German surrender, while Blunt later visited the Kaiser's former residence, Haus Doorn in Holland. There were good ostensible reasons for their mission, for valuable royal historic records and artefacts had been lodged with German relatives, but no doubt there were more recent papers, which could have caused embarrassment, for attitudes were very different in 1945 from what they had been in the late 1930s. Any suggestion that they would have indicated unpatriotic inclinations on the part of George VI or Queen Elizabeth is, however, risible. Having relatives behind the enemy lines could of course have disadvantages; when Buckingham Palace was bombed by a daring Luftwaffe pilot, George VI suspected that the pilot might have been a relative who had stayed at the Palace, for he seemed to have had a good knowledge of its layout.[2]

Perhaps alone among the royal houses of Europe, the House of Windsor, despite the unease caused by the eponymous duke's indiscretions, had 'a good war'. The King's almost painful sense of duty commanded respect, the Queen's charm won affection and the young princesses appeared the models of what daughters growing into young women should be. The decision of the King to remain in London during the Blitz (though he usually returned to Windsor in the evening), and his visits to bombed areas in the capital and other towns and cities, was important in sustaining morale. He spent the war in uniform, and Princess Elizabeth joined the ATS when she became eighteen. The royal family was seen to be enduring the discomforts and dangers of the nation as a whole, and this was underlined by both the bombing of Buckingham Palace and the Duke of Kent's death.

In many ways the Queen Consort was the key figure. The long love affair between her and the British public was to last until her death in the early twenty-first century, but the war had enabled her to fully demonstrate her talent and flair for queenship. Unusually for a queen consort, not of royal blood herself, she displayed a tact, timing and judgement in her public appearances unmatched by any member of the British or any other royal family in the twentieth century. That she had a better understanding of the British working classes than most sociologists is demonstrated by her insistence on wearing her best clothes when visiting the East End, and walking in her high heels among shabbily dressed people; the less perceptive might have considered this tactless, but her explanation exemplified her social insight: 'If the poor people had come to see me they would have put on their best clothes.'

Other monarchs had less 'good wars'. As we have seen, the states that today form Benelux all had constitutions that entrusted greater political responsibility to their monarchs than was the case in Britain. All three monarchs, Leopold III of the Belgians, Queen Wilhelmina of the Netherlands and Grand Duchess Charlotte of Luxembourg, viewed the worsening diplomatic situation of the late 1930s with apprehension, all hoped that war could be avoided and all hoped their countries could be neutral if it wasn't.

A victorious power at the end of the First World War, Belgium held to alliance with France and to the maintenance of the Versailles settlement, as modified by the Treaty of Locarno, until 1936. Germany's reoccupation of the Rhineland convinced Leopold and the Belgian government that a return to Belgium's traditional policy of neutrality provided the best hope of avoiding war, and accordingly Belgium withdrew from the military alliance with France. A pledge from Hitler to respect Belgium's neutrality was to prove a poor substitute for weakened defensive arrangements. The Grand Duchy of Luxembourg had, like Belgium, or most of it, been overrun by Germany in the First World War. Grand Duchess Charlotte, whose small country was bound to Belgium in an economic union, could do little, but like Leopold she put her trust in neutrality.

Queen Wilhelmina of the Netherlands, who had come to the throne at the age of 10, was an immensely experienced sovereign who had exhibited considerable ability and will-power in managing to keep her country out of the First World War. Despite the considerable power she exercised under the constitution, she became increasingly depressed during the 1930s by her inability to direct government policies in the circumstances of the severe problems the Netherlands faced in the shape of economic depression, the threat from Hitler's Germany and problems with the overseas Empire. Her husband, Prince Hendrik, a scion of the house that had governed the minor German state of Mecklenburg-Schwerin, was no great help to her, as he had become an alcoholic. She appears to have considered abdicating in favour of her daughter, Juliana, on several occasions.

Retrospective readings of the 1930s, which result in anyone who sought compromise or even reasonable relations with Nazi Germany or Fascist Italy being damned, and anyone who, however unrealistically, resolutely opposed them being praised, ignore the pressures, circumstances and public opinion of the time. All the Benelux monarchies were subject, not just to the largely pacifist public opinion that was general throughout western Europe, but to an awareness of military weakness, a widespread anti-Communism and not inconsiderable internal pro-German and pro-Fascist feeling. Nazi racial views accorded brotherly Aryan status to the Flemings, and both Leopold and Wilhelmina had to take account of Fascist and neo-Fascist sympathies and political parties. Criticism of the Benelux monarchs for not joining an anti-Nazi crusade, which was, as yet, unborn, is inherently anachronistic.

There was in the end not a lot that they could do to protect their countries, and much the same is true of the Scandinavian monarchs. The abortive plan by the Kings and Queens of Norway, Sweden, Denmark, Belgium and the Netherlands at the end of 1938 to call for an international conference of Britain, France, Italy and Germany to settle outstanding issues was an uncontroversial but hopeless gesture. Leopold expressed the essence of it in August 1939, when he called for Europe's leading powers to step back from the brink of war and submit their differences to negotiation.

Once war had begun, all the monarchs could do was to hope desperately that their neutrality might be respected. Only Gustav V, who had succeeded to the throne of Sweden in 1907, managed to keep his country out of the Second World War. In 1940, when German forces rolled across western Europe, Gustav played an important part in avoiding their entry into his kingdom. It was not, it is true, a heroic part, for it involved giving way to German demands, providing Germany with raw materials and allowing German troops to move along Swedish railway lines between occupied Norway and Finland, but his cabinet was with him, and there is little evidence that the vast majority of his subjects were not grateful to be kept out of the war.

Once attacked, monarchs and governments had to decide, first, how desperately to fight and, second, whether to stay with their people or go into exile. When, in April 1940, Germany invaded Denmark and Norway, the monarchs of the two Scandinavian countries followed opposite courses. King Christian X followed the advice of his ministers and ordered an immediate surrender; he also stayed in Copenhagen. King Haakon VII of Norway opted for a very different course, broadcasting an appeal to all Norwegians to resist the aggressors and, after a hot pursuit by German forces, boarding a British cruiser, which also carried Norway's gold reserves bound for Britain. Both monarchs were generally held to have had 'good wars', Haakon by heading the Norwegian government-in-exile, and Christian by staying put and helping to save his country from the worst excesses that the German occupation might have led to, including notably saving most of Denmark's Jews from the death camps.

Why then was Leopold III treated as a pariah by the Allies when he put up rather more of a fight than King Christian, and led a short-lived national resistance against the German invasion of his country before, similarly, deciding to stay with his people? In May German forces advanced into Holland, Luxembourg and Belgium. Luxembourg could not be expected to put up much resistance, and leaving the country in separate cars, the Grand Duchess and her consort, Prince Felix, made their way through France to Spain and then to Portugal, before embarking for North America. Within five days, Holland had capitulated, spurred on by the German bombing of Rotterdam, and Queen Wilhelmina was in Britain, whither she had been carried by a British destroyer, though whether this was entirely her wish has been challenged.[3] Belgium, to whose assistance British and French troops were sent, surrendered after eighteen days of fierce fighting, during which King Leopold had exhorted his troops to fight on, reminding them that on the line between Menin and Ypres they were fighting on the same ground as his and their fathers in the previous war. By 28 May, however, with British, French and Belgian forces in disarray, King Leopold overruled his cabinet and surrendered unconditionally, and said that his place was with his army and his people. This was a perfectly honourable decision.

The British government and the British press saw it differently. As Theo Aronson has written of Leopold's surrender:

> His surrender was cynically misrepresented by the Allied authorities as an act of gross betrayal. Needing an excuse

for the rout and subsequent evacuation of their own forces, they turned King Leopold into a scapegoat. His treacherous and totally unexpected surrender, they claimed, had left them dangerously exposed to the enemy. The 'Traitor King' had stabbed them in the back.[4]

Leopold's decision was popular with most of his Flemish subjects, though it was less well received in the French-speaking areas. He was, however, in a difficult situation, as his relations with the German occupiers, however necessary for the country's good, could easily be traduced as emanating from Nazi sympathies, especially as he was at loggerheads with a government-in-exile set up in London. His position was not helped when he announced in December 1941 that he had contracted a morganatic marriage with a commoner, Marie-Liliane Baels. A daughter was born to the couple the following July. There was no reason why the King should not, several years after the death of the popular Queen Astrid, have remarried, but the marriage was not well received in Belgium.

An interesting example of royal solidarity was revealed in 2019. The newly discovered diaries of the wartime Dutch Foreign Minister showed that, in 1945, Queen Wilhelmina of the Netherlands had sought, via the Vatican, to broker a deal by which top Nazis would be offered an escape route in return for King Leopold's release from the royal château in Belgium where he was imprisoned by Waffen SS guards. Wilhelmina apparently feared that the Belgian King and his wife would be killed by the Germans. They were eventually liberated by US troops on 7 May 1945, the day of Germany's surrender.

Victor Emmanuel III of Italy was, as a rather nominal king in the circumstances of Fascist Italy, in an unenviable position. The diminutive monarch had lost much of the popularity he had gained in the First World War. Having rather weakly allowed Mussolini to become head of government and then dictator, he retained some influence but little real power. His

dislike of Italy's ever closer alliance with Germany was shared
by most Italians and by some Fascists, including Count Ciano,
Mussolini's son-in-law. Victor Emmanuel's known disapproval
of Mussolini's desire to emulate the Führer was sufficient to
irritate the Duce, who increasingly talked of doing away with
the monarchy and sneered at the King, referring to him as
'that little midget', but Victor Emmanuel's influence was limited. Mussolini, who had reneged on his promised support for
Hitler at the time of the invasion of Poland and alternately
itched to join in the war and faltered when doubts as to Italy's
readiness set in, found it convenient to blame the King for
Italy's timidity. When, in early June, Italy did eventually declare
war after Germany's sweeping victories, Victor Emmanuel
could only sulkily rubber-stamp the decision and submit to
the humiliation of Mussolini becoming Supreme Commander
of the Forces in the Field.

The utility of the monarchy was, however, to be demonstrated as the expected easy victories failed to materialise, the
tide of war turned and Allied forces successfully invaded Sicily.
The removal of a head of state who commands the loyalty
of the armed forces is rarely accomplished peacefully, but
Mussolini was not head of state and the senior Italian generals had gone to war reluctantly. From 1942 there had been
rumours of plans for coups that would replace Mussolini and
allow negotiations for peace between Italy and the Western
Allies to take place. One such plan, which envisaged a coup by
Marshal Badoglio with the support of the armed forces, had
involved Crown Princess Marie Jose, a redoubtable woman
with left-wing views. By 1943, not only the general staff but
some members of the Fascist Grand Council were considering
a change of regime. In July 1943, the monarch, the army and
disaffected Fascists acted together: the Grand Council passed a
resolution critical of the regime, the King dismissed the Duce,
who was arrested as he left the Villa Savoia, and a new government under Marshal Badoglio was formed.

Undoubtedly, the fact that Italy had remained a monarchy made it easier for the Italians to get rid of Mussolini. In Germany by contrast, even when most generals had long given up hope of winning the war, it proved impossible to get rid of Hitler. Mussolini's overthrow did not, however, do much to strengthen the position of the Italian monarchy. In the first place, a great opportunity was missed, for with coordination between those who accomplished the Duce's dismissal and the Allies, the war in Italy might well have been shortened. A swift surrender followed by Allied landings in northern Italy before German reinforcements could be rushed into position might have avoided two years of hard fighting as Allied forces slogged up the peninsula. A combination of Allied insistence on unconditional surrender and Italian delays meant that Badoglio formally continued the war while negotiating with the Allies, thus allowing plenty of time for German troops to move into Italy. Had Victor Emmanuel declared the dismissal of Mussolini his final service to his country and then abdicated in favour of his son, Prince Umberto, the monarchy might have had a future, for the King had been associated with the Fascist regime for too long.

The position of the Balkan monarchs was unhappy. The countries and their monarchs were, as General Mihailovic put it, during the farce of his post-war trial at which he was condemned to death, caught up in the 'Gale of the World'. When Mussolini, jealous of German victories, attacked Greece and the Italian army was badly mauled by the Greeks, the victories of the Greek forces only postponed disaster for King George and his government. Hitler had to come to the rescue of his impetuous ally. Such a rescue could only come if German forces were able to move through Yugoslavia, and this presented the Yugoslav Regent, Prince Paul, with an invidious choice. He could either sign a pact with Hitler or put up a hopeless resistance to a German invasion. He wisely took the former path, but a coup in Belgrade overthrew the regency council and declared the seventeen-year-old King Peter II the country's ruler. A week later German troops invaded and Yugoslavia fell to pieces.

Prince Paul was the brother-in-law of the Duchess of Kent and had been a frequent visitor to Britain before the war. After the Belgrade coup, he was banished to Kenya, where he was kept under house arrest because of his alleged pro-German leanings. Essentially, he was blamed for putting his country's interests before Britain's. There had been nothing Britain could do to assist Yugoslavia. The Foreign Office and the press, however, demanded scapegoats, and, like Leopold, he was attacked as a traitor to the Allied cause and there was an outcry from super-patriots when Paul's wife, Princess Olga, came to Britain to comfort her sister, Princess Marina, after the death of the Duke of Kent.

The Balkan monarchs were damned if they did and damned if they didn't, damned by the British if they negotiated with Germany, and forced to flee their occupied countries if they stood in the way of German demands. King Peter was forced into exile in Britain. King George of Greece soon followed, for the British army was not able to save Greece from the invading German forces; nor was he fêted in wartime London, for the Foreign Office persisted in considering him untrustworthy.

Romania and Bulgaria were in just as impossible a position as Greece and Yugoslavia. Romania, with its rich oil fields, was the immediate cause of the breakdown of Soviet–German relations that preceded Hitler's invasion of Russia. King Carol and his governments had with some cunning managed to play off external pressures from the great powers, Britain, the Soviet Union and Germany, and from their hostile neighbours, Bulgaria and Hungary, as well as contain internal divisions between the army, the traditional political parties and the native Fascist movement, the Iron Guard, but by 1940 they were running out of options. The overweight

Romania that had emerged from the First World War was slimmed down, first when the Soviet Union took Bessarabia and then when by Hitler's *diktat* northern Transylvania had to be returned to Hungary. Carol was unable to prevent this, and in September 1940 he was forced by General Ion Antonescu to abdicate in favour of his son, who had previously been king for nearly three years. King Michael was forced to concede full powers to the nation's new strong man. When Germany invaded the Soviet Union, Romania threw in her lot with Germany. Whether any other decision was possible is debatable, but it was not King Michael's decision, and he first heard of his country's declaration of war from the BBC World Service.

King Boris of Bulgaria had many of the same problems as King Carol, save that, while both tried to avoid war, Boris was faced with the difficulty of his country's traditional close relationship with Russia; an influential section of Romanian opinion was prepared to regard a German alliance as the lesser of two evils, and hoped for the regaining of the Bessarabian province. Boris is quoted as saying that his generals were pro-German, his diplomats pro-British, his queen pro-Italian and his people pro-Russian.[5] To propitiate Hitler, Bulgaria followed the rather odd course of declaring war on Britain and the USA but refrained from declaring war on its neighbour, the USSR. This was, naturally, not enough for the Führer, and in August 1943 Boris was ordered to report to Hitler at Berchtesgarten. He was allowed to return to Bulgaria but died eleven days later. Had he been poisoned by his host? He was succeeded by his six-year-old son, Simeon.

As the tide of war turned, the positions of the Kings of Romania and Bulgaria can be compared to that of Emperor Karl of Austria–Hungary towards the end of the First World War. How were they to extricate themselves from an alliance and from a war that was proving disastrous for their countries when the troops of the ally were still in command of their immediate destinies? King Michael proved more determined and brave than ever Karl had been. He sent emissaries to the Allies suggesting a separate peace and even offered information on German military dispositions. There was no response.

In August 1944, King Michael acted decisively. He had Antonescu arrested and then broadcast to the Romanian people, announcing that Romania was no longer at war with the Soviet Union. This brought little immediate respite to Romania, for the Russians were determined to occupy the country, and carried on attacking Romanian forces, while an incensed Hitler ordered an air raid on Bucharest. For a short period Romania was being attacked by erstwhile foe and erstwhile ally. Nevertheless, King Michael had served his country well:

> Michael of Romania and his advisers had achieved a classic demonstration of the latent possibilities of monarchy. By all the rules of conventional wisdom the palace was virtually bereft of political power. In the event it had transmuted the often derided and sometimes perverted attitudes of ancient royal Europe – fealty, loyalty and a sense of honour – into mighty weapons with which they had reversed the policy of a seemingly irresistible occupying power and overthrown its government of collaborators.[6]

King Michael's (and Romania's) tragedy was that, though he wished to hold armistice talks with the British, it was Soviet troops that were within Romania's borders. There was little Britain could do to help the King, but the British government, despite George VI's support for his fellow monarch, was reluctant to even try. No doubt Churchill had already made up his mind to write off Romania as a Soviet satellite, a decision made evident by the 'Percentage Agreement' with Stalin in October 1944. King George wrote of Michael: 'I feel so differently towards [him] than the attitude taken up by the Government.'[7]

If Britain's record in the Second World War is overall a fine one, in that alone it stood up to Germany until *Barbarossa* and then Pearl Harbor brought fortuitous allies, its record in eastern Europe is less than admirable. It wrote off the interests of Poland, while it failed to recognise the problems and contexts of east European states that supported Germany because there was little other option and because they hated the Soviet Union. To ally with the Soviet Union on the basis of 'my enemy's enemy is my friend' was probably necessary, even though the Soviet Union was just as unpleasant as Nazi Germany, but the consequence of regarding the Soviet Union's enemies as Britain's enemies was the result of a purblind wartime state of mind, which in some circles meant fervent support for the tyrannical regime that was the Soviet Union. Just as Yugoslavian monarchism was written off because, without much real evidence, Tito was perceived as a greater threat to German hegemony than the royalist Chetnik forces, so, in an excess of short-term *realpolitik*, the interests of the monarchies of Romania and Bulgaria counted for nothing.

King Simeon of Bulgaria was only seven in 1944, and the country was governed by a pro-German regency council headed by his uncle Prince Kyril. Though Bulgaria had not declared war on the Soviet Union, Russian troops crossed the border. That the monarchy was doomed, as were non-Communist politicians, was made clear on the return to his native land of Georgi Dimitrov, leader of Bulgaria's Communist Party, from Moscow.

The impact of the Second World War and its aftermath on Europe's monarchies was to result in a further cull, which removed the Kingdoms of Romania, Bulgaria, Yugoslavia and Italy in the immediate post-war period. Only in Italy can the removal of the monarchy be seen as a result of the popular will expressed through a more or less fair referendum in 1945, which saw 59 per cent in favour of a republic. Victor Emmanuel had tarried too long. His son Umberto had only been king for a few weeks when the referendum was held.

He had a reputation as a playboy, but had presence and charm, and his wife, Marie Jose, a daughter of King Albert I of the Belgians, who, as we have seen, had plotted against Mussolini, was beautiful and charming. A longer period on the throne might have improved Umberto's chances, and, as it was, the result was relatively close, with southern regions voting in his favour.

The situation in Belgium was for long somewhat complex, as King Leopold, who had been held prisoner by the Germans and taken to Germany in 1944, was refused permission to return to his country by the Belgian parliament after his release by Allied troops. He had been at loggerheads with the Belgian government-in-exile since 1940, and these differences dominated Belgian politics throughout the late 1940s. The King established himself in Switzerland, while his brother Charles became Regent. Belgium was almost completely divided, with the left-wing parties opposed to Leopold and the Catholic Right supporting him, while French-speaking Wallonia and Brussels were against him and Flemish-speaking areas were behind him. In 1950 a referendum produced a 57 per cent majority in favour of Leopold's return, and a general election produced a majority for the Catholic party in parliament. This cleared the way for the King's return, but the country was so divided it seemed as though it was about to come apart amid demonstrations and riots. Leopold reluctantly agreed to abdicate in favour of his son Prince Baudouin, who would be known as Prince Royal until his twenty-first birthday a year later, when he would become king.

What remained in Europe along with the British monarchy, which emerged from the war with enhanced popularity, were the Benelux monarchies, the Scandinavian monarchies and the Greek monarchy, which had been restored with the aid of British troops.

Considering the vituperation hurled at a monarch like Leopold, who was accused of having come close to collaborating with the German occupation, and the fate of the royal house of Italy, the end of the Japanese monarchy might have seemed a foregone conclusion. Here was the head of state of a principal Axis power, who had presided over expansionist policies and whose armed forces, fiercely loyal to him personally, had committed numerous atrocities. Emperor Hirohito had become a hate-figure to the peoples of the Allied countries.

As we have seen, there is considerable controversy among historians as to the degree of Hirohito's responsibility for Japan's invasion of China in the late 1930s, and this is also true when it comes to his responsibility for the attack on Pearl Harbor and Japan's attempt at hegemony in the Pacific and the Far East. To the mass of his subjects and to British and American servicemen fighting Japanese soldiers, who fought tenaciously and savagely for their emperor, Hirohito appeared to be an absolute ruler. His real position was, however, much more circumscribed and reflected the ambiguities of the Japanese constitution and the convoluted decision-making process that characterised Japanese policy.

Establishing the degree of the Emperor's responsibility is not easy. Hirohito, whether in personal audiences he granted to ministers or at meetings and conferences, did not give much away. He often interrogated ministers and generals about policies and plans but he did not issue commands. Sometimes he was silent and his wishes had to be discerned from his expression or his gestures. At the conference in September 1941 when preparations for war with the USA, Britain and the Dutch East Indies were being made, Hirohito broke his silence to read a haiku that his grandfather, the Emperor Meiji, had written at the start of the Russo-Japanese War. Here was a cautious man whose mind had to be read.

Japan's attack on Pearl Harbor was a desperate move. Once Japanese actions in French Indo-China, and its demands upon the British in Burma and on the Dutch in the East Indies, had resulted in ever-tightening US embargoes on essential

Japanese supplies, then an oil-starved Japan had either to go
to war or give up the possibility of going to war. Pearl Harbor
bought time and allowed Japanese forces to make rapid and
wide conquests, but there was no real coordination with the
German ally, and Japan's lack of industrial capacity as compared to that of the USA meant that in the long term US
capabilities would increase while Japan's diminished.

Perhaps Hirohito's sins were those of omission rather than
commission. He was inextricably involved in the decision-
making process, but had neither the will nor the courage to
challenge the military. Once war had begun he was, naturally, desirous of victory. Like George VI, he wore uniforms
throughout the war, was briefed on its progress and sent
patriotic messages of encouragement to his servicemen. He
was not backward in giving advice to his commanders, and,
sensibly, bewailed the lack of coordination between army
and navy and, less sensibly, advocated stiff resistance rather
than strategic withdrawal as American forces advanced in the
south-west Pacific.

His prestige and potential influence were enormous. Had
he departed from his interpretation of his constitutional
role, he could, arguably, have ended the war sooner than the
late summer of 1945, though this might have risked a military coup. The war had long been lost, but he waited until he
was asked by his Prime Minister to decide whether the war
should be ended. Delay brought about the dropping of atomic
bombs on the two Japanese cities of Hiroshima and Nagasaki.
When Hirohito broadcast to his people, in high-pitched
court Japanese that many listeners found hard to understand,
announcing Japan's acceptance of all Allied terms for ending
the war, the orders of the Son of Heaven to surrender were
almost universally immediately obeyed.

Allied plans for Japan involved total demilitarisation and a
reordering of society and politics, which involved the abolition of state Shintoism, but what was to happen to the

Emperor? Opinion in the British government was divided as to whether a modified emperor system was essential for post-war stability, but the decisive voice was that of the American government, and in particular that of America's man on the spot, virtually Japan's ruler after the surrender, General Douglas MacArthur. Japan's temporary shogun decided that the reha-bilitation of Japan as a pro-Western democracy required the continuity provided by the Emperor, and that Hirohito had been more the prisoner of the militarists than the leader of the Japanese war effort. MacArthur was almost certainly wise in recognising the positive role of monarchy in bridging the past and the present and allowing change to take place under a cloak of continuity.

The other Asian monarchy of significance, Siam, or Thailand, as it had become known, played a purely passive role during the war years. The overthrow of the absolute monarchy in 1932 ushered in the rule of a series of military strongmen, the first of whom was Phibul Songkhram, who was a radical nationalist influenced by western Fascism. He had a great admiration for Japan, with which he concluded a close alliance that turned Thailand into a Japanese military base as soon as the Pacific War began. Rather like Mussolini, Field Marshal Phibul maintained the monarchy even though he would have preferred to dispense with it, but the boy king, Ananda, who ascended the throne in 1935, had virtually no influence. Though Phibul was temporarily disgraced by the defeat of Japan in 1945, this did not lead to the recovery of the monarchy. In June 1946 the young king was shot dead in mysterious circumstances; his body was found by his younger brother, Prince Bhumibol, who succeeded him. With another inexperienced and young king on the throne, Field Marshal Phibul was able to make his way back to power via a coup in 1947. A pattern of coups and further military strongmen set in, with Field Marshals Sarit and Thanom inheriting in turn a military government under a largely titular monarchy.

For the great majority of Asian monarchies, those which reigned because the European empires preferred at least the appearance of indirect rule, the Second World War was a disaster. It shattered the image of the invincibility of the empires as they were humiliated by Japan's victories, and encouraged radical and socialist nationalist forces, already extant in the inter-war period, which both sought to throw off their colonial masters and to get rid of the native monarchies, which had come to terms with colonialism and served under it. The empires came back, but, humiliated and weakened, not for long, and their successors were not usually those satraps of empire, maharajahs, princes, sultans and kings, who had ruled under them, but army officers and nationalist politicians from the echelons and classes created by the very imperialism they opposed.

The British realised first that the Empire was too difficult and expensive to preserve, especially as its ally, the United States, had little taste for empires and believed that former imperial possessions would be succeeded by democracies content to live under a *Pax Americana*. They scuttled precipitately from their principal possession, India, and despite the best efforts of Foreign Minister Ernest Bevin, proceeded, by means of cost–benefit analysis, to gradually rid themselves of the bulk of their vast Empire. The interests of satellite sovereigns did not usually figure in this analysis; the princes of India were shabbily treated by Mountbatten and then Nehru as their states were swiftly incorporated into India or Pakistan and their status abolished.

In Malaya, the British had, at least ostensibly, governed with a loose rein, relying on resident officers to advise the sultans. After the Japanese occupation, efforts were made to persuade the nine monarchies into a centralised Malayan Union. There was intense opposition to this, not just by the sultans but by many Malays who felt that their privileges vis-à-vis the Chinese and Indians, who had immigrated into the Malay

Peninsula, might be threatened by such a union. A rather looser Federation of Malaya was the result. With Malayan independence in 1957 came the complex system of a supreme leader, or Agong, elected by the sovereigns of the individual states that make up Malaysia, though in practice each sultan took it in turns to hold the post.

The Malay sultanates had to co-exist, not always easily, with Prime Ministers and political parties, but another sultanate, oil-rich Brunei, was able both to avoid absorption into Malaysia and to gain its independence from Britain with a constitution that enabled its Sultan, Omar Ali Saifuddin, to create an absolute monarchy supported by the generous welfare system that oil royalties made possible and by a Gurkha battalion of the British army.

The charismatic monarchies of Indo-China exercised a potent and persistent appeal, as the French had come to recognise, seeking to control and use indigenous dynasties and rule through them. The Second World War brought a series of kaleidoscopic changes. From 1941, the French colonial administrations, nominally under the aegis of the Vichy administration in France, were forced to allow the area to be occupied by Japanese troops. In 1945, in a last desperate throw as they attempted to stave off total defeat, the Japanese overthrew the French administrations and attempted to set up independent Asian states they hoped would be allies. Like the French, the Japanese recognised the importance of the monarchies. In Cambodia, King Sihanouk, urged on by Japanese advisers, proclaimed independence in March, and in Laos, King Sisavang Vong also declared independence in April. In Vietnam, the Japanese encouraged nationalist groups, including the Communist Vietminh, but it is noteworthy that when Ho Chi Minh declared independence after the Japanese surrender, he sought to clothe himself in the mantle of legitimacy by obtaining a 'voluntary' act of transmission of authority from King Bao Dai. The French were to make further use of Bao

Dai when they declared him Emperor in 1949. Even for their
enemies, the support or at least the acquiescence of monarchs was seen as essential. The return of the French and the
impact of the subsequent Communist insurgency in Vietnam,
which influenced nationalist and Communist movements
throughout Indo-China, faced monarchs with difficult decisions. Were they to be puppets of the French, or of nationalist
or Communist administrations, or seek to be rulers in their
own right? It took a man of some ability, like Sihanouk of
Cambodia, to fill all three roles at different times and survive.
Bao Dai only lasted until the French withdrawal from Vietnam
in 1954. The Laotian monarchs did not lack skill or support, and
survived in a country divided by civil war until King Savang
was forced to abdicate in 1976; the end of the monarchy came
not so much as a result of internal Laotian developments but
because the Communist victories in Vietnam and Cambodia
sapped the morale of the royalist forces.

The rather tough Dutch colonialists had inclined to a more
direct form of rule than the British or French, but in the words
of one historian 'had kept a number of Indonesian monarchies
half-alive as ceremonial camouflage for the far-reaching economic and administrative changes of colonialism'.[8] The very
obvious limitations on their independence made them an easy
target for nationalist movements and lost them the sympathy
of their people. The Dutch never really managed to restore
their pre-war authority, even though they had ruled in Java
longer than any other colonial power had possessed colonies
in the region. As nationalist forces took over, the sultans who
had served the Dutch were for the most part accorded no role
in post-independence Indonesia; an exception was the Sultan
of Jogya, for a while a minister in Sukarno's government,
who, still usually referred to as 'Our King' by the people of
Jogyakarta, was widely mourned on his death in 1988.

In the Middle East, the impact of the war upon the colonial
powers and upon the region's monarchies was not immediately

apparent, and the effects were delayed. The war was fought by the great powers, and Arab and the Iranian regimes had to accommodate themselves to it. Most, like King Ibn Saud, were benevolently neutral towards whichever side seemed likely to win. Britain, the dominant power in the region, acted forcefully against any tendency of its client monarchies to change sides. In Iraq, the monarchy and its able minister, Nuri Said, had remained steadfastly pro-British, but when Rashid Ali, supported by a faction of army officers, began to move Iraq towards a neutralist and then a pro-German position, Britain intervened forcefully, overthrowing the Rashid Ali administration and bringing back Nuri Said. In Egypt, close to the eye of the storm as General Rommel's army advanced in 1942, King Farouk, who had strong Italian links, proved an uneasy ally, while many army officers were deemed untrustworthy by the British Ambassador, Sir Miles Lampson. To install a satisfactory Egyptian government, it was found necessary to surround the royal palace with British tanks in February 1942. In Iran, whose oil fields were of major strategic importance, Britain and the Soviet Union acted together, the British occupying the south and the Soviets the north, forcing the Iranian government to accept Anglo-Soviet protection, an action that impelled the humiliated Shah, Reza Pahlavi, to abdicate in favour of his son. With the Allied victory in 1945, Britain emerged seemingly more than ever the dominant power in the region, but the fall of the Egyptian monarchy in 1952 and the bloody end to the Hashemite Iraq monarchy in 1958 owed much to the anger of army officers, always, as we have seen, a radical force in the Arab world, at the impotent or client nature of the monarchies during the war.

The wars of the twentieth century were not good for monarchies. If the First World War had dealt the institution a near-fatal blow, its successor had further thinned the ranks of the world's monarchs.

MIXED FORTUNES, 1952–1979

The year 1952 witnessed two contrasting images of monarchy. In Britain, the death of the much-respected monarch, King George VI, brought to the throne his daughter, Princess Elizabeth, now Queen Elizabeth II. She was 25, the same age as Elizabeth I had been when she came to the throne, and there was much talk of a new Elizabethan age. In Egypt, the golden boy who had become king in the early 1930s had become fat, corrupt and prematurely aged, and was known best in the Western press for his gambling and his appetites for food and young women. Such tastes had not been unknown to his predecessors, and were shared by some contemporary Arab sovereigns, but along with his inability to stand up to the British and in the context of puritanical Islamic revivalism and nationalistic army officers, Farouk cut an inappropriate figure. He was hustled off the throne in July and dispatched to a hedonistic exile on the Riviera.

King Farouk's comment that eventually there would only be five kings, those of Spades, Hearts, Clubs and Diamonds and of Great Britain, expressed not only his intimate acquaintance with the first four, but the common sense of the day about the fifth. The British monarchy was not just secure, respected and deeply loved, but it was the essence of Britain and Britishness. Farouk's analysis probably underestimated the security of the other monarchies of western Europe and that of the Japanese monarchy, but only in Britain was there no opposition of any consequence to the monarchy.

The popularity of the British monarchy was in part due to the particular characters and personalities of King George and Queen Elizabeth and their daughters, and the way in which the genuinely close royal family projected itself as at once very special and very normal. The royal family emerged from the war almost universally respected. There were, however, structural factors that supported the British monarchy. Constitutional practice had settled into an accepted formula from early in the reign of George V, and although the royal prerogatives occasioned intervention at times when governments lost the confidence of the House of Commons, or no party had a clear majority, the crown had largely managed to establish itself as above politics. Mid-twentieth-century Britain was both class-conscious and deeply conservative, a paradox only on the surface. Working people and the majority of the Labour movement sought to improve the position of the working classes in society rather than to demolish the class structure. The hereditary principle was in practice widespread, with male members of the working classes as well as the middle classes following in their fathers' footsteps; the sons of shipyard workers, ironworkers, printers and miners almost inevitably took up their fathers' crafts and trades. It was also a self-confident society, though a bit shabby and down-at-heel, with even the royal family suffering the rigours of rationing and reputedly 'eating Spam off a gold plate'; it had, nevertheless, won the war and looked forward to better times.

The monarchy was a symbol of continuity, past endurance and victory, while it also provided a dash of colour in the rather

dreary post-war world, as it did particularly with Princess
Elizabeth's marriage to Prince Philip of Greece, anglicised
into Lieutenant Philip Mountbatten RN and, the day before
the wedding in 1947, into the Duke of Edinburgh. The marriage did, however, result in a thinly disguised dispute over the
name of the dynasty. For Lord Mountbatten, as his most recent
biographer has written, 'the new regime signified the triumph
of the House of Mountbatten' and at dinner at Broadlands, his
country house, he went so far as to propose a toast to the new
dynasty, thus, when they heard of it infuriating both Queen
Mary and Queen Elizabeth, the Queen Mother.[1] The Queen,
advised by Churchill, however, announced the continuation
of the House of Windsor, thus seemingly side-lining her husband, while angering Lord Mountbatten who had so zealously
encouraged the match. Although the declaration was modified in 1962 to the effect that Mountbatten-Windsor would
be the family name but not be used by the immediate royal
family, the rebuff to the Mountbattens was seen by many
as a victory for the Queen Mother, who had not forgotten
Lord Mountbatten's once close relationship with the Duke
of Windsor.

Lord Mountbatten's influence on the royal family has been
the subject of as much debate among historians as his naval
record and his role as the last Viceroy of India. As assiduous in
promoting his own career and reputation as that of his lineage,
his influence over the education of Prince Charles has been
seen as unfortunate, while his desire for the limelight clearly
put him and the monarchy into danger when, in his later years,
he unwisely became involved in machinations against the
Wilson government.[2]

Prince Philip's problem was one faced by most male consorts and royal princes: how to find a dignified and purposeful
place in national life. They have a platform from which they
can promote their views and causes, but risk the outrage of
special interest groups if their views are controversial. Having

had to retire from a promising career in the Royal Navy, he turned his energy towards modernising the style of the monarchy during the 1950s and '60s but found his efforts resented by palace officials and by the Queen Mother, concerned to preserve the style of monarchy set by herself and George VI.

With the coronation of Queen Elizabeth II, the monarchy moved into top gear. The Festival of Britain in 1951 had celebrated Britain's past, present and future, and the new reign seemed destined to build upon its success and to symbolise hopes that austerity could be banished, that the fast-vanishing Empire could be succeeded by a positive Commonwealth and that Britain would continue to be a world power. The combination of youth, monarchy and the Queen's obvious sense of duty was irresistible, and via the coronation, which most people watched on the new medium of television, the nation rededicated itself.

Meanwhile, King Farouk settled down to his twilight of cards and call-girls. His exile and the end of the Albanian dynasty founded by Muhammad Ali owed something to his personal failings, but like most Middle Eastern monarchs, especially those under British patronage or tutelage, he had been beset by hostile internal forces. The failure of the Islamic world to compete with the West had, as we have seen, brought into being two somewhat contradictory forces – Islamic revivalism and an army-officer-led nationalism. The former had engendered in Egypt the Muslim Brotherhood, a movement that threatened Egypt's cosmopolitanism and its Coptic minority, but it was an army coup led by General Neguib, though Colonel Abdul Nasser was its heir, which brought the monarchy to an end. Although Egypt had always had an ambiguous relationship with the Arab world, the new regime found that its heady mix of nationalism and a brand of military socialism made it for two decades the natural leader of radical Arab aspirations, while the circumstances of the Cold War gave it diplomatic opportunities. Nasser's nationalisation of the Suez Canal and the eventual failure of the Anglo-French attack on Egypt and reoccupation of the Canal Zone due to American pressure increased his and Egypt's prestige in the Arab world enormously. The bloody *coup d'état* by army officers that overthrew the Iraq monarchy in 1958 owed much to Egyptian influence.

The outlook for Middle Eastern monarchies looked bleak. King Idris of Libya was ousted by Nasserite officers in 1969, and the Imam of the North Yemen was finally defeated by republican forces in 1970, after a long civil war. Against all expectations, the Kingdom of Jordan, under its brave and capable monarch, King Hussein, who succeeded after the assassination of his grandfather, King Abdullah, was to survive, as, in the Mahgreb, did the Kingdom of Morocco, where the monarchy had been the focus of opposition to the French. The combination of oil wealth sensibly invested in their economies and societies, British protection and close relations with Saudi Arabia ensured the survival of the monarchies of the states of the Persian Gulf, Kuwait, Bahrain, Qatar and the Union of Arab Emirates, together with neighbouring Oman.

The most important surviving monarchy was, however, the Kingdom of Saudi Arabia, where Islamic fundamentalism, American influence, royal autocracy and enormous riches from oil were blended into a unique mixture. Following the creation of King Ibn Saud or Abdul Aziz with assistance from the supporters of the Wahabi version of Islam, the desert kingdom remained poor until becoming oil rich after the Second World War as the US oil company Aramco came to dominate the economy.[3] It remained an absolute monarchy, but of a kind very unfamiliar to the West. As with other Arab monarchies, there was no tradition of primogeniture, and with rulers practising polygamy enthusiastically there were and are many possible successors to the throne. In 1932, when proclaiming himself king, Ibn Saud commanded that the succession should pass down through his sons, of whom there were forty-four.

Essentially the extended royal family rules, for the monarch requires the support of the family, needs to satisfy his relatives (there were several thousand princes in direct line of descent by the end of the twentieth century) and appoints them to the main posts in government and administration. The other constituency that has to be satisfied is the *ulema*, for the King is bound to govern under Islamic law and needs the advice of religious leaders to do so. Throughout the 1950s and 1960s the kingdom had the difficult task of staving off Nasserite Arab nationalism, retaining American support and protection and, as oil money flooded in, transforming the country's infra-structure and sucking in Western consumer goods, while still satisfying a puritanical religiosity. On the death of Ibn Saud in 1951, his son, Saud, became king. He did not prove an effec-tive ruler, and in 1958 he was persuaded to hand over effective power to his brother Prince Faisal, though he remained king. Reneging on this arrangement, he finally lost the support of the family, and in 1964 was forced to abdicate and was replaced as king by Faisal, who ruled until his death in 1975. The challenge of nationalistic republicanism was surmounted largely because the secularist Ataturk tradition clashed with the theocratic beliefs of much of the Saudi population, and because Egypt's military failures against Israel and the death of Nasser confounded the hopes placed in Nasserism. The continuing problem was how to satisfy an increasingly fierce Islamic fundamentalism while modernising state and society and remaining on good terms with the USA.

In some respects, the Kingdoms of Saudi Arabia and Iran were very similar: absolute monarchies, enriched by their great oil reserves, both were anti-Communist and sided with the West in the Cold War. The great difference was that, whereas the Saudi royal family were very careful to retain the support of the religious leaders, the Shah of Iran, Muhammed Reza Pahlavi, continued the policies of his father, Reza Khan, which can be described as a royal form of Ataturkism, a profoundly

secular modernisation programme from the top down. Like
Ataturk, he placed considerable faith in the role and the loyalty
of the army. Ataturk had been a Turkish nationalist as well as a
moderniser, but the Shah's nationalist credentials were much
weakened when, in 1951, his Prime Minister, Muhammad
Mossaddeq, nationalised the country's oil industry and was
then overthrown by a coup launched by the army and instru-
mented by the British and American intelligence services. The
Shah ruled successfully as an absolute ruler with the backing
of the army, and with considerable support from the growing Iranian middle classes, but an economic depression in the
1970s increased the popularity of the country's Shi'ite brand
of Islamic fundamentalism, always popular among the peasantry and urban poor. Islam has technically no Church, but in
a way that some Islamic scholars have seen as almost a heresy,
the Shi'ite religious leaders had become organised and hierarchical; they were also increasingly politicised and formed
an opposition to the Shah and his westernising policies. The
supreme religious leader, Ayatollah Khomeini, had launched a
revolt in 1963 and, ironically in the light of subsequent events,
had found sanctuary in Iraq, from which he coordinated
opposition to the Shah. From 1977, amid Iran's deteriorating
economic position, protests against the regime were orchestrated, and in 1979 the ailing monarch was forced into exile
as Khomeini returned. Absolute monarchy and westernisation
were replaced by an Islamic republic, the *Sharia* law and what
was effectively rule by a clergy.

The fate of the Shah both supported and ultimately confounded the analysis of Middle Eastern affairs by liberals and
socialists. Put briefly, this supposed that monarchy was conservative and reactionary and would in the great scenario of
history be replaced by modern, secular and probably socialist
regimes. The Iranian monarchy fell but was replaced by a far
more conservative and reactionary regime. The force of Islam,
energised by the reversals to its proclaimed destiny, had been

underestimated. The Saudi monarchy, opposed though it was to the Shi'ite form of Islam, learned the lesson.

The fates of the Saudi and Iranian monarchies make for an interesting comparison. The former saw the victory of the desert and fundamentalist Islam over the town and western style modernisation, but one supported by a traditional monarchy and incongruously fuelled by oil, the great propellant of modernisation elsewhere, while the failure of the Shah's 'white revolution', an attempt to modernise by utilising secularisation and an expanded urban society, ended in victory for the countryside and a conservative clergy.

In Asia the fortunes of monarchy were similarly mixed. The ultimate theocracy, Tibet, was invaded by Communist China in 1950, and the Dalai Lama, held to be the fourteenth incarnation of the first Dalai Lama, the religious and temporal ruler, managed to escape to India after an unsuccessful uprising in 1959. In 1973 the King of Afghanistan was overthrown and a republic declared. However, the two most important monarchies of Asia, Japan and Thailand, endured.

General MacArthur's view that the monarchy was essential to Japan was borne out in that the emperor system ensured a smooth transition from the defeated militaristic Japan to the dynamic economic power that developed after the end of the American occupation. Divested of the semi-godlike status in which it is unlikely he ever believed himself, and excluded from any political role, Emperor Hirohito continued in the eyes of most Japanese to epitomise the essence of the nation and its culture. The monarchy, despite public appearances and visits within the country and abroad by Hirohito, remained both closeted and ceremonial. It ceased to be grand and triumphalist as it had been from the Meiji period, but did not become a monarchy that, save for a few well-choreographed excursions by Hirohito, went in for 'walkabouts' or figured, save when royal marriages were in the air, in gossip columns.

In many ways it returned to its older traditions; it was *there*, if behind the screens, a vital national treasure and the spiritual and cultural embodiment of the national entity.

Many would have written off the Thai monarchy in the 1950s and 1960s as preserved by successive military juntas and dictators as a bauble necessary for the adulation of the common people. Were the military regimes to fall, it would assuredly be Communists or some sort of socialist regime that would succeed it. The military nationalists needed, though they did not necessarily want, the monarchy. Marshal Sarit, the most astute of the military-political leaders, built up the prestige of the monarchy, declaring Thailand's ideals to be 'King, Religion and Nation'. Cooperating and co-existing with the governments of generals, King Bhumibol cautiously extended his own power bases and popularity, retaining his support among the peasantry but attracting the expanding number of university students and graduates by his appeal to religion, patriotism and social responsibility. The late sixties and early seventies witnessed the strange and worldwide phenomenon of student revolt, an alienation of the fortunate from their very good fortune. In Thailand, students spilled onto the streets of Bangkok in 1973 in opposition to the military regime but in favour of the King. Bhumibol seized the opportunity to call a National Convention, and inaugurated a new era of democracy *and* royal power. As other neighbouring monarchies fell victim to Communism when the USA withdrew from Indo-China, the popularity and influence of the Thai monarchy increased.

The colonial powers retreated from their Asian possessions under a number of pressures: a consciousness of military and economic weakness, American pressure, nationalist opposition and a realisation that their electorates had little stomach for expensive wars to maintain them. They departed either abruptly, as with the British in India, gradually and with some dignity as with the British in Malaya, and after humiliating defeat, as with the French in Indo-China. In Africa, with the exception of the Mahgreb, where the French fought fiercely for Algeria, they wound up their African empires with all the haste of a business enterprise, realising that its more distant branches were no longer likely to make a profit, though the French hoped that rather than disposing of the branches they were really franchising them out. The Portuguese were unusual in maintaining their colonial possessions in-house until the directors were ousted and there had to be a quick sale. In the hurried wind-up of the African colonies, little thought was given to the chiefs, kings and emirs who had provided a buffer between the colonial subjects and their masters. For the most part, the sudden ending of empire in Africa, with all its mock-inheritance of parliaments, speakers and maces, left little space for monarchs, because it left them little power to dispense the patronage and protection that had been inseparable from their position. Loyalties to chiefs or kings lingered, but could hardly compete with populist political parties with their African socialisms and ministers with state largesse to dispense. A monarchy like that of Buganda, which proved obstinate, was easily dispensed with by Milton Obote's post-colonial regime. The one African monarchy that could claim a long history, the Ethiopian monarchy, much admired by socialists and liberals when Emperor Haile Selassie was ousted by Mussolini, was re-inaugurated after the Second World War, but fell after a bloody coup in which the Emperor, family and retainers were massacred. In black Africa monarchy only survived in pockets such as Lesotho and Swaziland, or was reluctantly tolerated by nationalist regimes that gave monarchies within their realms much less authority than had the British. The later and rather bizarre episode of the Central African Empire of Emperor Bokassa only lasted three years (1976–9). Beyond the fuzzy divide between black Africa and North Africa, the Kingdom of Morocco survived.

In comparison, most of the remaining monarchies of Western Europe had a smooth passage in the post-war and the

Cold War world. The Nordic and Benelux monarchies settled down into a cosy relationship with their subjects in which there was less of the theatre of monarchy than in Britain, though the supposed low-key character and almost bourgeois nature of the royal households was largely a figment of the imagination of the British press, which was forever picturing monarchs on bicycles mixing with subjects as they did their shopping. A pragmatic mix of social-democratic governments and ornamental monarchies characterised Sweden and Norway, though the Danish monarch continued to exercise rather more political responsibility. The Belgian and Dutch monarchs, however, played an active role in guiding their nation's affairs. King Baudouin soon re-established the consensus for the monarchy that had been destroyed by the arguments about Leopold's wartime role, and the monarchy became a unifying symbol in a country increasingly divided by language and between Walloon and Flemish aspirations. Queen Juliana took over from her mother, Queen Wilhelmina, on the latter's abdication as Queen of the Netherlands. It was Juliana who gave the Dutch monarchy the reputation of being a 'bicycling monarchy', for she was noted for her informal style. She brought the Netherlands through a difficult period, as the early years of her reign witnessed the surrender of the remaining Dutch colonies. She was not afraid to use her executive authority, and in 1973 she dispensed with an elected government for 209 days. Her reign was, nevertheless, not without its problems. There were complaints about her daughter Princess Beatrix's marriage to a German diplomat, for wartime memories were still vivid; then there was the strange business of Greet Hofmans, a faith healer who seemed to some in the 1950s to exert a Rasputin-like influence over Juliana before he was forced out by Prince Bernhard, who was himself associated with the Lockheed bribes scandal in the early 1970s and had to resign from his official appointments. Abdication or retirement from the throne had almost become a Dutch tradition, and in 1980

Juliana abdicated in favour of Beatrix, who, in a break with what had almost become another tradition, had sons.

Those seeking signposts to the future of monarchy in Europe could find contradictory indicators in Greece and Spain. The last surviving Balkan monarchy fell in 1967, when King Constantine launched an unsuccessful counter-coup to the takeover by the 'Colonels', a junta of army officers, and flew to Rome. If he had justified expectations that Constantine Karamanlis, who returned from exile to form a government on the overthrow of the Colonels in 1973, would ease his passage back, he was disappointed, for he was not allowed to return to Greece and a referendum abolished the monarchy by a two-thirds majority. Greece had been a torn country since the 'Great Division' of the First World War, and the civil war at the end of the Second World War had exacerbated hatreds. Constantine's fall owed something to his own lack of political expertise in the piranha pond of Greek politics, and a failure to act decisively due to a well-meaning desire to avoid bloodshed. He was also the victim of the maladroit behaviour of his mother, Queen Frederika, a granddaughter of the Kaiser and therefore an easy target in post-war Greece, of Greek history, and sheer bad luck. Greece, with its history of enforced abdications, had never provided a secure throne.

King Constantine's sister, Princess Sofia, had married Prince Juan Carlos of Spain in 1962. Few could have foreseen the reversals of fortune that resulted in Juan Carlos becoming King of Spain in 1975 while Greece had become a republic the previous year. In 1962 Juan Carlos's chances of becoming King were fairly remote. General Franco ruled Spain, and though sympathetic to the institution of monarchy was in no hurry to make way for an actual monarch. There were in any case quite a lot of claimants to the throne. Were Franco to restore the monarchy, whom would he choose to make king? Monarchists in Spain had been split since the nineteenth century between Carlists and supporters of the house that had reigned until rather ignominiously forced off the throne with the declaration of a republic in 1932. Carlists had fought for Franco during the civil war and had their own candidate for the crown, Don Javier de Bourbon-Parma. Juan Carlos's father, Don Juan, Count of Barcelona, was the third son of ex-King Alfonso, and though his father proclaimed him heir in 1933, the claims of an elder brother, Don Jaime, were later revived. From 1948, Juan Carlos lived in Spain under the aegis of General Franco, but there was never a certainty of his succession until 1969, when the Caudillo announced the establishment of a 'traditional, Catholic, social and representative monarchy', and that, bypassing the Count of Barcelona, Juan Carlos would in due course succeed to the throne. Juan Carlos's accession owed much to his ability and political judgement. As a British biographer has put it: 'Reigning monarchs are not often described as "self made", but in many ways Juan Carlos may be said to fit this description.'[4]

Juan Carlos's accession and his subsequent success in steering Spain peacefully from the authoritarianism of the Franco era towards a monarchy presiding over a parliamentary system was an impressive vindication of the virtues of constitutional monarchy. Without him, it is unlikely that a country deeply scarred by memories of the civil war would have had a non-violent transition. His role in aborting the attempted military coup in 1981 was only the most spectacular of his contributions to his country's well-being. The monarchies of the world had experienced mixed fortunes, but the Spanish example suggested there was a future for the institution.

PART FOUR

MONARCHIES IN THE CONTEMPORARY WORLD

ANNI HORRIBILES

When, in 1992, important sections of Windsor Castle were destroyed by fire, it seemed to many an ominous portent. The House of Windsor was in trouble. Queen Elizabeth saw the fire as the culmination of an '*annus horribilis*', coming as it did after sensational revelations about the marriages of the Prince and Princess of Wales and of the Duke and Duchess of York, and controversy over the immunity of the Queen from paying income tax. Elizabeth II remained enormously popular, and only a few left-wing intellectuals (who felt that the monarchy kept Britain back from being 'properly modern') and the incorrigibly envious favoured a republic, but there could be little doubt that the British monarchy was no longer accorded the respect and deference that had been the norm at the beginning of the Queen's reign.

There were many reasons for this. Britain had prospered in the last half of the twentieth century, but the hopes of coronation year for continued and unassailable great-power status had not been fulfilled, while, if the consumer society and the Thatcherite shake-up of the previous stable, if inefficient and stratified, society and economy, had produced benefits, they had also promoted insecurity, unease and a distaste for established authority. A further factor was that the 'family firm' that was George VI's household had done its job too well in promoting the royal family as the epitome of settled and stable family life, an image that had only occasionally corresponded with the lives of royalty in the past and did not mirror the lives of Queen Elizabeth's sister or children.

Even before the difficulties that became so prominent in 1992, the British monarchy had had to face problems as to how to adapt its image to changes in society, something it had done successfully in the past. The main questions concerned ceremony, remoteness and class. George V had, above all, been a dignified monarch, while George VI and, rather more so, his consort had successfully mixed dignity with flashes of the common touch. Queen Elizabeth II maintained the traditions of her father's reign; the monarchy was ceremonial and formal, though it communicated directly to its subjects by means of visits around the country and Christmas broadcasts. This was not enough for critics, friendly or otherwise, who from the late 1950s advocated a more informal and low-key monarchy and one less associated with the aristocracy. The troubles of the House of Windsor were made more newsworthy because of the position of the British monarchy as supposedly the most secure in the world and, as it had been for many decades, essentially above criticism.

From the 1950s onwards, the Palace pondered as to what should be done, with the Duke of Edinburgh championing modernisation and Queen Elizabeth, the Queen Mother, arguing against change. Much of the criticism was inappropriate. The gist of the attack from critics, such as Malcolm Muggeridge and Lord Altrincham, was that the monarchy was out of touch with contemporary Britain, was old fashioned with a style redolent of the days of the Empire, the Queen sounded upper class or priggish and the court was aristocratic and 'tweedy'. It was difficult to imagine a Queen who was not upper class, and it was perhaps the monarchy's business to be a little old fashioned. Robert Lacey has summarised the criticisms of the late fifties well:

> In retrospect the most striking thing about the criticisms of Altrincham, Osborne and Muggeridge was their irrelevance to the Britain of 'I'm alright Jack' and 'Never had it so good'. This obsession with the royal family was, in many ways, as unbalanced as that of the most bedazzled Crawfie addict.[1]

More attention should have been paid to the views of the Queen Mother, who was, after all, the great communicator of the family. This daughter of the Scottish aristocracy had a feel for the attitudes of the British public and realised that most people wanted a monarchy that was dignified and something special, and that the success of a popular gesture or an indication of warmth depended upon the backdrop of ceremony and formality. The problem was how to modify the monarchy, an institution that depended so much on its traditional and historic nature, without destroying it.

The solution was believed to be better presentation: to let the cameras in and to present the public with a more informal image of the royal family as 'ordinary' people; but also to show that the British monarchy was still capable of mounting ceremonies with pomp and display. The combination of the television documentary *Royal Family* and the investiture of Prince Charles as Prince of Wales in 1969 seemed to relaunch the monarchy.

The Silver Jubilee celebrations of 1977 had appeared to demonstrate that the nation, able to review twenty-five years of the Queen's reign, remained overwhelmingly loyal. Either the new projection of the monarchy had worked or perhaps it had been unnecessary. All over the country, galas and concerts in village halls, far more than London processions and formal ceremonies, testified to an enduring loyalty to the crown. The small platoons that made up the fabric of civil society, local territorial units, the British Legion, Scouts, Guides and the Women's Institutes demonstrated how deep-rooted support for the monarchy was. Ill fortune, if not disaster, was, however, to follow.

The consequences of the retreat from Empire, and the failure to provide a robust successor for it in the shape of the Commonwealth, had important implications for the monarchy, for Britain and for Her Majesty's other kingdoms. Before her accession, Queen Elizabeth had dedicated herself to the Commonwealth, but developments not under her control had weakened the links that bound that loose organisation together. Although the Empire of India had gone, the scramble to get rid of the colonies was only beginning at the time of the coronation, while few could have foreseen the degree to which links to what was often seen as the 'white Commonwealth' would have weakened by the late twentieth century.

The potential problems of the sovereign of Britain continuing to govern overseas kingdoms had never been properly addressed. There was a general acceptance in Australia, New Zealand and Canada in the mid-twentieth century of the importance of the traditional ties with Britain and a widespread loyalty to the crown. How best could such feelings be encouraged? The growing support among the British political elite for the incipient European Union was to be seen, with some justice, as a betrayal by Australia, New Zealand and Canada, and both Conservative and Labour governments paid little attention from the early 1960s to Commonwealth interests. Could, in such circumstances, independent nations continue their loyalty to a Queen overseas? There were possible options: Prince Charles could have served successively as Governor-General of the main Commonwealth states, or an official royal residence could have been established in each. Kings and queens have, however, proved reluctant to give responsibility to heirs apparent, and perhaps British governments did not really want to share their monarch with Commonwealth countries. The Governor-Generals, who were the Queen's representatives, had by the late 1960s become almost axiomatically citizens of the country concerned, a sensible development from one point of view, but one that inevitably made appointments subject to advice from the Commonwealth government concerned, and no longer the Queen's personal choice. This did not prevent a constitutional crisis when, in 1975, the Governor-General of Australia used his reserve powers to dismiss the Prime Minister, Gough Whitlam.

The Queen's personal fondness for the Commonwealth is, some have argued, the glue that keeps it going, for it is a heterogeneous body, all the more so now that nations that were never ruled by Britain have joined. The attachment to the Queen in the old Commonwealth states has proved surprisingly enduring in the face of declining economic and political ties, the rather ungrateful restrictions Britain placed on the rights of old Commonwealth citizens to enter and work in their 'home country' and the number of non-British immigrants who had settled in Australia, New Zealand and Canada. In Australia, in particular, there was nevertheless a vociferous and growing number who pressed for a republic, and many considered it only a matter of time before this aspiration was realised.

Pundits looking for problems that might confront the British monarchy in the late seventies were likely to mention potential trouble with the remaining royal prerogatives, which could present difficulties when governments were formed and no party had a clear majority in the House of Commons, possible demands for a less grand monarchy and the rumbling debate over the royal finances. They were less likely to mention sex and scandal, but these were the problems that were to shake the royal families of Europe around the beginning of the new millennium.

Walter Bagehot, in his highly influential book *The English Constitution* (1867), remarked that 'a family on the throne is an interesting idea'. He was thinking about the way interest, not only in Queen Victoria herself, but in the family and private life of the monarch, and indeed in all members of the royal family, had grown among the British public. At the beginning of the nineteenth century, monarchs themselves had been distant symbols, whom the vast majority of their subjects had never seen, but by the time Bagehot was writing, not only was the Queen an almost familiar figure, known by her visits to towns all over Britain, by articles in newspapers and by photographs in illustrated magazines, but people enjoyed a similar ersatz relationship with the royal family. The curtain on royal lives had been lifted and subjects, not just courtiers and ministers, had followed the progress of royal children from the nursery to their marriages, been fed gossip as to their personalities, followed their annual excursions to Osborne and Balmoral, and become well acquainted with their tastes in fashion or house furnishings as they grew older. There was a price to pay for this as Queen Victoria found out when she withdrew into privacy after the death of Prince Albert and there was outrage as it had become almost a duty for her to show herself to her people.

The trouble with a family on the throne is the trouble with families. They, or at least some of their members, don't fulfil expectations and Victoria and Albert had very high expectations. They had firmly turned their backs on the manners and mores of the Queen's uncles and her father and their times and set a high, perhaps unrealistically high, standard of respectability for their children and posterity. Ironically, it was a model of family life which the father of Victoria's 'wicked uncles' had previously attempted, unsuccessfully, to create.

It is intrinsic to a hereditary institution that sex, marriage and personal relationships are important and of wide interest. The most important block on sexual adventures had always been the need to ensure the legitimacy of the royal line, but this affected, principally, monarchs and their consorts and those likely to ascend the throne. In practice this usually meant that kings and crown princes could have mistresses, but that no doubts should be had as to the legitimacy of those born to a king or queen regnant or to those likely to succeed them. Nevertheless, if more junior members of royal families have more freedom, those of royal birth are royal for all of their lives, and their romantic and sexual affairs from their teenage years onwards take place on a public stage. This was once before a select audience but, more recently, before one much widened by the development of new means of communication. Meanwhile, commoners who marry princes or princesses find close attention paid, not just to their new incarnations, but to their past lives.

Sex and scandal had always been a factor for European royalty in the modern period. Rumour, gossip and slander about Catherine the Great's supposedly voracious sexual appetite and Marie Antoinette's alleged amours were spread far beyond court circles; the numerous affairs of the sons of George III provided fodder for cartoonists like Gillray and Rowlandson; Edward VII's extra-marital affairs, both when he was Prince of Wales and King, were well known; and, as we have seen, the homosexual inclinations of some of Kaiser Wilhelm II's intimate friends caused a major scandal.

So far as male royals were concerned, their heterosexual sex lives gave rise to gossip rather than scandal until relatively recently, and in the period between the Georgian and Regency cartoonists and the tabloid press of the late twentieth century gossip became muffled. It was hardly surprising that kings and princes had more sexual partners than merchants and labourers, for, like wealthy aristocrats of their day or the

film and pop stars and footballers of today, they had far greater
opportunities. There was indeed an expectation that princes
would err from pre-marital celibacy and even post-marital
monogamy, provided that their recognised children were the
result of their marriage. Walter Bagehot argued that the role of
the heir apparent was to taste 'all the world and the glory of it,
whatever is most attractive, whatever is most seductive'.[2]

Homosexuality was, of course, another matter, being both
a taboo and illegal until 1967. James I and VI's predilections
were, despite this, notorious, at least in court circles, while
Louis XI's brother, Philippe Duc d'Orleans, 'Monsieur', openly
flaunted his. In more recent times, several royals were bisexual,
as with Edward VII's eldest son, the Duke of Clarence, and
George V's youngest, the Duke of Kent, while King Ferdinand
of Bulgaria's sexual tastes were well known. Royal persons are
as much inclined to a variety of sexual appetites as the rest
of humanity; they have considerable opportunity to indulge
them, but they are closely observed. Homosexuality was,
nevertheless, likely to lead to serious scandal.

The major limitation upon the freedom of males close
to the throne concerned the choice of marriage partners. A
rash and unsuitable marriage could reduce the gulf between
sovereign and commoners, and the Royal Marriages Act
of 1772 was designed to prevent such marriages, as English
tradition did not recognise the continental solution of the
morganatic marriage. It did not, however, apply in the case
of the marriages of sovereigns. Even in the twentieth century
other European monarchies could be much more particular
than the British in these matters. When Prince Gustav Adolf
of Sweden, later King Gustav VI, married, as his second wife,
Lady Louise Mountbatten, there was opposition from the
court because she wasn't considered sufficiently royal. Even
in the twenty-first century, traditionalists disapproved of the
Crown Princess Victoria marrying a wealthy Swedish commoner. The Swedish, Danish and Norwegian constitutions all

include the stipulation that members of the royal family need permission to marry.

For royal females, the situation in regard to pre- or extra-marital affairs was rather different. A modern insistence on the equality of the sexes and repugnance against double standards has largely ignored the major reason for such standards, at any rate before the nineteenth century – inheritance. Both Mr Bull the butcher and Mr Rex the king were concerned that their heir should be *their* heir. The sad fates of George I's wife, Sophia Dorothea, and George III's sister, Caroline Matilda, who spent the last years of their lives confined to the castle of Celle for their adultery, testify to the harsh penalties for straying female consorts in the eighteenth century. The daughters of George III, confined by their father's fondness for them to 'the nunnery' within his court, nevertheless found sexual opportunities where they could; for those who didn't manage to escape via marriage, those opportunities were with equerries, as with Princesses Amelia, Augusta and Sophia. By the early nineteenth century, the penalties for royal female infidelity were less harsh, and Prince Albert's mother, Duchess Louise, though banished from Saxe-Coburg, was divorced by her husband and married her lover. Even among the daughters of Queen Victoria, brought up in the strictest of ménages, Princess Louise managed to have an interesting sex life. Her marriage to the Marquess of Lorne, reputedly a homosexual, was not a success. She had artistic interests and studied under the sculptor Edgar Boehm, and was, reputedly, under him in his studio when he burst a blood vessel and died.[3] In April 2004, Nicholas Locock appealed to the Court of the Arches against the refusal of Rochester Consistory Court to allow the exhumation of his grandfather's body; the purpose of the exhumation was to enable a DNA sample to be taken in order to test the claim that Henry Locock, supposed grandson of Queen Victoria's gynaecologist and born in 1867, was in fact an illegitimate child of Princess Louise.

Three developments during the twentieth century had a great impact upon what the wider world knew about royal marriages, amours and infidelities, and upon how they were viewed: the loosening of the restrictions and the moral codes, hitherto binding much of society to celibacy or monogamy; the enormous appetite of the media for scandal concerning the famous; and the widening of the social circles in which members of royal families moved.

It might seem logical that the more permissive society became, the more permission it would extend to its establishment, its elites or its celebrities, including royalty. The paradox is that the nineteenth-century working man or clerk, dedicated or consigned to celibacy or monogamy, would extend a generous tolerance to the robust and promiscuous sex life of the Prince of Wales. The reactions of women were rather different. Working-class and middle-class women, conscious of the dangers to hearth, home and family of errant husbands, tended to be more censorious of the amours of royal males and of their mistresses; it was the wronged wife who got their sympathy, though errant wives received little. Oddly, the reactions of the modern equivalents of both sexes are probably less tolerant, even if they are quite likely to be divorced and have had several sexual liaisons. In part this is the result of the intermittent attempts of many, but not all, monarchs since George III to portray the monarchy as the exemplar and model of family life; but it is also a result of a jealous populism, which argues that, 'If they are no better than me, why should they be more important than, or richer than, me?', a mixed mindset that confuses 'Why shouldn't I?' with 'Why should they?'. The sexual revolution of the late twentieth century has had some unexpected results.

The chapbooks of the early modern period, the sensational 'Secret Histories' and the radical cartoons and squibs of the early nineteenth century all delighted in covering the sexual and financial transgressions of British royalty, and there were

equivalent French publications. From the mid-nineteenth century, however, partly because of a greater respect for authority
and partly because it was less permissible to even mention
sex, except in the context of reports of legal cases, there was a
long hiatus in the coverage of the raunchier side of royal lives
or, indeed, the private vices and sexual proclivities of public
figures as a whole, save in coded terms or private gossip. The
discretion of the British press in not mentioning the liaison of
Edward VIII and Wallis Simpson until immediately before the
abdication is the best example. The mission of the investigative journalist of the late twentieth and twenty-first centuries
to expose was, conversely, unconstrained by loyalty, deference
or convention.

The troubles of the British monarchy in the last years of
the twentieth century were in part caused by the deliberate
projection of the image of an impeccable family life as one
of its central features. That image had been largely true of
the relationship between and the lifestyle of George V and
Queen Mary, though another description might have been
'dull', but it certainly reflected the happy domestic life of
George VI and Queen Elizabeth. If it reflected reality, it was
also a conscious image. The reason, of course, was 'David' –
the former Edward VIII – for after his abdication there was a
conscious projection of the new King and Queen and their
family as a contrast to the personality, tastes and lifestyle of
the previous, if short, reign of the exiled Duke of Windsor.
The new regime emphasised domesticity, Britishness and
tradition as opposed to the restless desire for modernity, the
resorts of the Riviera, and all things American of its predecessor. Above all it eschewed glamour, the third ingredient,
along with sex and scandal, seen as dangerous to the throne,
and one which Edward VIII had possessed in spades. It was
his film-star looks, his distaste for tradition, and his love of
the modern that had made him so attractive to the younger
generations in the twenties and thirties.

Royal persons with charisma, good looks and fashion sense had always fascinated the public, but had sometimes, as with Empress Elisabeth of Austria–Hungary, Queen Elizabeth of Romania and Edward VIII, been a mixed blessing to royal houses. Glamour, charisma and fashion sense had sometimes been an asset, but too often preceded disaster and the new regime eschewed it. George VI was a dignified figure, but lacked the charisma of his elder brother, while his consort, if charming and always well-dressed, never aspired to glamour. Not all members of the family fitted in with this style, with the Duke of Kent and his wife being notable exceptions, but the move towards a monarchy that was dignified, but less dashing, and content with family life and holidays at Sandringham and Balmoral, rather than Cannes, suited the times as war became more likely and, more so, after it began. The difficulties in establishing the new king should not, however, be underestimated, for the man who upon his abdication became the Duke of Windsor remained enormously popular and the media had to be instructed to help erase his life in exile. The chiefs of the five major newsreel companies mutually agreed that the wedding of the Duke to Mrs Simpson should be barred from every screen in Britain and in the year after the abdication there was a marked increase in the number of newsreel items featuring the royal family, depicting a united family going about their duties happily and honourably.

The style of monarchy which epitomised Britain during the Second World War continued into the austere post-war period, when dignity was combined with modesty. The phrase 'Spam served on a gold plate' exaggerated the degree that, at a time of rationing, the royal family shared the hardships of British society, while still preserving some of the glitter expected of monarchy, but a more expansive and fashionable way of life would not have been appropriate. This style survived largely intact until late in the century, seemingly immune, despite minor scandals, from the social changes transforming Britain. The problems it then confronted were, however, similar to those which had provided the context for its formation.

Later in the century, it became fashionable to talk of a 'royal soap opera', but, although there was enormous public interest in the life of the royals, as the success of the memoirs of the ex-governess Marion Crawford demonstrated, it made, until the eighties, for a fairly tame drama. Only Princess Margaret with her doomed love for Peter Townsend and marriage to Antony Armstrong-Jones added a touch of glamour and, subsequently, scandal. Yet, the reporting of Princess Margaret's life was an indication that the years when the press was discreet in its coverage were drawing to a close.

The late twentieth-century public demanded glamour and celebrity, though it usually found it manufactured in Hollywood, and wished to know every detail of the life of the glamorous. From the mid-nineteenth century, the public had demonstrated an appetite for every detail about royalty, whether the royals in question were beautiful, handsome and fashionable or not; when someone was both royal and glamorous, its curiosity knew no bounds. Hitherto, such information had been rationed, but suddenly no detail, however intimate, was to be private.

Edward, Prince of Wales and then Edward VIII, was, as we have suggested, the first royal superstar, but in an interesting reversal, in one of the most minor of European principalities, a film star became, if not a royal, a serene highness. Grace Kelly, star of, among other films, *High Society*, moved into royal society and married Prince Rainier III of Monaco in 1956. By accidents of history, the Grimaldi dynasty had remained rulers of a small enclave within France. The French government had control of important matters like foreign affairs and should Prince Rainier fail to produce an heir, the principality would revert to France along with its burgeoning casino industry, a fine harbour for the yachts of the rich and a permissive tax regime. On any scale but that of Hollywood and the popular press, the marriage, like Monaco, was unimportant, but we can find in the reception accorded to the supposed love affair of the Prince and the Actress, and the subsequent fortunes of the couple and their children, many of the essential features of the problems that were to bedevil more important royal houses.

Grace Kelly seemed the ice-cold blonde, a challenge to any leading man but a prize that could only be won by marriage. In fact, she had had a long string of affairs and was described by the columnist Hedda Hopper as 'nymphomaniac'. Far from being the result of compulsive mutual attraction, the marriage seems to have been the result of hard-headed bargaining; Grace Kelly became a princess and Prince Rainier received a dowry of $2 million from her affluent Philadelphian father. The marriage was stormy but produced three children. Prince Albert, who ascended to the throne in 2005, married the former Olympic swimmer Charlene Wittstock in 2011, but the sex lives and marriages of Princess Caroline and Princess Stéphanie afforded great enjoyment to newspaper and magazine readers who relish stories about celebrities behaving badly, and considerable chagrin to Prince Rainier in his lifetime. Princess Caroline's early marriages and affairs with unsuitable men were followed with the more traditional choice of her third husband, Prince Ernst August of Hanover. Her younger sister, Stéphanie, exceeded her sibling, enjoying numerous affairs with partners who included film stars, a barman, an elephant tamer and a footballer, and marrying first her bodyguard, whom she divorced when he was filmed enjoying the charms of a Belgian stripper, and then a Portuguese circus acrobat and juggler. Princess Grace didn't live to witness her daughters' escapades, as she was killed in a motor accident on one of Monaco's winding roads in 1982; there is still controversy as to who was driving at the time, Grace or Stéphanie.

In Britain such scandal would have appeared totally alien to the respectable House of Windsor, but it was all to come. A year before the death of Princess Grace, the heir to the British throne married Lady Diana Spencer. Serious and dedicated to his role as heir apparent and future king, though somewhat anguished and ill at ease in his public engagements, Prince Charles had heeded the advice of Bagehot, and the more immediate counsel of Lord Mountbatten, and tasted the pleasures of life in the shape of several lovers. This was hardly surprising, for most of his generation were enjoying the sexual liberation that had come with the sixties. The aristocratic and upper-class young were among the most enthusiastic. When it came to marriage, however – and the need to marry was becoming urgent as the Prince approached his mid-thirties – Mountbatten's advice was to find a virgin:

> choose a suitable, attractive and sweet-charactered girl before she has met anyone else she might fall for. After all Mummy never seriously thought of anyone else after the Dartmouth encounter when she was 13! I think it is disturbing for women to have experiences if they have to remain on a pedestal after marriage.[4]

Such a bride hardly resembled Lord Mountbatten's own wife, Edwina, consistently unfaithful to him, who had died in 1960, but he was thinking of a woman who would be a queen. He perhaps had in mind his teenage granddaughter, Lady Amanda Knatchbull, as a suitable candidate.

Eschewing both the traditional path of finding a bride among the Protestant royal houses of Europe and marriage to one of his girlfriends among his own age group and set, Charles followed Lord Mountbatten's advice and in 1981 married the twenty-year-old Lady Diana Spencer. This was not the first instance of Mountbatten's baleful influence on the monarchy, as his most recent biographer has revealed.[5] It was to be the most disastrous British royal marriage since George, Prince of Wales, married Princess Caroline of Brunswick in 1795.

Billed as a great love match, the marriage was to take the monarchy to new heights of popularity, for Diana brought glamour to it before miring it in gossip, scandal and embarrassment. For the Prince of Wales to marry the daughter of a long-established aristocratic family seemed a sound idea – after all, the marriage of the Prince's grandfather to a daughter of the Scottish aristocracy had been a great success – but it was soon clear that this was no love match and that Diana in no way resembled Queen Elizabeth, the Queen Mother. Charles had clearly proposed out of a sense of duty, while Diana was more in love with the idea of marrying the heir to the throne than with the actual heir. The notion that this was a story of innocence betrayed can be dispensed with; the Spencers moved in the royal circle and Diana's elder sister had been a girlfriend of Prince Charles. Diana had made the greatest catch, was in the limelight and in the lens of every camera and was determined to stay there. The Palace, which had promoted the marriage, had not done its homework well, and had failed to investigate the real background, personality and mental stability of its seemingly so-suitable candidate. The Prince, having done his duty, was soon dissatisfied with his emotional and demanding wife, and yearning for the woman he might have married had he not deemed her not marriageable material, Camilla Shand, by now married to cavalry officer Andrew Parker Bowles. For a few years all would ostensibly go well: an heir to the throne would be born and then a second son, but then there would be a great washing of dirty linen and the British monarchy would be back, *mutatis mutandis*, to George IV and Queen Caroline, and almost abreast of tacky Monaco.

Beautiful and fashionable royal women were nothing new, and from Queen Alexandra the British royal family had had their share. Princess Margaret had succeeded Princess Marina as the most glamorous royal and as a member of London's faster set. Nonetheless, neither had pursued publicity, while Diana loved it. She seemed to know instinctively what journalists wanted, sensed exactly what clothes would attract the greatest attention, and, like the Duke of Windsor in his younger days, played to the camera with her head slightly lowered and her eyes glancing shyly upward. Like Princess Grace, she was as much a 'celebrity', a word coming increasingly into use to describe film stars, models and the fashionable and international rich, as a member of a royal family. Like many an actress, she knew just how to upstage her leading man. The effect was to add glamour to the monarchy, but at the same time to narrow the distance between royalty and the rest of the fashionable world. She burst on the scene just at the time when one taboo that had come to set royal persons and the rest of society apart was cast aside: George IV had wished to, but since Henry VIII no senior member of the royal family had been divorced.

It is difficult now to imagine that, for many years, divorced persons were not supposed to enter the royal enclosure at Ascot, a rule that would today disbar so many members of the royal family. After a long struggle, not just with her conscience but with her conflicting desires and ambitions, Princess Margaret had decided in the early 1950s not to marry the divorced Group Captain Peter Townsend, an equerry to her father and sister. Townsend was a dashing war hero, but the love affair demonstrates once more the relatively small pool of young men that, even in the twentieth century, unmarried royal women had regular contact with; equerries or their equivalents have throughout the ages been the salvation or damnation of princesses. In 1960, Princess Margaret married Antony Armstrong-Jones, an upper-class and mildly bohemian photographer. London went wild on their wedding night, but by the late sixties the marriage had foundered amid speculation as to her relationship with Roddy Llewellyn, who was eighteen years her junior. It was a back-handed tribute to the public's interest in the royal family that the announcement of her divorce in 1976 pushed Harold Wilson's resignation as Prime Minister off the front pages of the popular newspapers.

Margaret's divorce was the harbinger of many other royal divorces. Like film stars and more and more ordinary people, royalty could end unsatisfactory marriages. Why weren't they content to take lovers and continue to be married? One answer was that the press and public wouldn't allow it, while the other was that contemporary mores had spread to the royal family. Princess Anne separated from her husband, Captain Mark Phillips, in 1989 and was divorced in 1992. Divorce might not be traditional, but the cause of the marital break-up was; she had become involved with an equerry, Commander Tim Lawrence RN, whom she later married. The Queen, far less hidebound than was reputed, seemed relaxed about this and hoped for her daughter's happiness in the new relationship.

She was certainly not relaxed about the other aspects of her *annus horribilis*: the deteriorating marriage of the Prince of Wales and that of her second son, Prince Andrew, who had married a rather too-jolly girl, Sarah Ferguson. Malcolm Muggeridge had coined the phrase 'the royal soap opera' back in the fifties, but soap operas had changed and become more 'raunchy' than he could have foreseen.

So far as the general public was concerned, all was well with the marriage of the Prince of Wales and Princess Diana until the early nineties, but it seems clear that from the mid-eighties the couple were increasingly at odds. Although appearances were kept up, by 1987 Charles was seeing Camilla Parker Bowles regularly and Diana had embarked upon a long series of affairs.

If the eighties saw the celebrity monarchy with the press dancing excitedly around it, the end came swiftly. After intense media speculation as to rows and infidelities, then and after the publication by the *Daily Mirror* of the famous photo-graph of the Duchess of York having her toes sucked by her supposed financial advisor, John Bryan, the Yorks announced their separation in March 1992 and preparations for divorce were initiated. Then came the publication of Andrew Morton's *Diana: Her True Story*, first serialised in the *Sunday Times* in June. The book revealed Diana's version of the failed marriage, her attempt at suicide and her self-harm, and the revelation of Charles's relationship with Camilla Parker Bowles. Behind the author was Diana herself, who had pro-vided Morton with extensive tapes. Few believed at the time that this could be so, that the wife to the heir to the throne could so betray her position in a welter of self-pity and anger, and Diana denied that she had had anything to do with it. She was perhaps only beginning to understand the consequences of her actions. The book's publication signalled the end of the marriage. It was followed by 'Squidgygate', the publication of a transcript of a telephone conversation between Diana and one of her lovers, James Gilbey, who referred to her affection-ately as 'Squidgy'. The formal separation of Charles and Diana was announced at the end of the *annus horribilis*; they were to be divorced in 1996.

The revelations continued, however. In 1993 transcripts of a further set of tapes, this time of conversations between the Prince and Camilla Parker Bowles, were published, first in America and then in Britain, and became known as 'Camillagate'. Charles, unwisely, agreed to cooperate with Jonathan Dimbleby in a TV film in which he admitted to his affair with Camilla. Diana then went on the BBC's *Panorama* and complained about her husband's misconduct, while admit-ting to her own affair with Major James Hewitt. The explosive 1995 interview, subsequently proven to have been obtained by BBC journalist Martin Bashir under false pretences, never-theless made the dissolution of the marriage inevitable. It was now war, not just between the Waleses and their respective journalist supporters, but between the sections of the public who supported one or other of the estranged couple.

If 1992–3 was a low point, there were further difficult years to come. A divorced Diana was not prepared to eschew the limelight and promised to present an even greater problem than the Duke of Windsor had once done. She showed a bewildering number of faces to the public: an icon of fashion; an ordinary mum on a millionaire's yacht; a Mother Teresa to the sick and unfortunate; and a woman wronged, albeit comforted by many lovers. The popular press, manipulating her and manipulated by her, took her side, as did a considerable and vocal section of the public. Her death in a car crash in Paris, alongside her lover Dodi Fayed, when she was, with uncanny irony, proceeding to the house that had once belonged to the Duke of Windsor, was followed by an extraordinary display of hysterical mourning at Diana's funeral as a genuine wave of grief was surfed by those who sought to make Diana a symbol for their own causes, discontents and unhappiness. As Robert Lacey has written, 'She was embraced by the public for motives that range from collusive fantasy to individual disfunction. For every bouquet of flowers laid to Diana there is a separate private story to be told.'[6]

It was more the funeral of a film star than a princess. The distinction between royalty and celebrity had become blurred. Some thought the crown itself was threatened. The monarchy had deep roots and would survive, but it was shaken.

One effect of the monarchy's decline in popularity was to provide wind for the sails of those who criticised the British monarchy for being grand and extravagant. The public had long been ambiguous about this, taking pride in the monarchy's ability to mount great state occasions with an efficiency and panache not usually found in modern Britain, and at the same time being quite prepared to say to opinion pollsters that the monarchy costs too much money. Then there was the question of the Queen's finances. George III had made what is, in retrospect, the great mistake of failing to press for the full hereditary revenue of the crown and accepting a woefully inadequate Civil List provision. He thus put himself and his successors at the mercy of parliament. If parliament entirely controls the royal finances, then the principle of the independence of the sovereign is in danger; though, as a leading constitutional expert has argued, 'the precise balance between these competing principles – parliamentary control and the independence of the sovereign – is a legitimate matter for debate and discussion'.[7]

There was also the question of income tax, which the monarch did not have to pay. The exemption from taxation of the sovereign and the Prince of Wales had been twentieth-century innovations, and Queen Elizabeth had hitherto strongly defended her tax-exempt status. In the new circumstances tactical retreats were felt to be in order. The Queen would pay taxes, though her heir would not have to pay inheritance tax. At the same time, it was agreed that government financing of the royal family would be confined to the most immediate members. The Palace had already made economies, but received little thanks for this, and the Civil List was frozen in 1990 and again in 1997. Further petty slights would follow, most famously the short-sighted decision not to commission a new royal yacht. The monarchy was 'down-sized'.

EUROPE'S 'ENGLISH SITUATIONS'

The other major monarchies of Europe, which the British press portrayed, often wrongly, as less grand and rich than the British, had, sensibly, not aspired to be the glamour or celebrity monarchy that the British monarchy became for a short while in the 1980s, and most had a press that was less sensational and more inclined to allow their royal families some privacy. They were not to escape, however, from gossip and scandal, most of which related to royal marriages.

No one really knows the wealth of the Queen or the British royal family, in part because it's very difficult to disentangle what belongs to the Queen as a head of state and what belongs to her personally, but it's unlikely that she is the richest monarch in Europe. The Netherlands' monarchs are almost certainly richer. Queen Beatrix of the Netherlands, as she was until her abdication in 2013, had a fortune estimated at over £2.5 billion, though at the behest of Prince Bernhard, *Forbes* reduced the estimate in their rich list to $250 million in 2004. Among the royal portfolio of investments is a considerable stake in Royal Dutch Shell. The allowances from the state for the immediate royal family are both generous and untaxed. The House of Windsor may well envy the House of Orange.

All has not, however, been placid for the Dutch monarchy, seen in Britain as low-key, democratic, bicycling and distinctly unglamorous, though it wields more power than the British monarchy. As we have seen, Prince Bernhard was caught up in a business scandal and resigned most of his official appointments in 1976, and there had earlier been initial opposition to Princess Beatrix's choice of a German husband. All Dutch monarchs since the nineteenth century have abdicated for health or personal reasons and there is no reason to doubt that Queen Beatrix's abdication was due to her age and a desire to make way for her son, now King Willem-Alexander, the first King after a long succession of Queens, while he was still comparatively young. The choice of marriage partners is a problem that bedevils modern European royalty. It can be argued that it's much safer to stick to other royalty on the grounds that princesses and princes have the background and experience that fit them for their roles, and that the British experience, with the significant exception of George VI's consort, Queen Elizabeth, points to the dangers of marriages with commoners. Yet in an age when royal offspring attend schools and universities, travel widely and mix with relatively broad sections of at least upper-class society, it becomes ever more difficult to insist on the old endogamous marriage list. Bridegrooms usually did have pasts, and brides now usually do as well. The idea that princes and those who have married princesses should pursue ordinary careers in business is acclaimed in theory, but in practice it is only service in the armed forces that protects princes from allegations of utilising royal rank for unfair business advantage.

Queen Beatrix is reputed to have said that she didn't want any 'English situations', but embarrassments have, nevertheless, arisen. When the then Crown Prince Willem-Alexander, having first had a Dutch girlfriend, whom he met while

studying at university, eventually became engaged to Máxima
Zorreguieta, an Argentinian, the engagement was controversial because her father had been a cabinet minister under the
Argentinian Junta.[1] It was agreed that her parents would not
attend the wedding in 2002. Prince Johan-Friso, second in line
to the throne, seemed to have made an uncontroversial choice
of bride in Mabel Wisse Smit, to whom he became engaged
in 2003. A former Balkans expert at the United Nations, she
had been vetted by the Dutch secret service and approved of
as a suitable bride, but allegations were then made that she had
once been the girlfriend of Klaas Bruinsma, a notorious crime
boss who was killed in a gangland shooting in 1991. As *The
Times* put it, 'Is fairy-tale princess really a gangster's moll?' It
was decided that Prince Johan-Friso and Mabel Wisse Smit
would marry, but that he would give up his place in the line of
succession to the throne. The younger son, Prince Constantjin,
and his cousin, Prince Maurits, have married Dutch upper-
class commoners without controversy. A rather unpleasant
and acrimonious royal feud arose, however, when Queen
Beatrix's niece, Princess Margarita, accused the royal household of trying to undermine her husband, Edwin de Roy Van
Zuydewijn, because he is a commoner. It was not his commoner status but rather his controversial business practices and
his unlawful use of the title 'Baron' that caused the trouble.
There was talk of taped telephone conversations and listen-
ing at keyholes, and the Prime Minister had to intervene to
vouchsafe the Queen's and his government's integrity. 'English
situations' *had* arisen.

King Willem-Alexander came to the throne in 2013. A
graduate of the University of Leiden, he served in the Royal
Netherlands Dutch Navy and is a qualified pilot; during his
mother's reign he regularly flew KLM flights and still does
occasionally. In many ways he is the epitome of the perfect
modern monarch for he, Queen Maxima and their three
daughters live a close family life. His interest and ability in sport

and in international water management are in tune with those of many of his subjects. There have, however, been populist demands for a reduction in the cost of the monarchy. In 2020 the Dutch government bowed to them and ordered a review. The cost of the monarchy to the state, £40.1 million, seems modest compared to that of Britain's, which is £84.6 million, until one considers that the Dutch monarchy has only three active members and the House of Windsor some sixteen working members, with the result that, in 2017–18, the British royal family carried out 3,793 engagements including overseas visits – far more than any European equivalent.[2]

That other major Benelux monarchy, Belgium, has never lacked royal scandals, though on the whole Belgium is a society with a discreet press and a code by which one does not pry into the financial or sexual details of others. The monarchy, like that of the Netherlands, continues to play an active political role, one which that scion of the House of Coburg, Prince Albert, Prince Consort of Britain, would have approved. The King is seen as above politics but has the essential role, in a country noted for the instability of its governments, of being able to intervene between politicians. King Baudouin and his Spanish wife, Queen Fabiola, were able to restore the consensus for the monarchy that had been destroyed by the events of the Second World War and provide one of the few unifying influences for a country split by national and language issues. Baudouin's strong Catholic convictions forced him into the odd position of what amounted to a temporary abdication, or a 'holiday from the throne', when he was faced with having to sign a bill to legalise abortion; the King's convictions were respected.

On Baudouin's death in 1993, there was no obvious successor, as many expected his brother, Prince Albert, seen as a man perfectly satisfied with his agreeable way of life and whose past was supposed to contain some scandal, to stand aside in favour of his son, Phillippe, or his daughter, Astrid. Albert, however, decided to shoulder the responsibilities of kingship, and he and his consort Queen Paola managed to preserve the dignity of both monarchy and state during a period in which many have seen Belgium as a rather dysfunctional society. In this period, to the enduring quarrels of Walloons and Flemings, there has been added a widespread suspicion of the integrity of politicians, bureaucrats, the police and judiciary, in the face of child-abuse scandals and a failure to monitor Islamic terrorist organisations.

The normally discreet Belgian press, or at least the Flemish half of it, made much of the discovery in 1999 that a young Belgian sculptress living in London was said to be the illegitimate daughter of King Albert. The Francophone press made less of this, but there were no official denials. The woman, Delphine Boel, was in her thirties, and Belgians tended to shrug this off as if it was an old scandal, but it embarrassed the royal household. Eventually, as her claim be the ex-King's daughter was shown by a DNA test to be clearly true, she was in 2020 granted the title of Princess of Belgium.

Crown Prince Phillippe's popular marriage to Mathilde d'Udekem d'Acoz in December 1999 helped to take the pressure off the initial scandal, and their grand wedding, attended by representatives of all Europe's reigning royal houses and many who were no longer reigning, together with the Crown Prince and Princess of Japan (for the Japanese royals had long been close to the Belgian Coburgs), reinforced the monarchy's position. Weddings almost always give a fillip to the popularity of monarchies, and that of Phillippe's brother, Prince Laurent, whose lifestyle and unmarried status had long intrigued Belgians, to British-born Claire Coombs in 2003 was also well received. King Philippe ascended to the throne in 2012 and the Belgians, not entirely happy with themselves or their divided country, seemed content enough with their monarchy, which remains a unifying institution.

In general, the Benelux monarchies remained both popular and politically powerful. Luxembourg may be a tiny state but

Grand Duke Henri, who succeeded on his father's abdication in 2000, has probably more political power than any European hereditary ruler, excluding the Prince of Liechtenstein; he both appoints the Prime Minister and shares executive power with the government. The monarchies exemplify a form of constitutional monarchy that gives much more positive political power to the ruler, along the lines of constitutional monarchy conceived by Queen Victoria's Prince Consort, than is exercised by British sovereigns.

Scandinavia is today seen as a rather austere vision of modernity: stripped-pine furniture, stripped-down monarchy and social democracy. Until well into the twentieth century, however, few monarchies were as traditional as these northern kingdoms in their insistence upon court etiquette and upon endogamous royal marriages. It is Sweden above all where constitutional monarchy has moved towards little but symbolic rule, as opposed to Denmark, where important prerogatives are retained, with Norway being more like Sweden, a monarchy presiding over what is essentially a republic. All three kingdoms have moved towards an informal style of monarchy, and, as with so many other European dynasties, they have relaxed their traditions when it comes to the marriage partners of the royal families. Sweden was, surprisingly in view of its reputation for sexual and social equality, relatively tardy about allowing members of the royal family to marry commoners, and it was not until 1980 that Salic law providing only for male succession was set aside.

King Carl XVI Gustav came to the throne in 1973. The previous year he had married Silvia Sommerlath, who had a German father and a Brazilian mother and was acting as Chief Hostess for the Olympic Games in Munich when he met her. With the change to the constitution, which not only permits women to come to the throne but gives them equal status in line of succession, the eldest daughter, Princess Victoria, is heir apparent, rather than her younger brother, Prince Philip.

The Swedish public and media long spared the royal family the intrusions of reporters and paparazzi, and Crown Princess Victoria was able to attend public-sector schools before going on to an independent high school and then to university in the USA. There have been signs that the attentions of the press have quickened, denying princes and princesses the freedom to live the ordinary and down-to-earth lifestyle that has long been proclaimed as the Swedish monarchy's pattern. The Spanish celebrity magazine *¡Hola!* and the Swedish magazine *Se Og Hør* began the trend, publishing stories and pictures of Princesses Victoria and Madeleine, and the rest of the Swedish press has followed. Princess Madeleine's attempt to live a normal life in London while she improved her English had to be cut short after she received incessant attention from paparazzi.

Queen Margrethe of Denmark was crowned the year before King Carl XVI Gustav became King of Sweden. Frederick IX had five daughters but no son, and Princess Margrethe's accession had been provided for by a referendum in 1953 in which Danes voted by a large majority to allow the succession of women. As we have seen, the Danish royal family is related to most of the main royal houses of Europe and is particularly close to the British royal family. Probably the best educated of European monarchs, and something of an intellectual, Queen Margrethe abandoned the family's tendency for ambitious dynastic marriages and married a French diplomat, Henri de Laborde de Monpezat, whom she met while at the London School of Economics; he filled the 'Prince Philip' role with slightly more discretion, but did not quite master Danish.

The Danish monarchy stands out from the other Scandinavian monarchies in two respects: its formality and its political power. Contrary to the view held by much of the British press, the monarchy is highly traditional and ceremonial, while the Queen receives a weekly report from her Prime Minister. The royal palaces befit one of Europe's oldest dynasties, and the Queen of this sea-going kingdom still has a royal yacht, the *Danebrog*.

If they have departed from tradition in not intermarrying with foreign royalty, the Danish royal family have continued to marry foreigners. Prince Joachim, the younger of Margrethe's two sons, married in 1995 the Hong-Kong-born Alexandra Manley, child of an Anglo-Chinese father and an Austrian mother. Beautiful and charming, she was seen as a 'Diana of the North', and the marriage was enormously popular. Crown Prince Frederik postponed his choice of marriage partner until 2003, when he became engaged to an Australian, Mary Donaldson; they married in 2004.

The Swedish and Danish royal families have managed to avoid what Queen Beatrix called 'English situations', but the same has not been true of the Norwegian royals. A branch of the Danish royal family, and a monarchy founded by the unlikely means of a referendum, as well as being one in which monarchs are not crowned but inaugurated, the dynasty had, like its Swedish counterpart, to confront and win over socialist and republican opposition. King Harald V, like so many other Scandinavian princes, married a commoner, but more unusually, a commoner from his own country, Sonja Haraldsen, daughter of a businessman. Their son and heir, Crown Prince Haakon, was to make a more controversial choice of bride. Mette-Marit Tjessem Høiby was a twenty-eight-year-old single mother with a history of involvement with Oslo's drug-fuelled house-party scene when she married Prince Haakon in August 2001. After the first shock of the engagement, Norwegian opinion seems to have rallied behind the bride, whose four-year-old son took part in the wedding ceremony. The support for the marriage was a tribute to the broadmindedness of Norwegian society but did raise the question as to whether there were any limits as to the pasts of royal brides. That there were some limits as to the choice of royal bridegrooms was demonstrated nine months later, when the Prince's elder sister, Princess Martha

Louise, had to renounce her royal privileges when she got engaged to literary dandy Ari Behn. The marriage did not last long and the couple divorced in 2017.

The restored Spanish monarchy looked secure at the beginning of the twenty-first century, with King Juan Carlos enjoying immense respect as the man who had led Spain from Franco's authoritarian rule to democracy without bloodshed.[3] One of the King's early decisions was not to reintroduce the grand and rather gloomy court, rigid with etiquette and tradition, that had for centuries characterised the style of Spanish kings. He made his home La Zarzuela, originally a hunting lodge on the outskirts of Madrid, rather than the royal palace in the city centre, which he used as his place of business. Physically brave and a lover of active sports, as well as fast cars, motor-cycles, helicopters, yachts and planes, he made few concessions to the obvious dangers of his position and was noted for dining out in restaurants and mixing quite informally with friends and subjects. This could be seen as an almost Scandinavian royal style if it were not for the unconscious dignity of his presence, for he was very much a king with a confident belief in monarchy.

The apparent security of the Spanish monarchy was not to last. The immense respect commanded by the king for his skilful handling of the fraught transition from Franco' regime to a more democratic Spain was to be eroded by sexual and financial scandals. It was well established that Juan Carlos was fond of women and had had several affairs since his marriage, something the Spanish newspapers long refrained from discussing, but the modern media are international, and in 1992 French and Italian newspapers published details of an alleged long-term relationship with a resident of Mallorca. This and other stories and rumours did not seem to dint his popularity. The marriage of Princess Elena to Jaime de Marichalar was accompanied by a declaration that his daughter would retain her rights to the succession despite having married a commoner, and the birth of a son to the couple seemed to secure the dynasty, even though the heir to the throne, Prince Felipe, Prince of the Asturias, had not yet married. Handsome, intelligent and well educated, he inherited his father's love of sport and new technology, and perhaps his fondness for beautiful women. The Spanish press is no longer as discreet as it was, for Spain is, after all, the home of the magazine *¡Hola!*, and it has eagerly charted the Prince's many girlfriends, film star Gwyneth Paltrow and Norwegian lingerie model Eva Sannum among them. The pressure on him to marry a royal princess was considerable, with his mother Queen Sofía, the daughter of King Paul of Greece, in particular, adamant that he should do so. His engagement to a divorced journalist, Letizia Ortiz, proved controversial, especially when *El Mundo* published photographs of a mural by a Mexican artist that contained a bare-breasted figure that was reputedly the Prince's fiancée. Nevertheless, the Spanish public seemed to have accepted the Prince's choice by the time of the wedding in May 2004.

It was the not-so-private life and financial dealings of Juan Carlos that was to destroy the prestige of royalty, bringing to an end the long period during which the monarchy had seemed more secure than any of the political parties. Indeed, 2012 has been termed Spain's own '*annus horribilis*'. The effects of the recession, which began in 2008 and was particularly severe in Spain, tested all Spain's institutions and fanned the flames of Catalan separatism, but a number of scandals made the monarchy particularly vulnerable. The worst of them was the accusation that the King's son-in-law, a commoner elevated to Duc de Palma de Mallorca, had been engaged in money laundering and had been using his royal connections in the pursuit of personal gain, a charge which aroused considerable anger at a time when the country was in recession. The others were new revelations about the King's romantic attachments and the publication in the press of photographs of Juan Carlos posing, gun by his side, in front of a recently shot elephant.

The Spanish public was well aware that the monarch had had a number of affairs and that he enjoyed shooting big game, but again the timing was wrong. While the Spanish were not noted for their support of animal rights, the photograph was, to say the least, not appropriate for the patron of the World Wildlife Fund.

Maybe, after his struggle to gain the throne and his major success in steering Spain skilfully towards constitutional monarchy after the Franco years, Juan Carlos had lost his touch. Perhaps he realised this, for in 2014 he abdicated in favour of his son, who became Felipe VI – though Juan Carlos's mistress, Corinna zu Sayn-Wittgenstein, claims that the abdication was more of a *coup d'etat*, mounted by Queen Sofia and the then Prime Minister Mariano Rajoy. The ex-King, who left Spain in August 2020 and is now living in Abu Dhabi, has been accused of having transferred over £59 million to Ms Sayn-Wittgenstein. He also faces charges relating to a £6.7 billion rail deal in Saudi Arabia. Complaining about her treatment by the Spanish public and press, Sayn-Wittgenstein has compared her position to that of Wallis Simpson. British precedents are indeed frequently invoked when it comes to the travails of European monarchies. Whether Juan Carlos will even be allowed to return to live in Spain is in doubt for it has been suggested that his son has now banished him from the kingdom. King Felipe now faces the formidable task of restoring the popularity the monarchy enjoyed during the earlier years of his father's reign.[4]

The collapse of the Soviet Union and its eastern European empire saw many royal exiles who had lost their throne in the wake of the Second World War re-evaluating their chances of regaining them. Former kings Michael of Romania and Simeon of Bulgaria intimated their availability as rulers, as did Prince Laka, son of King Zog of the Albanians. Even the Romanovs squabbled over who was the rightful pretender to the imperial throne of Russia. Both Michael, who is seen to have served Romania bravely, and Simeon, who was only a boy when he was forced to abdicate, were undoubtedly popular. Michael faced strong opposition from the post-Communist regime, which put its own interests above a restoration and placed obstacles in the way of his return. Simeon, by contrast, not only returned to his country but entered politics and served as Bulgaria's Prime Minister from 2001 to 2005. In 2020 he won a court case which gave him ownership of the royal palace, Tsarska Bistritsa. The possibility of these monarchs or their descendants (Michael died in 2017) restoring the throne in nations still divided and unstable after years of Communist rule seems remote, despite the respect in which they were held. Yet, as Jeremy Paxman has written, 'those countries in eastern Europe which were occupied by the Soviet Union after the Second World War … found that much of their history had ceased to exist along with their monarchies'.[5]

THE MIDDLE AND FAR EAST: MONARCHY AND RELIGION

Europe, we are told, is today very much a secular and post-Christian society, just as it is no longer a hierarchical society. Yet, if it has become accepted that princes or princesses may marry commoners of their own or other nationalities, and only tiny Liechtenstein now excludes women from the throne, it is still the general convention that the marriage partner must be of the religious denomination that is the tradition of the royal house, or must convert to that Christian denomination. In many cases this is stipulated in national constitutions, as with Denmark, Norway and Sweden, which insist that the sovereign must be a Lutheran, and Britain, which declares more loosely that he or she must be a Protestant. In other cases, it is axiomatic, if technically undeclared, that the sovereign should follow the religion of previous sovereigns. To the liberal mind this is a hangover from an intolerant past and an insult to other denominations or faiths within the national polity. This mindset is shallow and, with its mechanistic approach to monarchy as to other aspects of national unity and tradition, ignores the power of the past, which is a primary creator of national identity. The Dutch monarchy's origins and those of the state of the Netherlands itself are inextricably tied up with those of the Dutch Reformed Church, and even though there is a large Catholic population within the contemporary nation, for a king or queen not to be a member of the Reformed Church would be a denial of the national past. Only in Monaco and Liechtenstein do the constitutions declare that the sovereign must be Roman Catholic, but it is inconceivable that either a King of the Belgians or a King of Spain could belong to another religion and, in the latter case, King Felipe still formally has the title, though he rarely uses it, of His Most Catholic Majesty.

Islam and Monarchy

The question of a ruler who was anything but Muslim would, of course, never arise in any Islamic kingdom, for the creation of the conditions in which the community can lead good Islamic lives is part of the very purpose of the state. As queenship is a concept remote from Arab and Muslim traditions, and succession to the crown is much less securely tied to the eldest son of the reigning king, questions relating to marriage have not been important in the world of Islamic monarchies. Some forms of Islam can be puritanical and austere, but not in relation to sex so far as men are concerned. It is not just press censorship but rather social, cultural and religious traditions that have spared the remaining Islamic monarchies the sexual scandals and marital problems that have plagued their European counterparts. It was not so much King Farouk's well-known passion for call girls, but the westernised and public way in which he indulged in this and his other vices that made him a target of ridicule within Egypt. While many monarchs, emirs and sultans have largely continued with polygamous traditions, the late King Hussein of Jordan contented himself with several consecutive marriages on a modern Western pattern.

The problems of Islamic monarchies have largely been political and religious, or rather religious–political, for the two are entwined. As we have seen, the republican and secular form of Arab nationalism abated with the death of Nasser, leaving the opposed Baathist republics of Syria and Iraq, together with the Palestine Liberation Organisation, to uphold its traditions. The main problem at the beginning of the twenty-first century came from the resurgence of fundamentalist Islam. The Khomeini revolution, which overthrew the Shah of Iran, had been the first clear sign of the strength of an angry and vengeful Islamic movement, enraged by the weakness of Islamic societies in the face of Western power and further inflamed by Western influence within these societies. The Iranian revolution had many effects: it fanned anti-Western feeling throughout the Islamic world; it provided an Islamic republican model; and it exacerbated the old enmity between Sunni and Shi'ite. It thus provided problems for all Islamic monarchies, but particularly for Saudi Arabia, an Islamic kingdom with close connections with the USA trying to combine modernisation with traditional Islamic values.

The contradictions of Saudi Arabia are many, not least the spectacle of the princes of the royal house motoring to the Gulf states or flying to London to enjoy the pleasures and lifestyles of the Western world it is the mission of the dynasty to protect the kingdom against. In 1980, Westerners were shocked and horrified by a 'factional' TV dramatisation of the attempted elopement of a married Saudi princess and her lover, and their subsequent public execution, when they were respectively shot and beheaded for their adultery. If Saudi attitudes to women offend Western sensibilities, the presence of so many Westerners in the kingdom and the mild degree to which they are able to maintain Western and non-Islamic customs within the gates of their compounds infuriates the ultra-faithful. That American troops, including uniformed women, were stationed in the country that includes the holy places during and after the Gulf War was found especially insulting. Whether the Saudi monarchy can maintain a balance between ruling in consultation with the *ulema* and maintaining its close associations with the USA is, especially after 9/11 and subsequent Al-Qaeda bombings in the kingdom, a question with profound implications for all Islamic monarchies.

The very terms 'King' and 'Kingdom' are somewhat at variance with Saudi tradition. The emirs (the word means 'one who commands') who became kings in the post-First World War period did so largely to claim equality with Western monarchs. The Arab word for a king, *malik*, had not always carried positive connotations, and could stand for arbitrary personal rule. Arab kings have not gone in for coronations, in recognition of Muslim and Arab tradition, which sees the authority of the ruler as based upon an agreement between rulers and the ruled within the context of the enforcement of Islamic law. Kings have often preferred to be known by their religious title, 'Guardian of the Two Holy Places'.

The major problems facing the Saudi monarchy are Islamic fundamentalist terrorism, the challenge from Iran, and how to maintain a close relationship with the USA and other Western powers while maintaining religious and cultural purity. The former is a particular problem, given the fact that Islamic fundamentalism is inseparable from Saudi history and identity, and Wahhabism was a progenitor of terrorist groups such as Al-Qaeda and ISIS. The second is more straightforward in that hostility between Saudi Arabia and Iran represents the divide from Islam's earliest years between Sunni and Shia, but is complicated by the presence in allied Sunni states of Shia minorities. The third poses the problem as to whether strict obedience to religious doctrine is compatible with modernisation and alliance with the West.

With the death of King Abdullah in 2015, the usual problems of the Saudi succession system came to the fore. He
was succeeded by Salman bin Abdulaziz, who decided that
the man hitherto proclaimed as his heir was not fit to be his
successor and that the Crown Prince should be Mohammed
bin Salman. The decision was widely welcomed in the West
as the Prince, then twenty, was perceived as a moderniser
who would move the state towards greater democracy and
improve the position of women. Despite some modest
reforms, such as allowing women to drive unaccompanied
by a male relative, such hopes were dispelled by the assassination of journalist Jamal Ahmad Khashoggi, an opponent of
the regime, in the Saudi Consulate in Istanbul. It was widely
believed that the murder could not have taken place without
at least the tacit consent of the Crown Prince. The stability of the Saudi monarchy seemed shakier with its failure
to ensure the victory of the Yemeni government over Shia-
backed rebel forces and by the successful Iranian attack on
Saudi oilfields in 2019.

With the overthrow of the Iraq monarchy in 1958, it seemed
only a matter of time before the other Hashemite monarchy of Jordan went the same way. King Hussein, who had
seen his grandfather, King Abdullah, shot by an assassin, was,
however, to demonstrate an extraordinary ability to survive, despite the great disadvantage to the monarchy of the
enlargement of the country's population by Palestinians who
had little love for the Hashemite dynasty. His survival was
due to the loyalty of the Bedouin, his own courage and ability, and a more than fair amount of luck. With Hussein the
hereditary principle found justification, producing a leader
with as much ability and decisiveness as any Arab president
but, unlike most of his republican rivals, a man who was a
servant of his people. With his death in 1999, the odd character, by European standards, of Middle Eastern succession

systems was demonstrated when, just before his death, King Hussein put aside his younger brother, Hassan, who had been Crown Prince for many years, in favour of his son, who succeeded him as King Abdullah II. Abdullah proved an able monarch and the programme of economic liberalisation he launched proved successful in attracting foreign investment and generally improving the economy and standard of living of Jordanians, while he continued with his father's foreign policy of maintaining peaceful relations with Israel. Like the Arab world as a whole, the kingdom was shaken by the Arab Spring – a spring that did not precede a peaceful summer – and saw large-scale protests and demands for constitutional and economic reforms, to which the King acceded. Nothing is more dangerous than introducing reforms at a time of turbulence while maintaining strong control, and Jordan was also faced with the hostile forces of Islamic fundamentalist terrorism and civil war in neighbouring Syria, which resulted in its having to cope with a vast influx of refugees. No Arab monarchy (or, indeed, government) can be considered safe, but Jordan's monarchs have proved resilient.

With the Beys of Tunis and the Kings of Libya departed, Morocco remains the only kingdom in the Maghreb. Conquered by Arabs in the seventh century, it, unlike its neighbours, never quite became part of the Ottoman Empire and retained a qualified independence before the colonial period. With the end of French rule, it emerged in 1956 as an independent kingdom, and both an Arab and an Islamic state, which is a member of the League of Arab States. Aramaic is its official language alongside Berber, though French is the language of business and government. As with most Islamic monarchies, the King's role has a religious dimension signified by his title of 'Commander of the Faithful'. Although formally a constitutional monarchy, King Mohammed VI wields considerably more power than most constitutional monarchs. Though shaken by the Arab Spring it survives.

The Asian Survivors

The two most significant monarchies of East Asia, the Japanese and the Thai monarchies, present an interesting contrast to each other as well as to Western monarchies. The one remains largely withdrawn, continues to be surrounded by strict court ritual and fulfils an important but largely symbolic constitutional role. The other is politically important and very conspicuous, providing positive leadership in all aspects of Thai life. Both are intrinsic to the national identities of their countries.

The death in 1989 of Emperor Hirohito, the Showa Emperor and supposedly the 124th imperial ruler, was, unsurprisingly, the occasion of much comment as to the nature, purpose and future of the Japanese emperor system. His reign of sixty-three years had seen Japan's expansion and then its surrender, the American occupation and a new constitution devised to take from the Emperor his near-divine status and make Japan a democracy with a largely symbolic sovereign. Economic recovery and then heady economic growth had followed, and the so-called 'bubble economy', which briefly, with the Yen so strong and real estate prices so high, was supposed to value the grounds of the Imperial Palace as worth more than the State of California, was at its height at the time of his death.

How much did the monarchy matter? Was it a comforting link with the past, important to the older generation but largely irrelevant to the young? Was it, as many on the Left, both within Japan and abroad, saw it, an obstacle to genuine democracy and a revaluation of Japan's past? In modern Japan legitimacy was supposed to come from the will of the people rather than from the Emperor. Was the Emperor, like the King of Sweden, merely a symbolic gilding on a business-like, urban and increasingly secular society? Did he alternatively still represent the spirit of the nation?

The funeral of the Showa Emperor and the coronation ceremonies of his son and successor were themselves indicative of the priestly nature of the Japanese monarchy and controversial for some, who saw in them a denial of the secular nature of the Japanese state in that they demonstrated the close links between Shintoism, the state and the imperial family. The ceremonies and rituals also raised the question as to whether they contradicted Emperor Hirohito's 1946 repudiation of his divinity.

The most important ritual in the long succession of nearly sixty ceremonies that laid to rest Hirohito and brought Emperor Akihito to the throne was the *Daijosai*, or 'great food offering'. The essential content of this ceremony is as follows: after a year of mourning for the dead emperor, Shinto priests break tortoise shells and, according to the cracks that appear, pick two paddy fields, where sacred rice is planted. The rice having been harvested, the night-long ceremony takes place, with the Emperor, bearing the sacred regalia, entering a pavilion, specially built for the occasion, and awaiting the arrival of the gods of heaven and earth, to whom he offers food and partakes of it himself. What happens next can be told in two ways, one analogous to a Catholic peasant's understanding of the role of the host in the Eucharist, the other similar to a Jesuit academic's explanation to an Oxford undergraduate. Either the Emperor is mystically transformed into a temple maiden, has intercourse with the spirits, becomes pregnant and is reborn as a god, or, in a more sophisticated and essentialist description, the Emperor's night of prayer and meditation results in his transformation into one uniquely imbued with the spirit of the nation and fitted to guide its fortunes. The latter description surely expresses the universal essence of monarchy.

In Western societies the concept of a symbolic monarchy tends to suggest a diminished role for sovereigns, given the long history of kingship as wielder of executive power. For the Japanese monarchy, for so many centuries essentially symbolic, cultural and priestly, albeit the final source of legitimacy, the

move away from political power can be seen as a return to
tradition. As one Japanese writer has put it:

> Human society is a system of symbols, a realm in which
> symbolic meaning holds sway. The sacred meaning that
> attaches itself to the highest of a society's symbols is that
> which preserves the society's continuity and unity. This is
> true in any culture. The historical underpinnings of the
> imperial institution may be unique to Japan, but its spiritual
> underpinnings are universal.[1]

It is largely the priestly and cultural role of the monarchy
that has prevented it from becoming a public and casual
monarchy, a monarchy of walkabouts and banter and chats
with subjects. Every decade there are suggestions that the
monarchy may become less formal and more like the British
monarchy. Emperor Hirohito embarked on a series of visits
around the country in the immediate post-war years, took
on charitable duties, and visited factories and hospitals, but
after the end of the occupation he returned to a much more
private way of life. The then Crown Prince Akihito's marriage to Michiko Shoda in 1959 had seemed to herald a more
informal monarchy, and the couple attracted unprecedented
press publicity, but, although it was a most successful marriage, the pressure of court officials in favour of formality and
strict etiquette was successful in constraining further moves
towards informality. Japanese royals are able to be at their most
relaxed when abroad, especially when in the company of foreign royalty, such as the Belgian royal family, with whom they
have close ties. It was perhaps with this in mind that Crown
Prince Akihito decided that his son, Prince Naruhito, should
go to Oxford as a postgraduate. In 1994 Prince Naruhito,
by then Crown Prince himself, married Masako Owada, an
ex-diplomat educated at Oxford and Harvard, but even this
thoroughly modern career woman disappeared behind the

so-called 'Chrysanthemum Curtain' by which the Imperial Household Agency obscures the lives of members of the imperial family from public view.

The Agency's ability to control the media was well illustrated at the time of the pregnancy of Crown Princess Masako in 2001, when it managed to persuade the newspapers and magazines to keep relatively quiet about the pregnancy in the weeks before she gave birth. The frenzy of the media had been blamed for causing the Princess to miscarry in 1999. The birth of a baby girl, Princess Aiko, was well received, but presaged problems as to the succession, for the nineteenth-century constitution stipulates that only males can succeed to the throne, and the Crown Prince's brother, Prince Akishino, has only daughters. Considering that there have been empresses regnant in Japanese history, one would have thought that there would be little problem in altering the late nineteenth-century constitution, and indeed consultations have taken place with the royal families of Belgium, Holland and Denmark, all of which have passed laws to enable queens to reign.

The Japanese monarchy has been a cautious institution, which has maintained its dignity. The Household Agency has been much criticised for keeping the royal family apart from society as a whole, but it has avoided the pitfalls of over-exposure that the British royal family has fallen into. A rather secluded monarchy is perhaps in keeping with Japanese trad-itions. A more active monarchy, which expressed its views on social questions, would be contentious, and while a more informal and open monarchy would undoubtedly be initially popular, it would detract from the imperial dynasty's central symbolic role. The pressure on the Household Agency to relax the stifling protocol and isolation it inflicts upon the royal family is, however, mounting. It was much increased by the mental breakdown of Princess Masako after the birth of her daughter. Crown Prince Naruhito had in unprecedented statements talked of the transformation of his wife from a confident diplomat to an unhappy woman, a prisoner in her own home.[2]

When, in 2010, Emperor Akihito informed his advisory council that he would eventually like to retire, a further complication arose, for there was no provision in the constitution for the abdication of an emperor, even though several emperors had abdicated in Japan's long history before the Meiji period. Almost ignoring the Emperor's expressed wish, the Imperial Household Agency took no action and when, in 2016, the national broadcaster reported that the Emperor wished to abdicate, senior officials denied that there was any plan for him to do so. It took a rare televised address from Akihito to force the cabinet office to take steps to implement his wishes, leading to the passing of a bill by the National Diet in June 2017 allowing him to abdicate. The abdication, marking the end of Akihito's thirty years on the Chrysanthemum Throne, took place on 30 April 2019 and Akihito and his wife received the respective titles of Joko (Emperor Emeritus) and Jokogo (Empress Emeritus). On 1 May, Akihito's eldest son, Naruhito, acceded to the throne and Akihito's younger son, Akishino, became Crown Prince. The name of the new era, Reiwa, meaning 'beautiful harmony' (in succession to Heisei), had already been announced at the beginning of April and the lengthy and complex procedures leading to the enthronement in October began. On his accession the new Emperor stated:

> I swear that I will reflect deeply on the course followed by His Majesty the emperor Emeritus and bear in mind the path trodden by past emperors, and will devote myself to self-improvement. I also swear that I will act according to the Constitution and fulfil my responsibilities as the symbol of the State and of the unity of the people of Japan.

In contrast to Japan and to the general trend in the world's monarchies, the monarchy of Thailand has seen the power of the king increase substantially since the early 1970s. The military had, since the overthrow of the absolute monarchy in 1932, maintained the monarchy, not so much because they wished to but because they recognised the benefits of royal charisma and sought to exploit it for their own purposes. Regimes needed the apparent support of the monarchy for legitimacy and fed off its capacity as a patriotic and unifying force. King Bhumibol's reign started under a cloud owing to the fact that it was widely believed that he had killed his brother and predecessor with a single pistol shot, even though this was almost certainly an accident. For the first decades of King Bhumibol's reign the monarchy remained largely passive but from the 1970s he emerged as a powerful and positive figure, able to act as a buffer and a force for compromise between the military and democratic forces. In 1981 he faced down what was named the April Fools' Day Coup by leaving Bangkok and raising the royal standard at a military base, while in the 1980s and 1990s the monarchy emerged as the main force for unity in the kingdom and the protector of a democratic constitution. He effectively presided over the country's powerful groups, the military, and the financial and industrial elites, and retained the support of the urban and rural poor, who saw him as a paternalist.

In retrospect we can see King Bhumibol as a shrewd political operator who first flexed his muscles and then used his position to shape the course of national affairs. The military had sought to utilise the monarchy by building it up as an anti-Communist force, encouraging the King to make tours of the provinces, identify himself with religion and stress his role as the protector of the peasantry. At the same time the position of the army was progressively weakened by a decrease in US financial support after the end of the Vietnam War, and also by the withering of support for Thai Communism, an aim of the army's that, ironically, when realised, destroyed at least some of its *raison d'être*. Just as the military revolution of 1932 had been to some extent the work of new social groups, brought into being by the reforms and modernisation programmes of the Chakri kings, so the opposition to the military in the late twentieth century was in part caused by the development of new social classes, for which the students were the shock troops. Thailand saw rapidly alternating periods of elected government and of rule by military strongmen until the early nineties. The King, who in 1973, the year of Thailand's student revolutions, was in his forties and in the twenty-seventh year of his reign, was increasingly a key figure, needed by any section that aspired to form a legitimate government. Implacably anti-Communist, but at the same time pro-democratic, the King moved cautiously and was careful not to alienate the army.

The year 1992 saw the culmination of what had become a seesaw of military and then civilian governments when troops were ordered to fire on pro-democracy demonstrators. What has been called Thailand's 'Tiananmen Square' was followed by the abasement before the King of the Prime Minister, General Suchinda, and the leader of the demonstrators, Colonel Chamlong, who were both ordered to pull back from confrontation. An active monarchy had returned.

The new constitution of 1997 came into being in the circumstances of the Asian economic crisis of 1997/8. A mixture of royal paternalism and democracy by which the people are both enfranchised and protected by a framework of laws, the constitution gives a special place to the guiding hand of the monarchy. This is a form of democracy that overtly recognises pillars of the state, the army, the state bureaucracy, the Buddhist religion, and the throne itself.

The reasons for the powerful position of the monarchy go beyond the undoubted political achievements and great popularity of King Bhumibol. Though the hallowed nature of the monarch and the royal family is no longer emphasised, many subjects seem still to be influenced by the older views of God-Kings, while the number of great ceremonies associated with the monarchy's national and religious roles has increased. What was almost a cult arose around the adulation of the King's late mother, a commoner like the late Queen Elizabeth, the Queen Mother; her lying-in-state, which lasted for eleven months, and her cremation in 1996 were an orchestration of national mourning and reverence. With the ceremony and pomp with which it marks royal lifecycles, celebrating jubilees and the monarch's birthdays, and the enthusiasm with which the royal family embraces causes such as the environment and its conservation and places itself at the head of charities, the monarchy has, save for its active political role, much in common with its British counterpart in that it embodies the essence of the nation.

A new threat to the stability of Thailand emerged in the 2000s in the shape of the immensely rich mobile-phone magnate Thaksin Shinawatra and his Thai Rak Thai party, which promised populist reforms. Thai Rak Thai won electoral victories in 2001 and 2005, but a military coup in 2014 – the twelfth since 1932 – saw the dismissal of a caretaker government after six months of civil unrest and the establishment of a military government, the National Council for Peace and Order, headed by General Prayut Chan-o-cha, the Commander of the Royal Thai Army. The King may not have initially approved of the coup or the NCPO – at first, it was reported that he had merely acknowledged it – but he then proceeded to appoint General Prayut as Prime Minister and tacitly supported the exiling of Thaksin two years later. A national referendum on a new constitution, giving the military considerable authority, was held in 2016 and was approved by a 6 per cent majority. It seems clear that the monarch's authority played a considerable part in gaining public support for the constitution. Nevertheless, Thailand faced an uncertain future and had deep social and political divisions: between the countryside and the towns, between those who have prospered during the years of economic expansion and those left behind, between the military and political parties, and between the red-shirted followers of the ousted premier, Thaksin, and the yellow-shirted royalists.

A system of monarchy which gives considerable executive power to the monarch has advantages when the person on the throne is experienced and deeply respected. Even when the monarch is merely competent, but uses his powers cautiously, his position is protected by the dignity and mystique that surrounds his office. With the death of King Bhumibol in 2016 and the accession of his son, Maha Vajiralongkorn, however, many have questioned whether this less charismatic successor, who has a somewhat eccentric history, can preserve the power, influence and adulation that his father inspired. While he was Crown Prince, Maha rarely spoke in public or performed royal duties, and spent much of his time in Germany.

He has been described as something of a narcissist and, fond of alternating Ruritanian uniforms and tight jeans, his behaviour has often been bizarre. One authority on the Thai monarchy has seen him as a latter-day Caligula:

> In 2009 the then Crown Prince promoted his pet miniature poodle Foo Foo to the post of air chief marshal in which capacity he served until his death in 2015 at the age of seventeen. Foo Foo's cremation was preceded by four days of formal Buddhist mourning.[3]

The first years of his reign have drawn attention to the complex nature of the position of queens and consorts in Thailand. Kings were historically polygamous with consorts appointed in addition to queens, but until Vajiralongkorn, the title of consort had fallen into desuetude. One of his first acts was to declare his fourth wife, Suthida Tidjai, Queen, but he followed this by marrying his bodyguard Sineenat Wongvajirapakdi, and appointing her Consort, only to strip her of the title in 2019, apparently because of her ambition to become a second queen. The ex-Consort immediately became a non-person with her name removed from the palace website, until in 2020 the *Royal Gazette* announced that 'it will be regarded that she was never stripped of the royal consort title'.

The King seems determined to be a strong ruler. His image covers billboards in Bangkok and a video of him is played before film screenings in cinemas. Criticism of him is forbidden, and he has brought elite army units under his direct command. Somewhat bizarrely, he has continued the habit he formed when Crown Prince of spending much of his time in Bavaria, incurring the disapproval of Germany's then Chancellor Angela Merkel, who found having a foreign head of state ruling his country from her domains irregular.

The mystique of the Thai monarchy remains strong, however, and the alternatives of instability and military rule are unattractive. Whether even a distinctly eccentric king can destroy the concept of the monarchy as symbolic of the ethos of the nation and a unifying force remains to be seen, although the emergence of student protests and large demonstrations calling for a curtailing of royal powers suggest this is being put to the test.

The endurance in the very different ways of the Japanese and Thai monarchies stands out against a background of monarchical decline in the rest of Asia. Only in oil-rich Brunei – a 'Shellfare' state, as it has been termed, with some similarities to the Arab monarchies, which depend upon oil revenues – can we find another example of a stable monarchy. Like its Arab counterparts, Brunei has had its problems, not least in the financial misappropriations and sexual scandals attached to one member of the royal family, Prince Jeffri, but also the difficulties of reconciling absolute monarchy, Islamic virtue and Western influences. Enough of the vast oil revenues have, however, been spent on the infrastructure, health and education to keep the population prosperous and loyal, while the investment of much of the revenues may ensure future economic and political stability.

By comparison the Malay monarchies have seen their political influence decline, and even their symbolic positions questioned, during the long periods of office of Dr Mahathir Mohammad (Prime Minister 1981–2003 and 2018–20). A study of monarchies in South-East Asia has argued that:

> There could be no greater contrast than between Dr Mahathir's success in grinding down the residual royal prerogatives since 1983 and the subtle elaboration of the royal prerogative by King Bhumibol since 1973.[4]

Malaysia nevertheless remains a monarchy, though a distinctly odd one as the role of monarch is alternated between the monarchs of the nine different states which make up the federation. The powers of the incumbent, who is sometimes referred to as the King, are limited, with real authority residing in the office of Prime Minister.

This lack of royal power of these temporary kings may be something of a blessing to them considering the stormy and corrupt nature of Malay politics. If the lengthy periods as Prime Minister enjoyed by Dr Mahathir enabled him to diminish royal power, he also used his position during his first term in office to have his main rival, Anwar Ibrahim, sentenced to ten years in prison for sodomy and corruption before his own dismissal in 2003. The second term of the nonagenarian politician ended with his surprise resignation in 2020. He was at the time the oldest serving state leader. Despite the King's pardoning of Anwar in 2018 and Dr Mahathir's identification of him as his likely successor, complex wrangling and shifting party alliances resulted in another politician, Muhyiddin Yassin, becoming Prime Minister, albeit strongly opposed by Anwar.

The constitutional crisis brought the remaining powers of the present titular ruler, Yang di-Pertuan Agong, the ruler of Penang, into its centre. His role is to offer the office of Prime Minister to whomsoever he considers has sufficient support in the federal assembly to form a government, but his task is a formidable one for a number of reasons: the assembly is bicameral; all the states have their own governments and parliaments; and state elections, determining whom states send to the federal assembly, can shift the political balance. The situation is further complicated by the desire of ethnic Malays to have a federal government which represents their interests over those of other ethnic groups. Malaysian politics are as complex as its constitution. With reduced majority support in parliament, Muhyiddin and his cabinet submitted their resignation to the King in August 2021, thus continuing the political wrangling that has characterised Malaysian politics in recent years.

With the exception of Thailand, the monarchies of Indo-China were the victims of the Second World War and Vietnam War, with the Vietnamese and Laotian monarchies disappearing in the wake of the latter conflict. Cambodia remains technically a constitutional monarchy but it is, in practice, a corrupt one-party state with real power in the hands of its premier, Han Sen, once a member of the bizarre and murderous Khmer Rouge regime. That great survivor King Sihanouk hung on for long, being successively a protégé of the French, the Japanese and the French again, as well as an independent sovereign – sometimes absolutist, sometimes a constitutionalist, but always a populist. Even he, able to adapt to events, found it impossible to steer a consistent course. His prestige was useful even to that extraordinary and blackly bizarre movement the Khmer Rouge during its bloody period of rule, and the monarchy was restored in 1993. He reigned but did not rule in uneasy alliance with Hun Sen, who appeared to need the legitimacy the King gave to his Cambodian

People's Party's government, until Sihanouk's final abdication in October 2004. He was succeeded as king by Prince Sihamoni, a bachelor and aesthete, chosen by a 'throne council', but real power remains with Han Sen.

The two mountain kingdoms of Nepal and Bhutan, and what was the kingdom of Sikkim, have had a history of uneasy relations with their neighbours India and China. All bear the imprint of the great religions that originated in India and have the aura of theocracy. Nepal is the only Hindu kingdom, while Bhutan is Lamaist Buddhist, and Sikkim was, from the seventeenth until the late twentieth century, ruled by Buddhist priest kings. Nepal's links with India are close but not friendly, and Bhutan, which for long enjoyed the benefits of its isolation, has had to deal with unwanted immigrants and dissident guerrillas from India, while, as with Sikkim, its natural ties with Tibet have been cut by Tibet's absorption into China.

The tradition of divided authority is deep seated in the Himalayas. It was only in 1951 that the 100-year-old rule by a hereditary dynasty of Prime Ministers, which reduced the kingship to a symbolic and spiritual role, came to an end in Nepal.

Bhutanese history was even more complicated. From the seventeenth century, when Lamaist Buddhism came to Bhutan from Tibet, a monastic theocracy prevailed thereafter, with power shared between the premier spiritual authority, the Dharma Rajah, and the Deb Rajah, to whom civil authority was delegated, while ultimate authority resided in Tibet. The British, somewhat frustrated by the lack of an obvious ruler with whom to deal, supported Ugyen Wangchuk, a powerful provincial governor, who emerged in the early twentieth century as both Chief Abbot and 'Dragon King'.

In Sikkim, however, the priest kings, the Chogyal, established in the seventeenth century, continued to be the effective rulers after the kingdom became a protectorate of the Indian Empire. The dynasty continued to preside over a state with similar protectorate status in the early years of independent India, until it became nominally independent in 1975. Sikkim's situation was therefore similar to that of Bhutan, but with the complication that, although the official religion of the state was Buddhist, it had a large Hindu population.

All these kingdoms experienced strains and crises after Indian independence, with Nepal in particular seeing clashes between the absolute monarchy and more-or-less republican movements. Few could have foreseen, however, the Jacobean drama that took place in Nepal in 2001.

Princes and guns, like princesses and motor cars, have not mixed well. The Spanish Prince Juan Carlos accidentally killed his brother Prince Alfonso in 1956 while he was playing with a revolver, and there has never been a satisfactory account of the death of the young King Ananda of Thailand in a mysterious shooting accident in 1946. Such events pale in comparison to the massacre of King Bihendra and Queen Aishwarya of Nepal, two of their children and ten other relatives by Crown Prince Dipendra in June 2001. The motives of the Crown Prince, who strode into the room where his relatives were gathered and let rip with a sub-machine gun and then other guns, are obscure, though it is known that he was angry that his parents refused to allow him to marry the girl he wished to be his bride. He seems, in any case, to have been inflamed by whisky and marijuana. Having killed most of his family, he then retreated to his bedroom and shot himself. He survived for two days, during which, with bizarre fidelity to the hereditary principle, he was declared King of Nepal.

The Nepalese royal family had not previously been seen as dysfunctional and, indeed, Veronica Maclean, in her book *Crowned Heads*, had described a close and affectionate family who had stayed with the Macleans in Scotland and had entertained her generously on her visit to Nepal.[5] The effect upon the only Hindu kingdom in the world was, not surprisingly, traumatic. It greatly weakened the position of both the monarchy and the successor to the throne. King Gyanendra, an uncle of the regicide, who was absent the day of the massacre, was regarded with some suspicion and was unable to rehabilitate the tarnished image of a monarchy already beset by, of all things, a Maoist rebellion. The unhappy kingdom was beset by a tripartite struggle, with King Gyanendra's direct rule challenged by political parties, and both harassed by the Maoist rebels. In 2008 Nepal became a republic.

The recent history of the Bhutan monarchy has also been somewhat melodramatic. It includes the murder in 1964 of a Prime Minister, Jigme Palden Dorji, a member of a family that had long served as the monarchy's agent and conductor of foreign affairs – yet another example of the proclivity of Himalayan kingdoms to delegate responsibilities. The circumstances involved the tensions between King Jigme Dorji Wangchuck (ruled 1952–72), the Queen and the King's mistress, and the almost inevitable sequel was an attempt upon the King's life that was suspected to have been planned by the supporters of Palden and the Queen's household. The King's successor, Jigme Singye Wangchuck, gradually moved towards a more democratic form of government and abdicated in favour of his son in 2006, leaving it to him to oversee further democratisation. A major preoccupation with maintaining the country's culture, identity and religion in the face of immigration from India and Nepal has resulted in a national policy of insisting that non-ethnic Bhutanese adopt the native form of Buddhism and a hard line against illegal immigrants from Nepal and India has led to tensions both internally and with neighbouring states.

Shortly before his accession, the then Crown Prince had to be recalled from his studies in Britain to assist in operations against Indian secessionists, who were using Bhutan as a national base. Nevertheless, conscious that the stability of this theocratic kingdom depends both on relations with his powerful neighbours, India and China, both the former and present King have managed to steer a course between the two. For long a policy of keeping a distance from the more insidious influences of the modern world resulted in hostility to tourism, but under the present monarch, King Jigme Khesar Namgyel Wangchuck, the appeal of Bhutan for adventurous tourism has been recognised and regulated. Jigme continues to reign as Dragon King in what is probably the world's most isolated state and, along with Thailand, one of the last two Buddhist monarchies.

There would have been three, were it not for the fall of the Sikkim monarchy. The prospects for the Indian protectorate (as it became after the end of British indirect rule) appeared good as it had one of the region's higher per capita incomes and rates of literacy among Himalayan states. Its large Hindu population did, however, make for discontent with the Buddhist theocratic monarchy – a discontent fanned by the Indian government, which, although accepted by Jawaharlal Nehru, was resented by his daughter and successor Indira Gandhi, who had little time for a semi-independent monarchy, let alone one with a long relationship with Tibet and China, on India's frontier. Whether the deposition of the last Ghogyal monarch in 1975 was engineered by India is debatable. The last king was not a strong character and was formally deposed by the Sikkim Parliament, but the fact that India sent troops to put down loyalist opposition aroused suspicion of Indian involvement.

Many of the heads that have worn crowns in Asia have, indeed, been rather unsteady.

THE PERILS OF
CELEBRITY

It is paradoxical that public interest in the private lives of royal families, which Bagehot identified as an emergent strength because it 'brought down the pride of sovereignty to the level of petty life', has become a peril. The interest in a 'family on the throne' was undoubtedly an asset when confined to popular interest in royal lifestyles and rites of passage – particularly engagements and marriages – but it depended much on the restraint of the press when it came to misdemeanours or scandal. The rise of the celebrity monarchy and the realisation of the media that royal stories sell newspapers turned, from the late twentieth century, an asset into a problem. It is too simplistic to blame an intrusive media for revelations about the private lives of royals or for following effusive commentary with blasts of criticism. Princes and princesses seek to manipulate journalists and use them to build up their images and gain support for their causes, but then accuse them of intruding into their privacy when the publicity becomes unfavourable.

Aligned with the problem of relations between the public, the media and the royal families is the question of the tension

between tradition and modernity. The very idea of modernising a monarchy is arguably a contradiction, for a 'modern'
monarchy would not be hereditary, nor would it provide the
essential link between past and present. Monarchies are most
successful when they are one step, but not two steps, behind
social change, contemporary mores and opinions. They must
not be reactionary, but they become overly progressive to their
peril. For the most successful years of its recent history, the
British royal family has not been spectacular or glamorous,
and it must regret those more exciting periods in which it
has. The transformation of royal persons into celebrities poses
special dangers, as the career of Princess Diana demonstrated.
Monarchies stand for consistency, duty and what their subjects
have in common, but a lifetime presiding over public functions and limiting their public expressions of opinion to what
is acceptable to the majority of all ages, groups and classes is
not enormously attractive to young princes and princesses.

The British monarchy, long seen with some justice as the
most stable and secure in the world, seemed to have recovered
by the early twenty-first century from the divisions and the
emotional spasms that led up to Diana's funeral. Charles's relationship with Camilla Parker Bowles was gradually accepted
by the public, as was the eventual marriage of the couple,
while the two young princes, William and Harry, seemed
happy enough in their father's company. Diana, nevertheless,
cast a long shadow. Unlike their father, the princes were given
a conventional upper-class education at a prep school and
Eton and, though protected as much as possible, must have
been well aware that fellow pupils knew their family history.
William, by far the most able academically, proved protective
of his younger brother, who seemed a happy enough, if mischievous, boy. But the 'English [or rather British] situation' had
not yet run its course.

In his well-researched and very readable study of the brothers, Robert Lacey has pointed to factors that may have led to

the eventual breach between them.[1] One relates to the age-old problem thrown up by primogeniture, the gap between the heir to the throne and the 'spare', or second in line. 'Spares', usually male as until recently they took precedence, are very important until their elder sibling has an heir of his own and have, on several occasions, as with Henry VIII and George V, inherited the throne on the death of an elder brother. Once they have been moved further down the line of succession, however, their position and purpose are less clear. Princes and princesses – for Princess Anne is a model of how to handle this – have to work out a way of being a senior royal who is unlikely to succeed to the throne. Going into business is fraught with difficulty, as supposedly unfair competition is resented by rivals, as the Earl and Countess of Wessex found, while, perhaps misguidedly, the traditional route of a long military career has been discontinued. What is left is far from negligible: assisting the social and welfare role of the monarchy by heading and founding charitable causes, but not contentious ones; becoming honorary chancellors of universities; and generally enabling the monarchy to permeate public and civic life.

The recent scandal attached to Prince Andrew, Duke of York, points to the dangers posed by those who are clearly unsuited by character and disposition to the secondary roles thrust upon them, and little suited for those roles they are able to choose. Prince Charles has been quoted as saying that the trouble with his younger brother Prince Andrew is that 'he wants to be me'. Second-son syndrome apart, it is now hard to remember what a popular and gallant figure he was in the early 1980s, when he was on the front line of combat during the Falklands War and had the particularly dangerous role of a helicopter pilot assigned to the duty of acting as a decoy for missiles. If his fall from grace initiated by revelations of attendance at what the Italians call *bunga bunga* parties had echoes of previous princely scandals, what was significant was that only his ex-wife came to his aid, while institutions and regiments rushed to distance him from his erstwhile patronage. He had clearly been unwise in his friendship with a disgraced tycoon, but a long history of behaviour born of a sense of entitlement left him with few supporters.

The histories of his two nephews William and Harry point to the very different obligations and pressures exerted on first and second sons, and on their wives. William was, appropriately, the more conventional brother, already conscious of his future responsibilities, and the more academic. Both served in the armed forces but Harry saw combat in Afghanistan and promoted the popular cause of disabled veterans. Harry was, indeed, probably the more popular figure with much of the press, and he was seen as the mischievous younger brother who was allowed his minor lapses, such as appearing in decidedly non-PC clothing at a fancy-dress party and without any at another in Las Vegas. William's marriage demonstrated a further step away from royal endogamy, or even, as with his great-grandparents, marriage between royals and aristocrats, for Kate Middleton was upper middle class, but she proved adept in swiftly and gracefully adapting to her new role. Harry's marriage to Meghan Markle, a divorced mixed-race American actress, was more daring and innovative, and was widely acclaimed as increasing the monarchy's appeal to a multi-ethnic society. What was not appreciated at the time was the Prince's deep dislike of criticism by and intrusion from the press, and the determination of the couple not to be restrained by the conventions and lifestyle that had come to be the norm for the House of Windsor. Disaster was to follow.

If the different future roles of William and Harry were a significant factor in the relations of the two brothers – with the elder learning from his father, but probably more so from the Queen, the responsibilities he would inherit – another may well be the different effects of their mother's legacy. Diana,

whatever else she had been, was not a role model for a future
monarch, for she had rebelled against the restrictions and inhibitions that becoming royal placed on her. If Lacey is correct
in seeing Harry gradually coming to resent his brother's advice
and guidance, it may be seen as a replay of his mother's rebellion. The turning point, we are told, was William's sensible but
almost fatherly advice – when his brother appeared bowled
over by Meghan Markle – not to be in too much of a hurry,
but to wait a while. William himself, though Kate Middleton
was clearly his chosen girl, had waited some time to make sure
she had the qualities of a future queen before getting engaged
to her. Harry was looking not for a princess but for a woman
in his mother's image. The well-leaked disagreement over
which tiara from the royal collection Meghan should wear
at her wedding – at which, when the bride-to-be was told
she could not have her first choice, Harry reportedly said,
'What Meghan wants, Meghan gets' and the Queen allegedly
rejoindered, 'She gets the tiara that she's given by me' – was a
warning of trouble ahead. The somewhat wayward younger
brother and dashing army officer that had endeared himself to
the British public was to reinvent himself or be reinvented as
a social crusader.

There is no better example of the rapidity of the change
from raptured applause to constant criticism than the speed
with which the reputations of the Duke and Duchess of Sussex
were demolished and criticism took over. Their engagement
and wedding had been accompanied by a sympathetic press
and public acclaim, but this changed with their decision to
take legal action against a British newspaper for intruding
on their privacy and with rumours circulating of Meghan's
demands for special treatment and inability to get on with her
staff. Soon, as one commentator put it, the couple's every move
seemed 'fraught with controversy and hullabaloo. Despite their
environmental campaigning and their laughable pledge not to
have more than two children for the sake of the planet, the

couple have made it perfectly clear that their comfort, their privacy and their ease of passage are not going to be compromised for any cause no matter how green or noble.'[2]

Much of the criticism from the British press was, no doubt, unfair, but the Duke's action of going to court against a newspaper detracted attention from a successful African tour that cost the British taxpayer £245,000. Essentially, the unwritten bargain between royalty and the media by which reporters and cameramen are given access to get their stories and pictures, and the royals benefit from the coverage, broke down. Given the circumstances of his mother's death, his attitude to the media seemed understandable, if obtuse, but to sue appeared to be what an American celebrity, rather than a British prince, would do. It also became obvious that the newly married couple had little taste for the lifestyle of the monarchy, the annual calendar of long visits to Sandringham and Scotland, and what has been termed its 'Balmorality'. On the whole, the British public does not begrudge the royal family their breaks from duty and rather likes the image of a family devoted to country sports, horse riding and wet Labradors, perhaps because most would prefer to holiday on a Spanish beach. There are, however, limits to a taxpayer-funded life and, although there is room for a degree of private life within it, royalty is not offered the self-indulgence available to the merely rich and famous.

The announcement by the Duke and Duchess of Sussex at the beginning of January 2020, on their return from a holiday in Canada, that they intended to step back from their roles and duties as senior members of the royal family, came, nevertheless, as a bombshell. In the words of the *Daily Mail*'s royal correspondent, they 'had pressed the nuclear button'. Although negotiations with the palace as to their roles and duties had been in progress, it was clear that the Queen had not been informed and nor had other members of the family. The implications were serious, and their intentions widely

seen as self-indulgent. In their statement the couple declared
their intention 'to become financially independent, while
continuing to fully support Her Majesty The Queen', but
how were they to achieve this financial independence and
give the Queen their full support while ceasing to fulfil the
roles she had assigned to them? Previous attempts by British
royals to earn money had not only been unsuccessful, but
had proved an embarrassment, for whatever business interests they pursued were inevitably seen as a misuse of their
royal positions and therefore unfair to competitors. Their
plan to balance their time 'between the United Kingdom
and North America' seemed impractical and headstrong, and
had numerous implications: who would be responsible for
their security in the USA and, if by 'North America' they
meant Canada, would the Canadian government be prepared
to take responsibility? An even more fundamental question
concerned the incomes and privileges they received from the
British taxpayer, the security protection from Scotland Yard
and the financial support provided by Prince Charles and
the Duchy of Cornwall. Would Frogmore Cottage, expen-
sively renovated for them, stand empty while they lived in
North America?

The Queen had, in her Christmas broadcast, referred to
2019 as a 'bumpy year', but the new year seemed likely to
prove a second *annus horribilis*. Could an acceptable solution
to the Harry and Meghan problem be found, or would it
result in the couple wandering the world restlessly in a repeat
of the exile of the Duke and Duchess of Windsor – or what
might have been the fate of Princess Diana, but for her tragic
death? The perils of celebrity had once more proved a curse.
Royals are celebrities from their birth and may be said to have
celebrity thrust upon them, but with it come responsibilities
and limitations. Prince Harry should have understood this, as
should 'David', Prince of Wales, but Meghan, who achieved
her own celebrity as a modestly successful actress, had probably

never done so, as was the case with Wallis Simpson, until it was too late.

The monarchy is resilient, and an awkward compromise was found by which the couple would retain but not use their HRH titles, and Prince Harry's honorary positions, including those in the armed services, would be removed. Support for their lifestyles from the public purse would be reduced, but the Prince of Wales would continue to give them financial support. To have satisfied the Duke and Duchess completely would have placed an unfair extra burden upon the Prince of Wales, the Cambridges and other members of the royal family, especially if this involved giving the couple the right to choose only the duties they enjoy.

Within days it was clear that such a compromise was a chimera. Prince Harry, clearly disappointed with the outcome of his discussions with his family at the meeting called by the Queen, flew back to Canada, where his wife awaited him. The major worry in the royal family, as it was expressed by the British press, was of a replay on a minor scale of the fate of the Duke and Duchess of Windsor: an embittered royal couple roaming the world restlessly and seeking a semblance of the position to which they feel entitled. That there was no reconciliation became even more evident with the couple's move to California and the publication of the book *Finding Freedom* by Omid Scobie,[3] who was widely believed to have gained his information from close associates of the Sussexes; nevertheless, the book was later criticised as 'full of mistakes' by the Duchess's lawyer in her ongoing legal tussle with the *Mail on Sunday*, a court action which went against the Palace's tradition of ignoring critical press articles.

The announcement that they had signed a deal with Netflix to produce TV programmes and films seemed to suggest that their future lay in personal celebrity and in the US rather than in Britain or in the royal family. If the news that they were to pay for the renovation of Frogmore Cottage and would not henceforth receive an income from Prince Charles seemed to suggest an attempt to regain favour with the British public and the royal family, Prince Harry's comments on the US presidential election suggested a total and reckless break with the royal tradition of not interfering with politics, as well as his subservience to his wife's interests and views. As the distinguished biographer of the Queen Mother and the Duchess of Windsor Hugo Vickers commented, 'I wish Prince Harry would cease to be a mouthpiece for his wife.'

Instead, immersion in Californian celebrity culture provided the Sussexes with new platforms to jointly voice their complaints about their alleged mistreatment at the hands of the royal family and the British press. The Oprah Winfrey TV interview of Meghan and Harry in March 2021 was highly controversial, particularly with respect to accusations of racism within the royal circle and claims that the couple were denied both material and mental-health support. It's difficult not to make comparisons with the 1995 *Panorama* interview in which Princess Diana gave her side of the story as to her life within the royal family. A key difference, however, despite her personal unhappiness, lay in how she so significantly contributed to the work of the monarchy through her extensive charity involvements, including the championing of unpopular causes. In attempting to perhaps have it both ways, the Sussexes have hastily abandoned their inherited and adopted roles and yet continue to trade on their royal connections from across the pond and beyond. The planned publication of the Duke of Sussex's memoirs in 2022 will inevitably cast a shadow during the Queen's Platinum Jubilee year.

There is little doubt that the monarchy was shaken by the Sussexes' departure and subsequent actions and that it had implications for the rest of the royal family. One result was renewed calls for a 'slimmed-down' monarchy. This step has been taken in Sweden and is reputedly favoured by Prince Charles, but, as has been argued, what George VI called the

'family firm' is already somewhat slimline with the departure of Prince Andrew from prominent duties. Visits to
Commonwealth and other nations are an important duty for
senior royals, but for more junior members of royal families,
their duties are assigned to them by the monarch and royal
household, or else, more satisfactorily, are chosen either themselves or because the duties are in line with the person's own
interests, abilities and sympathies. Most of such appointments
involve visits of a less glamorous nature to cities, towns, factories, universities and charities around Britain. In general,
the system works well enough, for there are always numerous
organisations, institutions and charities eager to have a royal
patron. A team of royals enables royal influence across a large
swath of national life and enable the 'welfare monarchy' to
have many arms. Usually, it only founders when the match
between patron and organisation is unsuitable or the patron
less than arduous or tactful.

The Duke and Duchess of Sussex's taste for American-style
celebrity and its freedoms contrasts with the more mundane,
but valuable, royal duties performed with tact and poise by a
whole team of members of the royal family, among the most
diligent of which are Princess Anne and the often-overlooked
Princess Alexandra of Kent. The spirit of the 'family firm'
endures, and although a few of the less useful junior members
of the British royal family might usefully be dispensed with, it
would not suit the British style of monarchy, for an extended
royal family is one of its attractions; its reach to its subjects
would be diminished without the numbers to fill all those
positions of heads of charities, university chancellorships and
presidents of professional organisations.

It may well be the Queen, the longest-reigning monarch,
who best embodies the ability of the British monarchy to be
a unifying and impartial force above politics, reaching beyond
the political and metropolitan elite. Prince Charles, despite his
tendency to preach his favourite causes, many of which now

have mainstream support, has, with the support of the Duchess of Cornwall, much of this quality and has prepared himself well for his future role, as Prince William and his wife are also doing. Without the monarchy, Britain would be a drearier country, but its ruler needs a supporting cast.

The death of Prince Philip, Duke of Edinburgh, at Windsor on 9 April 2021 was a personal tragedy for the Queen and occurred at a particularly difficult time for the royal family. At the age of 99, Philip had been the longest-serving royal consort in British history, supporting the Queen for more than six decades of her reign. When he retired from royal duties in 2017, he was said to be patron, president or a member of more than 780 organisations. As many commentators remarked at the time of his funeral, despite his original outsider status and secondary role as royal consort, his had been a life of duty and service to his Queen, Country and Community.

15

HAS MONARCHY
A FUTURE?

Walter Bagehot proclaimed that a republic had emerged in
Britain under the cloak of the monarchy. We can also distinguish under the cloak of many republics the patterns of
government established under monarchies. Many have pointed
to the ghosts of the British constitution in that of the USA, as
King, Lords and Commons were replaced by President, Senate
and House of Representatives. A president may only, as it was
determined in 1951, serve for two terms, but he is assuredly
king for his time. In Paris an elected temporary king wields
enormous power and is accorded the respect of a Bourbon
without the lineage.

The distinction between republics with directly elected
presidents and those whose presidents are appointed by
governments or parliaments is too little remarked upon. Only
the former can be said to rule and it would be an unfair quiz
question that asked contestants to name two presidents of Italy
or Germany, although the names of elected presidents of major
countries are usually familiar. When de Gaulle called a referendum on his proposal for a directly elected president in 1962, he

was accused by the Left of emulating Napoleon III or restoring absolute monarchy, but few can doubt that the constitution of the Fifth Republic has been more successful than that of the Fourth. Elected presidents are, in practice as well as theory, heads of state, or sovereigns, and not just tradition, but a basic human need demands that there be something sacred about a sovereign; he or she needs to be seen as an embodiment of the nation and to be in many respects above the political fray, in the midst of which they were elected. Thus, we have the special place accorded to the 'Chief' in the USA, surrounded as they are by a style and ceremony that recall imperial as much as republican Rome. Elected in hard-fought and divisive contests, US presidents, nevertheless, enjoy conventions of universal respect, prerogatives and immunities; a president may be impeached but they have the ability to pardon themselves and others for acts committed during their term of office; they also enjoy an afterlife as somehow forever a president. Similarly, a French president has legal immunities (rather useful, as many, such as Jacques Chirac, have found) and live for their term in the context of a style and grandeur associated with a monarch.

Although it contradicts a central conception of monarchy, which is intimately linked to the hereditary principle, we can see with elected presidents something of older forms of kingship, which were often legitimised by acclamation or even, as in Poland, by election. By comparison, presidents appointed by governments or parliaments lack either power or charisma. The two most useful forms of contemporary government seem to be either elected presidencies, which have inherited many of the attributes of monarchy, or monarchy itself, albeit monarchy that has shed a greater or lesser part of its political power but, via its links with national pasts and continued prestige, manages to maintain the concepts of legitimacy and sovereignty.

For nations that have well-established parliamentary systems and in which the executive role of Prime Ministers supported by parliamentary majorities has long been accepted, the question of an alternative to monarchy involves invidious decisions. The Australian referendum on the continuation of the monarchy in 1999 illustrates the dilemma. Here was a nation in which the majority seemed to agree that its monarchy, located in another country, once the 'mother country', was no longer suitable for a nation both independent and searching for a new identity. The monarchy was, however, retained, in part and for the moment, because of affection for the Queen and because of positive appreciation of the monarchy, but also because of the want of an acceptable substitute. What form should a new constitution take? Any elected head of state would compete with and overawe Prime Minister, parliament and the states of the federal system. A head of state with limited power, appointed by a complex process, would fail the tests of charisma and authority, could hardly aspire to epitomise the nation, and would be regarded as a political placeman.

The degree to which many centuries of monarchical rule have bequeathed the legacy of the expected style and charisma of leadership and particular notions of the relationship between ruler and subjects to successor republics is a vital factor in many states. Historians and political scientists have pointed to the legacy of the Tsars in Russia in creating a proclivity towards strong personal rule and a suspicion of the idea of legitimate opposition that antedate the years of Communism and survive their passing. Re-elected with a huge majority in 2004, Vladimir Putin's inauguration in the splendour of the Kremlin as President of Russia was reminiscent of a Tsar's coronation, with its pomp and the formations of cavalry in the uniforms of regiments that fought against Napoleon in 1812. The Republic of Indonesia, it has been argued, has inherited from the royal rulers of the past particular expectations of post-colonial rulers and is 'a polity without a monarchy yet still infused with ideas of monarchical origin and a yearning for the golden age of a just king'.[1] In many

instances the overthrow of monarchy has led to its replacement by a charismatic ruler in whom great sections of the
population can discern attributes previously associated with
kingship: a paternalist care for the interests of the people, a
strong protector of the nation and the personal dispenser of
justice. If in some instances this tendency can co-exist with
electoral democracy and simply mean that such a president or
member of a political dynasty can be elected time and time
again, it can also lead to dictatorship, sometimes even hereditary dictatorship, as with North Korea or Syria.

Although a worldwide survey of existing monarchies still
finds absolute and near-absolute monarchs, it is clear that for
economically advanced and liberal societies the only model
that has a future is constitutional monarchy. Its advantages
over not only other forms of kingship but over other forms
of government are considerable. It acts as a brake on the
powers and ambitions of Prime Ministers and on the tyranny
of the majority, while most importantly it enables the sacred
functions of national leadership to be concentrated in one
individual who is not a politician.

The division between what Bagehot saw as the dignified
and the efficient aspects of government is essentially a more
profound divide between the spiritual and the secular roles
of government. As we have seen, these roles were in the
past often, but not invariably, combined in kingship. There
were in fact an enormous variety of ways in which, within
different cultures, these roles were fulfilled, ranging from a
sharp division between secular and religious authority, as with
Tokugawa Japan, and a complete concentration of power
in one individual, as with imperial China. In early modern
Europe, the tendency was towards the absorption of religious
authority by kings and emperors, while in late modern Europe
kings had increasingly to share power over the estates of their
realms. If we define 'spiritual' power broadly to mean not just
'religious' authority but the idea of monarchy as possessed of

a special legitimacy in terms of sovereignty, and possessed of a capacity to express the essence of the national community as it has developed over time, then, in a more secular age (in the West and to a great extent in Asia) the case for a division of roles is strong. Perhaps only for the USA can the argument be made that the Presidency effectively embraces both the need for a practical governor and someone who expresses nationhood and sovereignty, but then America is perhaps the only state to have managed to reify its constitution. And yet, in election years at least, there are tensions, as in 2016 and 2020, while threats of impeachment threaten to become almost traditional.

The difficulties of elected presidents in putting themselves forward as symbols of continuity and consensus are obvious, while, as we have seen, presidents appointed by an indirect process lack either effective power or the aura of sovereignty. Monarchy effectively binds together past and present; by reminding a nation of what it has been, it assists it to decide what it is. It also reminds ordinary families of their own histories. Few people would recollect that they were born or their grandmother died on the date that Ted Heath, or even Margaret Thatcher, became Prime Minister, but very many find parallels between their lives and major events in the life cycles of monarchs.

Effective constitutional monarchy is not merely symbolic. Its utility is important and consists of its restraining influence in times of internal crisis, the cautious exercise of its prerogatives and its social role. It enables change to take place within a frame of continuity. The monarchy was a major factor in Britain's smooth transition to mass democracy, and it is dubious whether Japan would have moved from militarism to become a stable parliamentary democracy after 1945 without its monarchy. The importance of a monarch as the final fount of authority for the armed forces is demonstrated by the Thai monarchy's success in putting an end to a long period of

military rule, although the continued support of the military
is essential to its survival. The degree of political power that
monarchies retain varies considerably, with, even in Europe,
the Dutch, Belgian and Danish sovereigns having a much
more interventionist role than does the British Queen. Yet
Queen Elizabeth's remaining prerogatives are essential both
symbolically and in practice, for who else could be trusted to
intervene impartially in a constitutional impasse?

Tinkering with Britain's largely unwritten constitution has
seen the introduction of a hitherto alien concept, a Supreme
Court – to its supporters a buttress to the rule of law but to
its denigrators the beginning of rule by lawyers. The implications for the royal prerogatives were little discussed until the
Court ruled in 2019 that a decision by the Queen to approve
a prorogation of parliament, taken on the advice of the Prime
Minister, was invalid as the Queen had been misled. Amid the
consequent furore, few raised the point that to suggest that a
monarch, on the throne for so many years and who had dealt
with so many Prime Ministers and crises, could have been
misled was an implicit criticism of the monarch and was a
modification of the prerogative. Effective constitutional monarchy is not synonymous with powerless monarchy and the
prerogatives are important. It may be that the British monarchy has been, since the mid-twentieth century, fortunate
in having rarely to intervene in the political sphere and even,
perhaps, too cautious about doing so. It is clear that its symbolic role and immense social influence are its major strengths,
but in times of crisis the head of state needs to be prepared to
intervene, cautiously.

The fundamental importance of the social influence of
monarchies and the position of monarchs as uncontested leaders of civil society has only recently been properly recognised.[2]
It is a crucial barrier against the expansion of the state and
of politics into all areas of life. The support that most monarchies, often following the British example, give to charitable

causes is a positive, not just in its obvious effect of increasing the amount of money raised and thus ensuring that society rather than merely government does something for the sick, the afflicted and the otherwise unfortunate, but in its bonding effect between diverse social groups. Royal influence in general penetrates to institutions and a range of activities, to society's small platoons, that are thankfully beyond the reach of the supposedly 'efficient' part of the constitution. The paradox is that in a constitutional monarchy the head of state, having distanced himself or herself from politics, can be head of a wider community than the formal state.

Monarchy has demonstrated considerable ability to change and adapt, but the future of even constitutional monarchy must, nevertheless, be seen as in some doubt in the long term. Kings were able to adapt to and thrive with the nation state, but if the future model for the state is the 'market state'[3] in which the final justification of the state is economic efficiency and the ability to satisfy the aspirations not of subjects or citizens but consumers, wage-earners or 'stakeholders', will such states have a place for monarchs? Mass democracy found a place for traditional institutions, but the market state with a yardstick for utility and profit may not. The link monarchies provide between national pasts and present identities may be less valuable if interest in the past declines and identities become vague or contested. Aristocracies have lost much of their status, and, without aristocracies, monarchies are in the lonely position of being the only hereditary institutions in societies. In response to the decline of social deference and of automatic respect for authority, monarchies have tended to become less formal and remote, with the consequent danger of losing magic and charisma. Finally, the decline of religious belief in some states may pose a threat to their monarchies' sacerdotal role; even if the next British coronation follows the hallowed format, the sense of awe at the process of anointment and crowning that the 1953 coronation induced in the nation may be absent. Monarchies may be able to surmount such problems. The decline of formal religion does not mean that the need for a spiritual dimension to life and to communities has gone, while the need for the present to secure its identity by reference to the past remains.

Most of the monarchies that have survived the cull of the twentieth century seem relatively secure. In East Asia Japan's 'Emperor system' faces little overt opposition. While the Thai monarchy has the problem of an eccentric and unpredict-able sovereign, it has surmounted many crises in the past, and the populations of the European monarchies seem content enough with their constitutional monarchies for the fore-seeable future. The rage of Islamic fundamentalism seems a double-edged sword so far as the continued existence of the Arab monarchies are concerned in that it has removed the threat of nationalist republicanism but faces the problem of how to accommodate religious extremism.

All the monarchies of Europe and, despite tight censorship, several of their Middle Eastern counterparts, have had to deal with scandals, most of them relating to money or sex, though republics like France and Italy have probably seen more and juicier of the same ilk. Queen Beatrix of the Netherlands warned against 'English situations' after the scandals sur-rounding the break-up of the marriage of Prince Charles and Princess Diana, which has now been followed by the farci-cal antics of Prince Harry and his wife, but most European monarchies have since experienced such embarrassments. One reason is, of course, that investigative journalism has no inhibitions and, if the British tabloids were the pioneers, the European press has shed its previous circumspection and the internet knows no bounds. Another vital reason is that royalty have become international celebrities.

Modern monarchy, it is often remarked, is well suited to nations that are content with their pasts and their identities, and it may well be that it has been the perseverance of monarchy that has enabled many such nations to heal and overcome the divisions and traumas of their pasts. The Belgian monarchy suggests that there is a case for monarchy as the most important cohesive influence for a state deeply divided on ethnic and linguistic lines. The initial success of the restored Spanish monarchy indicates that the wounds of a traumatic recent past may be healed by a monarchy whose associations with nation and state cover so many centuries, with the caveat that a decisive and sensitive monarch is required for this to happen, and that greed and scandal can quickly erode previous esteem. The appeal of monarchy is indeed multi-faceted: it suits nations that are relatively homogeneous, in that the population may identify with a past of which the monarchy is a present symbol; but monarchy's older role, as above race and ethnicity and as an inclusive institution for all who pledge loyalty, can make it an effective defender of minorities.

However, we would be purblind not to face the fact that in the last hundred years the number of monarchies has greatly diminished. Is this because monarchy fails to express the needs and aspirations of many societies or because an increasing number of contemporary states and their societies fail to have the qualities or aspirations – stability, cohesion and pride in their pasts and origins – that make monarchy a suitable expression of their identity? As we have seen, defeat in war and the associated loss of confidence in the system of government perceived as responsible led to the end of several monarchies extant in the early twentieth century. States which emerged after the dissolution of great empires tended to have an ambiguous relationship with their colonial pasts, even when their very names and territorial boundaries had been created in those pasts, and they often saw monarchy as an institution incompatible with their desire for new beginnings and identities.

More generally, much of modern thought values theory over empiricism and change over continuity, which makes it difficult to accept the inevitable contradictions and compromises of human society. Constitutional monarchy may appear a compromise between the principles of kingship and those of representative democracy in that it limits the powers of both, or a contradiction between the concepts of the sovereignty of the people and the sovereignty of a dynasty. Kings have, however, always ruled within limits imposed by God, providence or tradition, and kingship has equally also contained to varying degrees a spiritual and a secular dimension. Constitutional monarchy imposes in the name of the king or queen those limits on governments as well as monarchs, while in a mechanistic world it maintains the spiritual and cohesive elements of national identity. Contradictions or the reconciliation of opposites are essential to the workings of human society. We would be the worse without monarchy.

NOTES

Introduction
1. L.L. Blake, *The Royal Law* (2000) p. 101.
2. W.M. Spellman, *Monarchies 1000–2000* (2001) p. 12.
3. G. Coedes, *The Making of South-East Asia* (1966) p. 220.
4. Declan Quigley, 'Royalty's rhyme and reason', *The Times Higher Education Supplement*, 5 April 2002.
5. See Sir J.G. Frazer, *The Golden Bough*, 9 vols (1890–1951).
6. Spellman, *Monarchies*, p. 74.
7. Reinhard Bendix, *Kings or People: Power and the Mandate to Rule* (1980) p. 22.
8. John A. Hall, *Powers and Liberties: The Causes and Consequences of the Rise of the West* (1986) p. 76.
9. Nicholas B. Dirks, *The Hollow Crown* (1987) p. 7.
10. Spellman, *Monarchies*, pp. 18–19.
11. Anthony Reid, 'Charismatic Queens of Southern Asia', *History Today*, 53/6, June 2003.
12. Arno J. Mayer, *The Persistence of the Old Regime* (1981) p. 8.
13. Quoted in N. Henshall, *The Myth of Absolutism* (1992) pp. 131–2.
14. Robert Tombs, *The English & Their History* (2014) p. 239.
15. David Cannadine, 'The British Monarchy *c.* 1820–1977' in Eric Hobsbawm and Terence Ranger (eds), *The Invention of Tradition* (1983); T. Fujitani, *Splendid Monarchy: Power and Pageantry in Modern Japan*

(1998); and Maurizio Peleggi, *Lord of Things: The Fashioning of the Siamese Monarchy's Modern Image* (2002).

16. Whether or not Bolivar was inclined to monarchist ideas is contro-versial, but the case that he looked to monarchist solutions to Latin America's problems has been made by Salvador de Madariaga in *Bolivar* (1952).

17. Mark J.Van Aken, *King of the Night: Juan José Flores and Ecuador, 1824–1864* (1989).

18. See K. Schultz, *Tropical Versailles: Empire, Monarchy, and the Portuguese Royal Court in Rio de Janeiro, 1808–1821* (2001).

Chapter 1

1. Barrington Moore Jr, *Social Origins of Dictatorship and Democracy* (1967) p. 174.

2. See Mark C. Elliott, *The Manchu Way: The Eight Banners and Ethnic Identity in Late Imperial China* (2002).

3. Jonathan D. Spence, *Emperor of China: Self Portrait of K'Ang-Hsi* (1988) p. xii.

4. Benjamin A. Elman, *A Cultural History of Civil Examinations in Late Imperial China* (2000).

5. It was a testament to the underlying unity of China that in the British colony of Hong Kong it was only when the news of the overthrow of the Emperor came through that students at the University cut off their queues, the symbol of their submission to the Manchu.

6. Derek Massarella, *A World Elsewhere: Europe's Encounters with Japan in the Sixteenth and Seventeenth Centuries* (1990) p. 12.

7. David Montgomery Earl, *Emperor and Nation in Japan* (1964) p. 12.

8. Hugh Cortazzi, *The Japanese Achievement* (1990) p. 175.

9. Moore Jr, *Social Origins*.

10. Fujitani, *Splendid Monarchy*, p. 9.

11. Richard Storry, *A History of Modern Japan* (1960) p. 35.

12. Fujitani, *Splendid Monarchy*.

13. *Ibid.*, pp. 13–14.

14. Donald Keane, *Emperor of Japan: Meiji and his World, 1852–1912* (2002).

15. W.G. Beasley, *The Modern History of Japan* (1981) p. 131.

16. Keane, *Emperor of Japan*, pp. 348–50.

17. *Ibid.*, pp. 513–22.

18. Roger Kershaw, *Monarchy in South-East Asia: The Faces of Tradition in Transition* (2001) p. 10.

19. C. Geertz, *Negara: The Theatre State in Nineteenth-Century Bali* (1980).

20. Coedes, *South-East Asia*, p. 220.

21. Sir Richard Winstedt, *Malaya and its History* (1949) p. 27.

22. See Peleggi, *Lord of Things.*

23. See C. Campbell Orr (ed.), *Queenship in Britain: Royal Patronage, Court Culture and Dynastic Politics* (2002).

24. Peleggi, *Lord of Things*, p. 14.

Chapter 2

1. See Hall, *Powers and Liberties*, pp. 85–110.

2. Spellman, *Monarchies*, p. 117.

3. Malcolm E. Yapp, '1900–21: The Last Years of the Qajar Dynasty' in Hossein Amirsadeghi (ed.), *Twentieth Century Iran* (1977) p. 2.

4. Philip Magnus, *King Edward VII* (1964) p. 127.

5. Yapp, 'The Last Years', p. 4.

6. Bernard Lewis, *The Emergence of Modern Turkey* (1961) p. 13.

7. Spellman, *Monarchies*, p. 140.

8. *Ibid.*, p. 23.

9. Harold Nicolson, *Monarchy* (1962) p. 251.

Chapter 3

1. Brian Moynahan, *The British Century* (1997) p. 16.

2. See David Cannadine, *Ornamentalism: How the British Saw Their Empire* (2002).

3. Kershaw, *Monarchy in South-East Asia*, p. 4.

4. Cannadine, *Ornamentalism*, p. 43.

5. *Ibid.*, p. 9.

6. Lawrence James, *Raj: The Making and Unmaking of British India* (1997) p. 322.

7. Carol A. Breckenridge, 'The Aesthetics and Politics of Colonial Collecting: India at World Fairs', *Comparative Studies in Society and History*, 31/2 (1989) p. 126.

Chapter 4

1. Giles MacDonogh, *The Last Kaiser: William the Impetuous* (2000) p. 13.

2. I. McAlpine and R. Hunter, *George III and the Mad Business* (1969). John C.G. Röhl, Martin Warren and David Hunt, *Purple Secret: Genes, 'Madness' and the Royal Houses of Europe* (1999).

3. Princess Louise had a hearty Hanoverian sexual appetite, while the Marquess had a limited appetite for heterosexuality. It was said that 'the only thing that was wrong with Princess Louise was that she ran after anything in trousers and that the Marquess had the same problem'.

4.   Benedict Anderson, *Imagined Communities: Reflections on the Origin and Spread of Nationalism* (1991) pp. 204–6.
5.   See Eugene Weber, *Peasants into Frenchmen: The Modernisation of Rural France 1870–1914* (1976).
6.   George IV almost certainly went through a marriage ceremony with Mrs Fitzherbert, but as the marriage was contrary to the Royal Marriages Act, their union was not legal.
7.   Gordon Brook-Shepherd, *Royal Sunset* (1987) p. 3.
8.   Mayer, *Old Regime*.
9.   Gonzalo de Reparaz, *Alfonso XIII y sus complices* (1931), quoted by Gerard Noel, *Ena, Spain's English Queen* (1984) p. 34.
10. John C.G. Röhl, *The Kaiser and his Court* (1994) p. 10.
11. Botho Eulenburg, quoted in MacDonogh, *The Last Kaiser*, p. 203.
12. Friedrich von Holstein, 2 December 1894. Quoted in MacDonogh, *The Last Kaiser*.
13. Holstein to Philipp Graf zu Eulenburg, 27 November 1894, quoted in Röhl, *The Kaiser and his Court*, p. 2.
14. Dominic Lieven, *Nicholas II: Tsar of All the Russias* (1993) p. 261.
15. *Ibid.*, p. 260.
16. Dominic Lieven, *Empire: The Russian Empire and its Rivals from the Sixteenth Century to the Present* (2003) p. 158.
17. Pieter M. Judson, *The Habsburg Empire: A New History* (2016)
18. Brook-Shepherd, *Royal Sunset*, pp. 250–1.
19. David Cannadine, 'The British Monarchy, *c.*1820–1977', in Eric Hobsbawm and Terence Ranger (eds), *The Invention of Tradition* (1983) p. 133.
20. See for instance Campbell Orr (ed.), *Queenship in Britain*.
21. See Joan Haslip, *The Lonely Empress: A Biography of Elizabeth of Austria* (2000).
22. Röhl, *The Kaiser and his Court*, p. 20.
23. Brook-Shepherd, *Royal Sunset*, pp. 27–32.
24. Lewis, *The Emergence of Modern Turkey*, pp. 183–4.
25. Brook-Shepherd, *Royal Sunset*, p. xix.
26 . Norman Angell, *The Great Illusion: A Study of the Relations of Military Power to National Advantage* (1910).

Chapter 5
1.   Annika Mombauer, 'The Origins of the First World War' in Arthur Marwick, Clive Emsley and Mombauer, *Europe in 1914* (2000) p. 187.
2.   Edward Crankshaw, *The Fall of the House of Habsburg* (1963) p. 391.

3. Kenneth Rose, *George V* (1984) p. 167.
4. Spellman, *Monarchies*, p. 236.
5. Mayer, *Old Regime*, p. 304.
6. Sean McMeekin, *July 1914 Countdown to War* (2013), and Christopher Clark, *The Sleepwalkers* (2012).
7. Margaret MacMillan, *The War That Ended Peace* (2013) p. 331.
8. There is a case that Germany lost the war on the economic front not because of the Kaiser, but because of the generals, who insisted on taking control of the economy, with disastrous results.
9. Hannah Arendt, *On Revolution* (1963) p. 15.
10. Holger Afflerbach, 'William II as Supreme Warlord' in Annika Mombauer and Wilhelm Deist (eds), *The Kaiser: New Research on William II's Role in Imperial Germany* (2003) pp. 195–217.
11. Matthew Stibbe, 'Germany's "Last Card": Wilhelm II and the Decision in Favour of Unrestricted Submarine Warfare in January 1917' in Mombauer and Deist (eds), *The Kaiser*, pp. 217–35.
12. Theo Aronson, *Crowns in Conflict: The Triumph and Tragedy of European Monarchy 1910–18* (1986), pp. 132–3.
13. *Ibid.*, p. 168.
14. Rose, *George V*, p. 216.
15. *Ibid.*, p. 225.
16. Niall Ferguson, *The Pity of War* (1998) pp. 436, 462.

Chapter 6
1. Ferguson, *The Pity of War*, pp. 168–73.
2. Lieven, *The Russian Empire*, p. 57.
3. For the latter, see Barbara W. Tuchman, *The Proud Tower* (1966) and George Dangerfield, *The Strange Death of Liberal England* (1935).
4. Robert Conquest, *Reflections on a Ravaged Century* (1999) p. ix.
5. Ferguson, *The Pity of War*, p. 435.
6. Misha Glenny, *The Balkans 1804–1999: Nationalism, War and the Great Powers* (1999) pp. 351–2.
7. Geoffrey Hindley, *The Royal Families of Europe* (2000) p. 55.
8. *Ibid.*, pp. 98–9.
9. Glenny, *The Balkans*, p. 413.
10. R.R. James (ed.), *'Chips': The Diaries of Sir Henry Channon* (1967) p. 89.
11. See Susan Williams, *The People's King: The True Story of the Abdication* (2003).

Chapter 7
1. Robert Lacey, *The Kingdom* (1981) p. 160.
2. As Robert Lacey, *The Kingdom*, has shown, the Government of India and the British Foreign Office had different priorities and often disagreed in their policies towards Arabia.

Chapter 8
1. Stephen S. Large, *Emperor Hirohito and Showa Japan* (1992) p. 7.
2. *Ibid.*, p. 10.
3. Edward Behr, *Hirohito: Behind the Myth* (1989) p. 54.
4. *Ibid.*
5. Herbert P. Bix, *Hirohito and the Making of Modern Japan* (2000).
6. Large, *Emperor Hirohito*.
7. Kershaw, *Monarchy in South-East Asia*, p. 35.

Chapter 9
1. L. Picknett, C. Prince and S. Prior, *War of the Windsors* (2002) pp. 172–3.
2. Aronson, *Crowns in Conflict*, p. 46.
3. See Picknett *et al., War of the Windsors*, p. 171.
4. Theo Aronson, *The Royal Family at War* (1993) p. 27.
5. Hindley, *Royal Families of Europe*, p. 90.
6. *Ibid.*, p. 123.
7. Aronson, *Royal Family at War*, p. 172.
8. Kershaw, *Monarchy in South-East Asia*, p. 4.

Chapter 10
1. Andrew Lownie, *The Mountbattens: Their Lives and Loves* (2020).
2. *Ibid.*
3. Robert Lacey, *The Kingdom: Arabia and the House of Saud* (1981).
4. Charles Powell, *Juan Carlos of Spain: Self-Made Monarch* (1996).

Chapter 11
1. Robert Lacey, *Majesty* (1977) p. 268.
2. W. Bagehot, *The English Constitution* (1963 edn) p. 96.
3. Caroline Dakers, *The Holland Park Circle: Artists and Victorian Society* (1999) pp. 128–9.
4. Philip Ziegler, *Mountbatten* (1985) p. 867.
5. Andrew Lownie.

6.   Lacey, 'The Beautiful and the Damned', *Sunday Times*,
     26 September 1999.
7.   Vernon Bogdanor, *The Monarchy and the Constitution* (1995) p. 185.

Chapter 12

1.   This row was similar to the controversy when Prince Michael of Kent
     married Baroness Christine von Reibitz and it was revealed that her
     father had been a major in the SS.
2.   Valentine Low, *The Times*, 26 September 2020.
3.   See Charles Powell, *Juan Carlos of Spain: Self-Made Monarch* (1996).
4.   Matthew Campbell, *Sunday Times*, 9 August 2020.
5.   Jeremy Paxman, *On Royalty* (2006) p. 269.

Chapter 13

1.   Nishibe Susumu, 'Defending the Dignity of the Symbolic Emperor',
     Japan Echo, 18/2, Summer 1989.
2.   *The Times*, 9 June 2004.
3.   Francis Pike, 'Thailand's Caligula', *The Spectator*, 12 September 2020.
4.   Kershaw, *Monarchy in South-East Asia*, p. 160.
5.   Veronica Maclean, *Crowned Heads: Kings, Sultans and Emperors: A Royal
     Quest* (1993) pp. 213–37.

Chapter 14

1.   Robert Lacey, *Battle of the Brothers: William, Harry and the Inside Story of
     a Family in Turmoil* (2020).
2.   Jan Moir, 'By Royal Disappointment', *The Spectator*, 24 August 2019.
3.   Obid Scobie and Carolyn Durand, *Finding Freedom* (2020).

Chapter 15

1.   Roger Kershaw, *Monarchy in South-East Asia*, (2000) p. 80.
2.   See in particular F. Prochaska, *The Rise of the Welfare Monarchy* (1995).
3.   The concept of the market state is described by Philip Bobbit in *The
     Shield of Achilles* (2002).

BIBLIOGRAPHY

Aken, Mark J.Van, *King of the Night: Juan José Flores and Ecuador, 1824–1864*, Berkeley, University of California Press, 1989

Anderson, Benedict, *Imagined Communities: Reflections on the Origin and Spread of Nationalism*, Verso, 1991

Angell, Norman, *The Great Illusion: A Study of the Relations of Military Power to National Advantage*, Heinemann, 1910

Arendt, Hannah, *On Revolution*, Allen Lane, The Penguin Press, 1963

Aronson, Theo, *Crowns in Conflict: The Triumph and the Tragedy of European Monarchy 1910–1918*, John Murray, 1986

——, *The Royal Family at War*, John Murray, 1993

Bagehot, W., *The English Constitution*, Oxford University Press, 1963

Beasley, W.G., *The Modern History of Japan*, 3rd edn, Weidenfeld & Nicolson, 1981

Behr, Edward, *Hirohito: Behind the Myth*, Hamish Hamilton, 1989

——, *The Last Emperor*, MacDonald, 1987

Bendix, Reinhard, *Kings or People. Power and the Mandate to Rule*, Berkeley and Los Angeles, University of California Press, 1980

Bix, Herbert P., *Hirohito and the Making of Modern Japan*, Duckworth, 2000

Blake, L.L., *The Royal Law*, Shepheard-Walwyn, 2000

Bobbit, Philip, *The Shield of Achilles*, Allen Lane, The Penguin Press, 2002

Bogdanor, Vernon, *The Monarchy and the Constitution*, Oxford University Press, 1995

Breckenridge, Carol A., 'The Aesthetics and Politics of Colonial Collecting: India at World Fairs', *Comparative Studies in Society and History*, 31/2, 1989

Brook-Shepherd, Gordon, *Royal Sunset*, Weidenfeld & Nicolson, 1987

Campbell Orr, C. (ed.), *Queenship in Britain: Royal Patronage, Court Culture and Dynastic Politics*, Manchester University Press, 2002

Cannadine, David, 'The British Monarchy *c.* 1820–1977' in Eric Hobsbawm, and Terence Ranger (eds), *The Invention of Tradition*, Cambridge University Press, 1983

——, *Ornamentalism: How the British Saw Their Empire*, Allen Lane, The Penguin Press, 2002

Coedes, G., *The Making of South-East Asia*, Routledge & Kegan Paul, 1966

Conquest, Robert, *Reflections on a Ravaged Century*, John Murray, 1999

Cortazzi, Hugh, *The Japanese Achievement*, Sidgwick & Jackson, 1990

Crankshaw, Edward, *The Fall of the House of Habsburg*, New York, Viking Press, 1963

Dakers, Caroline, *The Holland Park Circle: Artists and Victorian Society*, New Haven, Yale University Press, 1999

Dangerfield, George, *The Strange Death of Liberal England*, Constable, 1935

Dirks, Nicholas B., *The Hollow Crown*, Cambridge University Press, 1987

Earl, David Montgomery, *Emperor and Nation in Japan*, Seattle, University of Washington Press, 1964

Elliott, Mark C., *The Manchu Way: The Eight Banners and Ethnic Identity in Late Imperial China*, Palo Alto, Stanford University Press, 2002

Elman, Benjamin A., *A Cultural History of Civil Examinations in Late Imperial China*, Berkeley and Los Angeles, University of California Press, 2000

Ferguson, Niall, *The Pity of War*, Allen Lane, The Penguin Press, 1998

Frazer, Sir J.G., *The Golden Bough*, 9 vols, Macmillan, 1890–1951

Fujitani, T., *Splendid Monarchy: Power and Pageantry in Modern Japan*, Berkeley, University of California Press, 1998

Geertz, C., *Negara: The Theatre State in Nineteenth-Century Bali*, Princeton, Princeton University Press, 1980

Glenny, Misha, *The Balkans 1804–1999: Nationalism, War and the Great Powers*, Granta Books, 1999

Hall, John A., *Powers and Liberties: The Causes and Consequences of the Rise of the West*, Penguin Books, 1986

Haslip, Joan, *The Lonely Empress: A Biography of Elizabeth of Austria*, Weidenfeld & Nicolson, 2000

Henshall, N., *The Myth of Absolutism*, Macmillan, 1992

Hindley, Geoffrey, *The Royal Families of Europe*, Constable, 2000

James, Lawrence, *Raj. The Making and Unmaking of British India*, Little Brown, 1997

James, R.R. (ed.), *'Chips': The Diaries of Sir Henry Channon*, Weidenfeld & Nicolson, 1967

Keane, Donald, *Emperor of Japan: Meiji and his World, 1852–1912*, New York, Columbia University Press, 2002

Kershaw, Roger, *Monarchy in South-East Asia: The Faces of Tradition in Transition*, Routledge, 2001

Lacey, Robert, *Majesty*, Hutchinson, 1977, and revised edn, Time Warner, 2002

——, *The Kingdom*, Hutchinson, 1981

Large, Stephen S., *Emperor Hirohito and Showa Japan*, Routledge, 1992

Lewis, Bernard, *The Emergence of Modern Turkey*, Oxford University Press, 1961

——, *What Went Wrong? The Clash between Islam and Modernity in the Middle East*, Weidenfeld & Nicolson, 2002

Lieven, Dominic, *Nicholas II: Tsar of All the Russias*, John Murray, 1993

——, *Empire: The Russian Empire and its Rivals from the Sixteenth Century to the Present*, Pimlico, 2003

McAlpine, I. and R. Hunter, *George III and the Mad Business*, Allen Lane, The Penguin Press, 1969

MacDonogh, Giles, *The Last Kaiser: William the Impetuous*, Weidenfeld & Nicolson, 2000

Maclean, Veronica, *Crowned Heads: Kings, Sultans and Emperors: A Royal Quest*, Hodder & Stoughton, 1993

Madariaga, Salvador de, *Bolivar*, New York, Pellegrini & Cudahy, 1952

Magnus, Philip, *King Edward VII*, John Murray, 1964

Marwick, Arthur, Clive Emsley and Annika Mombauer, *Europe in 1914*, Open University Press, 2000

Massarella, Derek, *A World Elsewhere: Europe's Encounters with Japan in the Sixteenth and Seventeenth Centuries*, New Haven, Yale University Press, 1990

Mayer, Arno J., *The Persistence of the Old Regime*, Pantheon, 1981

Mombauer, Annika and Wilhelm Deist (eds), *The Kaiser: New Research on William II's Role in Imperial Germany*, Cambridge University Press, 2003

Moore Jr, Barrington, *Social Origins of Dictatorship and Democracy*, Allen Lane, The Penguin Press, 1967

Moynahan, Brian, *The British Century*, Random House, 1997

Nicolson, Harold, *George V: His Life and Reign*, Constable, 1952

——, *Monarchy*, Weidenfeld & Nicolson, 1962

Noel, Gerard, *Ena, Spain's English Queen*, Constable, 1984

Packard, Jonathan M., *Sons of Heaven: A Portrait of the Japanese Monarchy*, Macdonald, 1988

Peleggi, Maurizio, *Lord of Things: The Fashioning of the Siamese Monarchy's Modern Image*, Honolulu, University of Hawaii Press, 2002

Picknett, L., C. Prince and S. Prior, *War of the Windsors*, Edinburgh, Mainstream, 2002

Powell, Charles, *Juan Carlos of Spain: Self-Made Monarch*, Macmillan in association with St Antony's College, Oxford, 1996

Prochaska, F., *The Rise of the Welfare Monarchy*, New Haven, Yale University Press, 1995

Quigley, Declan, 'Royalty's Rhyme and Reason', *The Times Higher Education Supplement*, 5 April 2002

Reid, Anthony, 'Charismatic Queens of Southern Asia', *History Today*, London, 53, June 2003

Röhl, John C.G., *The Kaiser and his Court*, Cambridge University Press, 1994

——, Martin Warren and David Hunt, *Purple Secret: Genes, 'Madness' and the Royal Houses of Europe*, Corgi Adult, 1999

Rose, Kenneth, *George V*, Weidenfeld & Nicolson, 1984

Ruoff, Kenneth J., *The People's Emperor: Democracy and the Japanese Monarchy 1945–1995*, Cambridge, Mass., Harvard University Press, 2001

Schultz, K., *Tropical Versailles. Empire, Monarchy, and the Portuguese Royal Court in Rio de Janeiro, 1808–1821*, Routledge Inc., 2001

Spellman, W.M., *Monarchies 1000–2000*, Reaktion Books, 2001

Spence, Jonathan D., *Emperor of China: Self Portrait of K'Ang-Hsi*, New York, Vintage Books, 1988

——, *The Search for Modern China*, Hutchinson, 1990

Storry, Richard, *A History of Modern Japan*, Penguin Books, 1960

Susumu, Nishibe, 'Defending the Dignity of the Symbolic Emperor', *Japan Echo*, 18/2, Summer 1989

Tomes, Jason, *King Zog: Self-Made Monarch of Albania*, Sutton Publishing, 2003

Tuchman, Barbara W., *The Proud Tower*, Hamish Hamilton, 1966

Weber, Eugene, *Peasants into Frenchman: The Modernisation of Rural France 1870–1914*, Palo Alto, Stanford University Press, 1976

Williams, Susan, *The People's King: The True Story of the Abdication*, Allen Lane, The Penguin Press, 2003

Winstedt, Sir Richard, *Malaya and its History*, Hutchinson, 1949

Yapp, Malcolm E., '1900–21: The Last Years of the Qajar Dynasty' in Hossein Amirsadeghi (ed.), *Twentieth Century Iran*, New York, Holmes and Meier, 1977

Ziegler, Philip, *Mountbatten*, Sidgwick & Jackson, 1985

INDEX